'Ecstatic Sound'

'Ecstatic Sound'

Music and Individuality in the Work of Thomas Hardy

JOHN HUGHES

Ashgate

Aldershot • Burlington USA • Singapore • Sydney

Published by

Ashgate Publishing Limited
Gower House, Croft Road
Aldershot
Hants GU11 3HR
England

Ashgate Publishing Company
131 Main Street
Burlington VT 05401–5600
USA

Ashgate website: http://www.ashgate.com

John Hughes has asserted his right under the Copyright, Designs and Patents Act, 1988, to be identified as the author of this work.

British Library Cataloguing-in-Publication Data
'Ecstatic Sound': Music and Individuality in the
        Work of Thomas Hardy. – (The Nineteenth Century)
        1. Hardy, Thomas, 1840–1928 – Criticism and interpretation.
        2. Music in literature.
        I. Title.
        823.8

US Library of Congress Cataloging-in-Publiction Data
Hughes, John
        'Ecstatic Sound': Music and Individuality in the
        Work of Thomas Hardy/John Hughes
        p. cm. – (The Nineteenth Century)
        Includes bibliographical references and index (alk. paper)
        1. Hardy, Thomas, 1840–1928–Knowledge–Music.
        I. Title. II. Nineteenth Century (Aldershot, England).
        ML80. H24 H84 2001
        823'.8–dc21   2001022827

ISBN 1 84014 633 8

This book is printed on acid free paper

Printed and bound in Great Britain by MPG Books Ltd, Bodmin, Cornwall

Contents

The Nineteenth Century General Editors' Preface   vii

Acknowledgments   ix

Introduction   1

1 'Souls Unreconciled to Life'   23

2 'Those Unaccountable Sensations'   63

3 'The Beats of Being'   105

4 'Till Time Seemed Fiction'   155

5 'Let Every Man Make a Philosophy for Himself out of His Own Experience'   201

Bibliography   233

Index   243

The Nineteenth Century General Editors' Preface

The aim of this series is to reflect, develop and extend the great burgeoning of interest in the nineteenth century that has been an inevitable feature of recent decades, as that former epoch has come more sharply into focus as a locus for our understanding not only of the past but of the contours of our modernity. Though it is dedicated principally to the publication of original monographs and symposia in literature, history, cultural analysis, and associated fields, there will be a salient role for reprints of significant texts from, or about, the period. Our overarching policy is to address the spectrum of nineteenth-century studies without exception, achieving the widest scope in chronology, approach and range of concern. This, we believe, distinguishes our project from comparable ones, and means, for example, that in the relevant areas of scholarship we both recognize and cut innovatively across such parameters as those suggested by the designations 'Romance' and 'Victorian'. We welcome new ideas, while valuing tradition. It is hoped that the world which predates yet so forcibly predicts and engages our own will emerge in parts, as a whole, and in the lively currents of debate and change that are so manifest an aspect of its intellectual, artistic and social landscape.

Vincent Newey
Joanne Shattock

University of Leicester

Acknowledgments

I would like to thank the colleagues at the Cheltenham and Gloucester College of Higher Education who have helped during the writing of this book. Peter Widdowson and Simon Dentith are in many ways responsible for the thriving research ethos which the English School now enjoys, and for the system of study leaves from which I benefited at a crucial stage. I am grateful to Peter Widdowson also for his benign guidance on Hardy matters, and for his meticulous reading and commentary on an earlier version. Roger Ebbatson and Alan Brown were similarly and typically generous in offering their time to reading the draft through, and both made many valuable suggestions which I have incorporated. I would like also to thank Maggie Wheel in our library for her efficiency and good humour on many occasions over inter-library loans.

Outside the College, there are many other people I wish to acknowledge. Although my D Phil thesis on Hardy was on a very different topic, I remember with gratitude and pleasure the contributions made by my various supervisors, in particular John Bayley, Valentine Cunningham, and Patricia Ingham. I would like to thank Vincent Newey at Ashgate for approving this project, Ruth Peters and Celia Hoare for their exemplary editorial work, and Erika Gaffney for the professional and helpful way in which she controlled the various pre-publication stages. Two editors, Ken Newton at *English* and Simon Curtis at *The Thomas Hardy Journal*, allowed me to reprint work here that has previously appeared in their journals. Roger Ebbatson and John Schad invited me to give papers on work in progress. On a more directly personal level, I have enjoyed encouragement and stimulus from a number of people, including my brother, David, and the following close friends: Sarah Wood, Martin Aske, Mark Ford, Clare Hanson, Manzu Islam, and Michael Carrington. Finally, above all, I would like to thank Joanna, and to dedicate the book to our two boys, Ashley and Joseph, who were both born during the period the book was being written.

Introduction

John Bayley's discussion of 'The Darkling Thrush' in *An Essay on Hardy* identifies an inimitable principle of disunity at work in the poem, which he takes as a key to Hardy's characteristic effects in both the poetry and the prose. Bayley writes:

> Throughout his work, the ways in which we are absorbed into it, moved, delighted, are never co-ordinated, never really unified.[1]

Bayley's sustained reading of the poem locates unconsciously produced separations of metaphor and description as the means by which the poem is held between the world of human meanings and consolations, and the bleakly inhospitable winter scene:

> The thrush's song is the climax of this whole tendency; and the thrush himself, in his shrivelled and unkempt physical presence, its leading man. The metaphors are now of religion, of joys and consolations; and we recognise that the poem itself, like not a few of Hardy's, has come to suggest the progression and cadence of a hymn. But the blessed hope appropriate to a hymn is in complete obliviousness of such a song as the bird is singing - its 'happy goodnight air' - a line whose unexpectedness, among the comparatively formal sobriety of the poem's diction, always brings the tears to my eyes. (*An Essay on Hardy*, p. 38)

For Bayley, the 'joy illimited' and hope of the bird's singing are all the more moving for their incongruity and unexpectedness. At this moment, the listener's response is divided between an unillusioned consciousness of things, and a reawakened sense of joy and communion that is oblivious to this. The bird's song signals possibilities that the tentative conclusion of the poem seems concerned to remark, and incorporate, even as it suggests at the same time that such possibilities are unactualisable:

> [...] I could think there trembled through
> His happy good-night air
> Some blessed Hope, whereof he knew
> And I was unaware.[2]

So Bayley's discussion is informed by the ideas that the bird's song involves an absent-mindedness at odds with the scene around, and that it transmits a sense of happiness that is both real and insistent, as well as unsustainable within this surrounding physical environment at the end of the century. The song provokes a response, a surprise by joy that the speaker in the poem, fervourless and leaning upon the coppice gate, is painfully aware that he is unable to live up to and translate into a lived experience.

This discussion anticipates important features of the argument which follows, above all that the uses of music in Hardy's work are in many aspects marked by an ambivalent attitude such as Bayley suggests. Music is seen to evoke a response to life that is inseparable from what gives life value, as well as incompatible with Hardy's vision of personal and historical circumstances. Within the sardonic, parodic and ironic operations of the fiction, for instance, and the gaps between memory and actuality in the poetry, music works to evoke necessary potentials of individuality and community. It awakens hopes that are set in a kind of counterpoint to the deadening types of disappointment to which they are subject in what the plots of the fiction, and the scenarios of the poems, ultimately confirm as reality. Music is in this way an important contributory factor to the rhythm of experience in the fiction, particularly the later fiction, configured as it increasingly is in terms of repeated, disjunctive, open-ended intervals of hope, inspirations of personal expression, that are belatedly pulled into the ironic, spiralling repetitions of plot. I want in this book to explore various aspects of this use of music, and the way it operates unconsciously, involving sensation to invoke an ideal dimension of relatedness outside of consciousness, and consciousness's reflective sense of chronology, personality, and context. The study of music in these texts provides a way of seeing how they open and close between different and disjoined dimensions of time and experience, and allows for an access into what are seen as the fundamental, even constitutive, affective dimensions and concerns of Hardy's writing. As this suggests, this book presents itself less as a study of the representation of music in Hardy's fiction and poetry simply, than as one that explores the connection between music and emotion within his work.[3] The aim thereby is to approach Hardy's abiding concern with individual expression, and his recurrent themes - time, community, and love - through this connection.

With respect to these affective features in Hardy's work, for instance, it is doubtful that there is any poem of Hardy's, even the most explicitly grief-stricken, which, for all its conscious sense of loss, does

not secrete within itself coexisting, and primarily unconscious, elements
of joy or ecstasy. Another remark of Bayley's, along the lines that
disappointment is a characteristic effect of form in Hardy, suggests
Hardy's often unsparing treatment of human aspirations.[4] At the same
time, though, it suggests the opposite, the extent to which Hardy's texts
depend on pursuing fugitive effects of pleasure, and presentiments of
happiness. Hardy the poet, like his fictional characters and his readers,
is constantly overtaken by this elating sense of the possible, by
moments of enthusiasm that imply a distinctive conception and
evaluation of life. Given the broad range of ways in which music's
'insistent calls of joy' function in Hardy's work (*Complete Poems*, p. 876),
this Introduction offers itself as a kind of overture, indicating some of
the main questions and motifs which are developed in the book as a
whole.

It follows that this study of Hardy's representation of music, and
its intimate relations to his practices of writing, inevitably involves one
in a suspicion of many of the received negative images of Hardy and
his work.[5] Instead of seeing Hardy merely as a poet grimly and
retrospectively fixated on transience, for example, one emphasizes that
he is also in primary ways an artist of the moment, with all its chancy
transitions, its expressive intervals, its speculative quests and
sympathetic projects. Music is peculiarly important in this context, since
for Hardy the response to music clearly constitutes one of the most
fundamental revelations of human individuality and emotion. In terms
of the rationale of this book, these remarks suggest why the significance
and function of music in Hardy's work go beyond its biographical
importance for the man himself, or its dramatic importance as an
element in countless scenes. Musical incidents never lost their binding
fascination for Hardy's imagination, since they offered him a dramatic
paradigm for those creative, affective and meditative augmentations of
the self that his work repeatedly represents, and produces. This remains
the case, however much the texts also depend on exploiting the often
fatal discordance between their sense of such possibilities, and the
novelist or poet's ultimate conclusion that the significance and promise
of such experiences are ultimately undone by the little ironies of life,
and the satires of circumstance.

Thus, to examine the elements of joy in 'The Darkling Thrush' is
not to deny the prevailingly sombre mood of the scene in the poem, nor
the dominant tenor of its conclusions and imagery. Indeed, because of
these features Peter Widdowson has pointed out that it is a poem which
has been deployed as a kind of model case, by those with an interest in
the ideologically limiting construction of Hardy as a pessimist. The

poem is taken as one which 'legitimizes the continued acceptance of despair as a reasonable - perhaps even exemplary - intellectual position'.[6] On this reading, scepticism, and age cannot attain to any 'blessed Hope', and the only lyres in the poem are the broken ones made up by the tangled bine-stems. Nonetheless, as Widdowson also emphasizes, Hardy's poetry in general can be seen as shot through with the 'opposite [...] capacity: to embrace happiness, hope, futurity, self-determination'. My concern here is to stress how this opposite strain manifests itself even in 'The Darkling Thrush' in various ways, contributing to the circulation between incommensurable attitudes and moments of experience that defines Hardy's poetic vision. While there is in the scene nothing to endorse the inconvenient and inconsequential promptings of joy that arise from the bird's 'carolings', the interesting fact is that the poem appears equally to encompass the contrary truth that these promptings are irresistible. They can be neither dismissed nor finally comprehended. Accordingly, the song of the bird sets up an oscillation, between the inspired and the grimly literal, that is evident in many and minute ways in the poem, as in the four lines below. There, the intricate felicities of sound and suggestion of the first two lines yield, in the last pair, to a more down to earth appraisal, a returning sense of the separated and drained elements of the scene:

> So little cause for carolings
> > Of such ecstatic sound
> Was written on terrestrial things
> > Afar or nigh around[...]

Further, it is certainly true that in hundreds of poems, and in nearly all the fiction, music provides a kind of *topos* for the scenes and plots which play out, arrange, these discordances of different qualities of feeling and of thought. Music recurrently, if temporarily, brings about an enhanced sense of individuality and affinity.

From such a viewpoint, it is a certain play of feeling and response which is seen to produce a poem, as Hardy seeks to convey the fluctuating qualities of an incident. By the same token, such an activity of writing brings about for a poet like Hardy a re-affirmation of his vocation. Hardy finds his own individuality through what he writes about, and the logic of this remark could even apply to the way in which the aged, wind-blown, thrush is itself a beleaguered figure of lyrical inspiration and tradition, a kind of alter-ego or counterpart whose song draws out Hardy the poet. The song of the thrush signals to Hardy the writer, because there remain within him characteristic susceptibilities and gifts of articulation which still find their echo within the insistent accents and movements of the bird. Whether the 'happy goodnight air' is really a song of hope or not, the poem is itself (for all its counterposed elements of an explicit disenchantment), a joyful manifestation of the ways Hardy's inimitable capabilities can surprise and displace the mind's conscious attitudes in a self-celebrating exercise of verbal accuracy:

> At once a voice arose among
>> The bleak twigs overhead
> In a full-hearted evensong
>> Of joy illimited;
> An aged thrush, frail, gaunt, and small,
>> In blast-beruffled plume,
> Had chosen thus to fling his soul
>> Upon the growing gloom. (*Complete Poems*, p. 150)

The bird's independent existence and his song appear not merely to move the poet, but to move him characteristically to a complementary artistic expression. The song transcends the poet's power of comprehension, but it reawakens his powers of response and writing. In this respect, there is a clear connection, as well as analogy, between the mysterious song of the bird, and this rediscovery which it entails in the poet of his own equally enigmatic capacities, not only of feeling, but of inspiration. What becomes important is not what the song means to the poet so much as what it *does* to him. And what it does, above all, unsought, is to evoke an affect of joy which in turn passes into the writing. Music binds together bird, poet and reader though transmissions that are as indubitable as they are unaccountable.

In such ways for Hardy self-expression operates out of unconscious moments of emotional connection or identification. Hardy's greatness in this respect resides in this ability to turn back and capture such fleeting and subliminal sensations of correspondence, and to place them at the heart of his writing. To take one more straightforward example of this, in a note dated May 30 1877, and reprinted in the *Life*, Hardy wrote:

> Walking to Marnhull. The prime of bird-singing. The thrushes and blackbirds are the most prominent, - pleading rather than singing, and with such modulation that you seem to see their little tongues curl inside their bills in their emphasis. A bullfinch sings from a tree with a metallic sweetness piercing as a fife.[7]

The birds' singing is once again an occasion both *of* art, and *for* art, as the moments of Hardy's attention are solicited by the implorings of the thrushes and blackbirds, and the intense notes of the bullfinch. The phased exactitude of language is accordingly the mark of a writerly concentration which seeks above all to render that inwardness with the birds which distinguished his sense of the encounter itself. Metaphor or simile are in this case for Hardy powers of nuance, not of interpretation. The writing strives to pass on the distinct qualities of the birds' tones as they strike the ear. Once again, the language articulates the physicality of Hardy's connection with the scene, recording his sense of its value, and perpetuating it in the reader. Indeed, it is even possible to indicate the main outlines of the book's argument in relation to this modest note, since it demonstrates clearly enough how, for Hardy, qualities of the individual spirit are forced into emergence by sensation and emotion. Creative thought, self-expression, are intimately a matter of opportune contingencies. As in 'The Darkling Thrush', the writing begins with the writer's sense of the possibilities of relation which seize him in the moment.

In pursuing this account of how Hardy's work investigates the unconscious basis of individuality in automatic responsiveness, in sensation and passion, I have found there to be suggestive connections and parallels between his work and the philosophical and aesthetic texts which came increasingly to interest him. Chapter Five probes Hardy's reading of such texts in detail, but of immediate interest here are the concrete ways in which Hardy's writing has its own philosophical dimensions, as it enacts and stages issues which were to surface time and again in the philosophy of his time and after. Hardy's work can even be described as a form of empiricism, as Gilles Deleuze has argued, insofar as thought for Hardy essentially has a bodily condition, and an external milieu.[8] The immediacy of music, as it dynamically associates bodies - as well as notes and sounds - within the uncertain time of the present, offers an image, as well as an occasion, for this notion of thought. So too, musical experience, as Hardy describes it, implicitly affirms a corresponding evaluation of life based on unconscious desire, and the associative work of the senses and the sympathies, rather than on *a priori* rational principles or moral prescriptions. In developing such points, it will be one strand of my argument to tease out the philosophical potentials of Hardy's work - the epistemological, aesthetic, ethical and political lines of enquiry enveloped within the pensive texture of Hardy's verse and prose.

Above all, this probing of the philosophical implications and suggestions of Hardy's writing is, to bring out the extraordinary power and fertility of his mind. At points, the clearer articulation of these features of Hardy's work will involve incidental references to a range of philosophical and literary theoretical works, both those which Hardy himself read, and those which have assisted in the readings offered in this book. While Gilles Deleuze is my primary reference in this latter respect, it would be possible to cite many other thinkers. For instance, Mikhail Bakhtin was concerned throughout his life with opening up literary and philosophical thinking of subjectivity to the pre-reflective, practical, interpersonal, activity of selfhood. Like Deleuze, Bakhtin was concerned with probing the gap between lived events and cognitive representations of them, with what Michael Holquist calls 'the sheer quality of happening in life before the magma of experience cools, hardening into igneous theories, or accounts of what has happened'.[9] In the very early, philosophically-orientated work, *Towards a Philosophy of the Act*, Bakhtin is concerned with 'aesthetic' moments (in perception, and implicitly in art itself) where an effect of inclusive and empathetic movement breaks up the static integrity of the subject-object relation:

> An essential moment (though not the only one) in aesthetic contemplation is empathizing into an individual object of seeing - seeing it from inside in its own essence. This moment of empathizing is always followed by a moment of objectification, that is, a placing *outside* oneself of the individuality understood through empathizing, a separating of it from oneself, a *return* into oneself [....]
> I empathize *actively* into an individuality and, consequently, I do not lose myself completely, nor my unique place outside it, even for a moment. It is not the object that unexpectedly takes possession of me as the passive one. It is *I* who empathize actively into the object: empathizing is *my* act, and only that constitutes its productiveness and newness (Schopenhauer and music). Empathizing actualizes something that did not exist either in the object of empathizing or in myself prior to the act of empathizing, and through this actualized something Being-as-event is enriched (that is does not remain equal to itself). (*Towards a Philosophy of the Act*, pp. 14 -15)

Ignoring for the most part the main thrust of Bakhtin's book as a technical incursion into Kantian philosophy, there are two especially useful points of intersection between this passage and the argument of this book.[10]

In the first place, Bakhtin's remarks suggest that artistic creativity and originality can in an 'essential' respect be conceived of in terms of an activity of thought that eludes the epistemology of the rational subject, and which has its basis in the truancies and empathetic projections of quotidian perception and feeling. In terms of our examples so far, the compelling sense of the birds in each case has little to do with a considered, cognitive relation to them, though much to do with a spontaneous sense of empathy that in turn generates an answering response in the reader, as well as involving for the writer an enlarged sense of self. A comparable moment occurs in *A Pair of Blue Eyes*, as Stephen and Elfride walk back to her home:

> Her blitheness won Stephen out of his thoughtfulness, and each forgot everything but the tone of the moment.
> 'What do you love me for?' she said, after a long musing look at a flying bird. (*A Pair of Blue Eyes*, p. 111)

His 'musing' on the flying bird in a way answers her question, since, as a case of empathy in this sense, it involves a contagious imaginative matching of the kind that drew him to her.[11] The bird's fluidity of movement attracts Stephen's look, as Elfride's own physical vitality and exuberance of movement had first attracted him:

> She looked so intensely *living* and full of movement as she came into the old silent place that young Stephen's world began to be lit by 'the purple light' in all its definiteness. (*A Pair of Blue Eyes*, p. 75)

The metaphysical and ethical overtones of such incidents of empathetic connection can be detected time and again in relation to music in Hardy's work. This is because music is seen by Hardy not simply as another vehicle for the transports of the soul, but also as an analogue for it. The soul, for Hardy, is itself an affair of resonances, reverberations, correspondences, expressive traits; and it betrays recurrently through its physical means its ideal nature, its individuality not merely compatible with, but inseparable from its altered states and qualities of feeling. Like a piece of music, the soul is actualized physically, and is essentially dependent, as in the scenes from *A Pair of Blue Eyes*, on the externality and agency of those individuals and events which revive it: through such associations and accidental incarnations it reveals, on the one hand, differing tones and aspects, new suggestions and effects; and, on the other, it reveals its virtual essence that insists behind these variations like their enigmatic and unrepresented theme. One could be tempted to say on this basis, in line with current critical parlance, that self-hood in Hardy's fiction is 'performative', so long as it is stressed once again, how necessarily involuntary, interpersonal and accidental such manifestations of self-hood are.

In the second place, Bakhtin's larger argument can also be seen as at least suggesting that it is a necessity of art to capture and recapitulate the play of meanings, the possibilities of relationship and expression, which appear obscurely encoded in affective and sensory experience. For the reader of Hardy's poetry, these spontaneous movements of mind and feeling, and their divisions from the workings of reflection, are played out in endless ways, and in the forms of expression as well as the forms of content. In terms of content, we saw above how reading 'The Darkling Thrush' involved entering into the momentary delight or reverie of the speaker, before finding that these possibilities are denied by reflection.[12] In terms of expression, too, the reader finds that a corresponding reduction attends the possibilities of the poem's language - all those singular, variable and unresolved aspects of significance and sound which tend to flicker or fade inconsequentially amidst the gathering gloom of the critic's returning conscious sense of fact, commentary and paraphrase.

At this point it is possible to offer an outline of the four main chapters that follow, in terms of this broad problematic between self-conscious subjectivity and what Hardy calls the 'soul'. Chapter 1 looks at Hardy's idea of how the soul is expressed physically, through bodily sensations and changing affective states, and it concentrates on how this is evident in the fiction. The discussion traces the shifting role of music in the development of Hardy's tragic vision: briefly, in the earlier fiction, music is a positive accessory to the narratives of love and community which are offered, whereas in the later novels and tales, it tends to take on a more symbolic function, confirming and defining the developing tragic view. Chapter 2 looks at Hardy's examination in the fiction of different aspects of the effects of transport brought about by music. The discussion pursues the underlying conception of unconscious experience involved, and a range of inter-related issues - ethical, epistemological and aesthetic - which arise out of the readings. It links these issues with related general topics, most importantly perhaps, Hardy's fictional representation of sexual difference. In the two chapters on the poetry which follow, there is a corresponding concentration in each on a particular way in which the conscious self is surprised or perturbed by the reanimating potentials of music. In Chapter 3, the main topic is inspiration, in Chapter 4, it is memory. In both chapters, Hardy's relations to other poets and the reader become important: in the one case in terms of ideas of influence; in the other in terms of ideas of literary tradition and posterity. Similarly, in both chapters, Hardy's own uses of sound and management of metre become considered according to these different emphases.

With respect to these issues of poetic creativity, technique and tradition, one can consider how the thrush (battered and worn though he is) figures through his song the inevitable uplift for the lyric poet as he is once again brought to write. John Lucas, asks of Hardy, and as it were against a general conception of the prevailing modes and tones of his work, 'why shouldn't he rejoice in the sheer delight of making'[?], and reminds us of how Florence Hardy:

> told one visitor to Max Gate that her husband was upstairs writing a miserable poem 'and thoroughly enjoying himself'.[13]

The excitement which the bird produces in the poem connects Hardy with those earlier poets who were also summoned by birds, and whose modified tones, rhythm and diction echo variously within 'The Darkling Thrush'. The poem is, however mutedly, a bugle-call, signalling to a virtual community made up of the readers and poets it addresses, as well as of those earlier poets to whom it responds. In many ways, musical ideas - such as these to do with sound, making, song - indicate aspects of how poetry itself has the power, in common with music, to transcend the constraints of identity and time. Working in their common medium of sound, both poetry and music call on powers of expression which are both utterly individual, and yet which in essential ways by-pass the consciousness of the artist.

Chapter 5 revisits more explicitly, and in a different context, many of the philosophical issues raised by the account of Hardy's work in terms of this see-saw between sensation and reflection, between inspiration and sober reason. Certainly, the lowering of the spirits which is characteristic of conscious deliberation in Hardy's work, suggests one reason why Hardy tended in his moments of philosophical stock-taking to be increasingly and regretfully drawn to a defensive philosophical scepticism, even pessimism. Michael Millgate, noting how in mid life 'the general direction' of Hardy's thought was 'becoming increasingly pessimistic and disenchanted', cites a telling passage, written in May 1886:

> Reading in the British Museum. Have been thinking over the dictum of Hegel - that the real is the rational and the rational the real - that real pain is compatible with formal pleasure - that the idea is all, etc., but it doesn't help much. These venerable

philosophers seem to start wrong; they cannot get away from a prepossession that the world must somehow have been made to be a comfortable place for man. If I remember, it was Comte who said that metaphysics was a mere sorry attempt to reconcile theology and physics.[14]

Hardy's pessimism was predicated, one might say, on a similar conviction of a split between the world of objectivity, and the world of feeling. Undoubtedly he would have been impervious to any Hegelian attempt to redeem this, by subsuming the excitations and commotions of the heart within an idealist philosophy centred on the rational mind. But neither does Hardy's pessimism mean, as some have argued, that he is a sort of literary Schopenhauer, since his gloomy, often sententious, reflections are the product not of a consistent metaphysics, but of a cast of mind characterized, as Bayley put it above, by his vision of experience as divided and uncoordinated. In general, Hardy was temperamentally distrustful of the closed-off nature of philosophical systems, of theories and attitudes which dictate presumptuously to experience. A typical moment of sceptical rumination occurs in a letter in 1915. He closes with the statement, as against those who would counter 'Herbert Spencer's doctrine of the unknowable':

> I am utterly bewildered to understand how the doctrine that, beyond the knowable, there must always be an unknown, can be displaced. (*Life*, p. 370)

However, while Hardy's was not a philosopher's mind, it was as Deleuze suggested, a philosophical one. For all the obvious cautions which must attach to his labelling of Hardy as an empiricist, the label has the merit of drawing together some of the constitutive ways in which Hardy's mind works.[15] Specifically, it can direct attention to how the writing itself, through its material media, constantly releases implications, stimulates questions, encompasses possibilities, at the same time as its scenes depict how thought is generated from events of sensation and feeling. Where philosophy describes or explains an empiricist conception of mind, Hardy's writing can be said to dramatize and produce it, enacting a creative form of thinking that preserves its essential relations to the possibilities of the immediate. In this context, Chapter 5 concentrates on those contemporaneous philosophical thinkers whose anti-rationalist work Hardy was interested in, figures such as William James, Schopenhauer, Bergson, von Hartmann, and others. These are writers whose concern resides fundamentally with achieving a higher level of consciousness about the unconscious intelligence, and emotion.

One can illustrate the connections between such a way of thinking of experience, and the experience of thinking, so to speak, that we are offered by reading Hardy the poet, by turning to another very short poem about a bird and its music. 'The Caged Goldfinch' is a poem in which philosophical questions and possibilities throng and multiply, providing the obvious topic of the poem - the inescapable facts of the caged bird's suffering - with a rich atmosphere of suggestion:

> Within a churchyard, on a recent grave,
>   I saw a little cage
> That jailed a goldfinch. All was silence save
>   Its hops from stage to stage.
>
> There was inquiry in its wistful eye,
>   And once it tried to sing;
>   Of him or her who placed it there, and why,
>   No one knew anything. (*Complete Poems*, p. 436)

Outrage as to the bird's plight in the poem, and the sickening sense of horror we share at what we assume to be its imminent death, alternate with curiosity as to who placed it there, and with speculation as to the deceased's love for the bird.[16] In this way the poem, through the types of mystery and ignorance which are implicit in the situation, starts to proliferate lines of reading and response which do not cancel each other out, but which spread out into a more generalized and inclusive sense of the disharmonies of existence. These resonating possibilities ramify and connect within the overall affective dimension of hopelessness which the poem sets up. Intense distress seems to condition the desire to understand, for the onlookers and the reader, as well as for the bird even, since its predicament has divided it from its innate capacities for expressiveness, for movement and song and interaction. It has been forced into 'wistful' and pathetic inquiry, as the onlookers are caught in unresolved and fascinated musing. The potentially joyous matching of thrush and hearer that underlay the other poem has here become determinedly tragic.

Bleak as 'The Caged Goldfinch' is, though, it implies in a negative way another kind of unity of diversity. This is the saddened community of those who are shocked involuntarily into thought and feeling by the bird:

> Of him or her who placed it there, and why,

No one knew anything.

We imagine individuals lingering for a moment, out of an obscure necessity to exchange some remarks corresponding to their sense of all that is disquieting and somehow implicating about the scene. Contrary feelings of shame and indignation whirl around in the atmosphere of bafflement and dismay. Consequently it seems for the onlookers that their remarks, like their actions, are in themselves desultory, inadequate and inconsequential. There is so much to say, and nothing to be said. Those who stand by the scene, like those who read about it, are caught between staying and turning their backs on something that cannot be helped. Nevertheless, as this indicates, Hardy's poem depends for its full effect on renovating certain innate powers of sympathy. These condition an enlarged sense of inquiry, even as, at the same time, the situation seems in itself, in another aspect, merely dispiritingly hopeless and brutally simple.

In such ways ethical, social and epistemological lines of questioning begin to be mobilized by the bird's plight, as in other poems about the suffering of birds, poems like 'The Puzzled Game-Birds', 'The Blinded Bird', or 'The Bird-Catcher's Boy'. In these cases, human indifference, perversity, and cruelty are more markedly and incontrovertibly elements of the scenario, so much so that 'human' and 'inhuman' become almost interchangeable terms. Pained as they are, the poems seem designed to reverberate with philosophical questions. In the first of these poems, for instance, the simple word 'house' in the phrase, 'If hearts can house such treachery' vibrates with the Nietzschean possibility that civilization merely provides a kind of domestic front for all kinds of internalized violence which in turn sustain it:

> They are not those who used to feed us
> When we were young - they cannot b ? -
> These shapes that now bereave and bleed us?
> They are not those who used to feed us,
> For did we then cry, they would heed us.
> - If hearts can house such treachery
> They are not those who used to feed us
> When we are young - they cannot be! (*Complete Poems*, p. 148)

In these respects, Hardy's 'moments of vision' are also 'visionary moments': the intense emotion that attends the registration of facts opens up alternative possibilities of value and the ideal. Like music, the poems offer expansions of thought and sympathy, working through the manifold and elliptical promptings of feeling rather than through merely cognitive certainties. In so doing, they bear out Edward Thomas's suggestion, apropos of 'Song to an Old Burden', that Hardy's verse possesses for the reader 'something which the intellect alone cannot handle'.[17] There is a useful comparison here with James Ireby's description of Jorge Luis Borges's conception of the aesthetic phenomenon as deriving from a disturbing emotion, and as consisting in the '"imminence of a revelation that is not yet produced": a kind of expanding virtuality of thought, an unresolved yet centrally focussed multiplicity of views'.[18]

Before closing this introduction with some remarks about the fiction, it is useful to consider the larger issue of critical reading which is raised by this immediate discussion (as well as by the main topic itself, that of Hardy's uses of music in both the poetry and the fiction). This issue announces itself in so far as Hardy's poetry, for all its textual open-endedness, appears to me to be resistant to most of the critically available, theoretically governed, modes of reading that similarly would connect up philosophical issues of the subject with the contrary and incommensurable 'materiality' of the unconscious and the text itself. One can contrast, for instance, the approach in this book with a highly suggestive book by Daniel C. Melnick which too deals directly with music, *Fullness of Dissonance: Modern Fiction and the Aesthetics of Music*. Broadly, Melnick's account construes the discordances of nineteenth- and twentieth-century texts in terms of modernist (and proto-modernist) aesthetics of dissonance. In matters of theory, Melnick draws mostly on Theodor Adorno's *Introduction to the Sociology of Music*:

> Dissonance, in Adorno's conception, constitutes a key modernist strategy designed to oppose and overcome what he calls 'the deceptive moment' in the reception of conventional art: the moment in which the 'self-limited' audience is made to feel 'in accord with all, accepted and reconciled by all,' a moment designed falsely and uncritically to seem 'to fulfil men in themselves, to train them for consent' within the order of modern society.[19]

It would be true to say that a poem like 'The Darkling Thrush' refuses to underwrite such simple messages and effects of reconciliation, and preserves something like what Melnick calls a 'dynamic joining of utopian yearning with critical negativity' (*Fullness of Dissonance*, p. 9), as it hovers between hope and gloom. For Melnick, then, dissonance is a kind of master-figure (or anti-figure) for literary texts which give:

form to a declaration of ongoing process and tension, to the refusal to resolve, to the denial of the sense of conventional ending in harmony. (*Fullness of Dissonance*, p. 8)

However, could we dismiss the positive unfoldings of selfhood and mind in these poems as 'deceptive moments', of ideological mystification, or as 'utopian yearnings'? Further, Melnick's account appears in terminology and tone itself overly programmatic, even apocalyptic, when put alongside the scrupulous and watchful provisionality of a Hardy poem. Alternatively, it could be said that a deconstructive reading, such as Paul de Man practised, might trace in Hardy's writing a problematic of reading which could be made to correspond to this sense of the sceptical and provisional. However, once again there would seem to be a discrepancy between the conclusive sense of the intractable which would ultimately emerge from such a reading - applied, for instance, to 'The Darkling Thrush' - and the pleasure involved in the text, the real and undeflectable sense of joy which it stages, and transfers to the reader, as we have seen, through the subdued virtuosity and variations of its language. Adopting a de Manian mode might lead to ascetic talk about a poem's 'pathos' or the poet's 'predicament', but this would swallow up Hardy's productive kinds of unknowing and self-division. The parenthetical sense of hope whose necessity is at the heart of the poem could not survive the labyrinthine workings of de Man's *a priori* - the mutual interference of rhetoric and grammar which provides thought, for de Man, with its unhappy linguistic condition.

As against this Heideggerian metaphysics (or anti-metaphysics), then, Deleuze's work has offered what have seemed to me alternative, and useful and workable, ways of considering the image of mind that operates in Hardy's writing. For Deleuze, thought is materially conducted through the senses: affects and sensations, states and intensities of the body correspond to the mind's connection to its outside, as the various faculties of thought are forced into operation. Deleuze's key idea of 'becoming' is fundamental, as a conceptualization of the ways individual bodies are linked, destructively and creatively, by physical relations. Music can offer a specific case of this general concept in practice, since it produces effects of correspondence between individual bodies, catching them up into a larger passage or rhythm, and compounding their powers of relating and sensing. The listeners or performers participate in an event which works outside of the customary limits and traits of conscious identity, and produces new motifs of self-expression and thought. Thus, self-hood is confirmed primarily as self-improvisation or self-differentiation, as 'individuation' in Deleuze's use of the term.

To apply this general idea of becoming to our running example, the imaginative premiss of 'The Darkling Thrush' could be said to lie in this mystery of the echo which the bird's far-flung song finds in the poet's 'soul'. The relation of poet and bird is more a matter or resonance or attunement - of physical correspondences which indicate and embody ideal possibilities of relatedness - than of intelligible communication. Within the poem, the irreducible differences in kind - between man, bird and the elements of the landscape - nonetheless become the condition of a response of fellow-feeling which is in itself utterly unfathomable, as well as utterly ordinary. Certainly, from a philosophical point of view (as with 'The Caged Goldfinch'), all kinds of questions about identity, humanity, nature, congregate in the poem, as we have suggested, but more fundamentally than this, the poem's scene and language are concerned with the production of what Deleuze would call 'a bloc of becoming', where:

> it is not one term which becomes the other, but each encounters the other, a single becoming which is not common to the two since they have nothing to do with one another, but which is between the two, which has its own direction, a bloc of becoming, an a-parallel evolution. (*Dialogues*, p. 7)

'The Darkling Thrush', that is, is a poem in which Hardy is intrigued, in the first place, by the ways in which the bird's very unknowability - its obliviousness to the poet himself, its different type of feeling - is the condition for an unpremeditated encounter of sound in which the poet finds, nonetheless, a characteristic inspiration and affective summons.

The last point to stress about this conception of becoming is that it makes the body the primary instrument of thought, and relegates reflective consciousness to being merely a secondary effect of thought, a relative and centripetal function of interior rumination. In this aspect, we could link this belatedness of cognition (*vis-à-vis* affective responsiveness and sensibility) in the poem to the larger sense of belatedness which afflicts the poetic persona in 'The Darkling Thrush' at the end of the year (as an old man, a post-Romantic, post-Christian, post-nineteenth-century, poet).

In turning to the fiction, similarly, the study of Hardy's representation of music allows for an examination of the non-rational bases of experience in corporeality and sympathy. The essential importance for Hardy himself of this latter idea is suggested by the double-underlining of the word, 'sympathise', in the following quotation from Trollope in the notebooks:

> No novel is anything, for comedy or tragedy, unless the reader can <u>sympathise</u> with the characters.[20]

Although there are various forms of Hardyan narrative sympathy (and empathy) the following extract usefully introduces common elements. In Chapter 13 of *Tess of the d'Urbervilles*, after the initial unhappiness of her pregnancy, Tess goes to church, taking a back seat so as to escape the attentions of young men:

> She liked to hear the chanting - such as it was - and the Old Psalms, and to join in the Morning Hymn. That innate love of melody, which she had inherited from her ballad-singing mother, gave the simplest music a power over her which could well-nigh drag her heart out of her bosom at times.[21]

and it continues:

> When the chants came on one of her favourites happened to be chosen among the rest - the old double chant 'Langdon' - but she did not know what it was called, though she would much have liked to know. She thought, without exactly wording the thought, how strange and godlike was a composer's power, who from the grave could lead through sequences of emotion, which he alone had felt at first, a girl like her who had never heard of his name, and never would have a clue to his personality. (*Tess*, p. 81)

Tess's impressionability as far as music is concerned is identified with a forgetfulness of circumstances, as she is momentarily absorbed in it before people in the church begin to whisper about her. Again, music is identified with a power to overcome time, as Tess feels the enduring influence of this 'old favourite', and ponders the paradoxes by which, through his music, a composer can conquer mortality. For the reader, this absorption on Tess's part finds an answer in a kind of mingling in her enjoyment which seems to dissolve our difference from her. Our objective sense of her predicament yields to a participation within the feelings and impressions associated with music. Her affectibility has further aspects, identified as it is with what seem essential features of her individuality, revealed in her 'innate love of melody', here rekindled in the midst of harsh circumstances. It is also involved firmly with Tess's sense of her own participation in other lives: with her mother's own love of music that has been passed down to her; with the

communal activity of singing in the Church; and with the inner life of
the composer which is expressed in music in ways described as defiant
to strict logic:

> She thought, without exactly wording the thought, how strange
> and godlike was a composer's power, who from the grave could
> lead through sequences of emotion, which he alone had felt at
> first, a girl like her who had never heard of his name, and never
> would have a clue to his personality.

Although Tess is initially enclosed in her sense of her predicament, the
narrative restores our sympathetic connection with her, largely by this
representing of her experience of music as itself a form of imaginative
and interpersonal connection.

Even in this scene, then, the writing works out of a disjunction
between a forlorn and unsparing sense of circumstances hanging over
the scene, and a forgetful, enlivening, response to an ideal sense of
things which is associated with music. Although, in truth, the
predominant aura of the scene is tragic, the narrative follows
movement of feeling by which the grimly determined aspects of the text
and its narration, and the customary forms and demarcations of
subjectivity, are momentarily displaced. Of course, within the world of
the novel, Tess's aspirations and feelings are condemned to remain
within the realm of the merely possible, and are subject to crushing
extinction on the part of custom and violence. However, the point, as
with the earlier discussions of the poems, it that the feelings, and the
possibilities of association which they embody, are real and crucial to
living.

This sense of perpetual, yet tragic, readiness appears also to be
what Hardy responds to most deeply about Tess's predicament, and
perhaps what was particularly in his mind when he conceived of her as
a 'pure woman'. Indeed, the tragic for Hardy is just this division
between possibility and fact. It is a division which is conceived, from
the aesthetic meditations of the mid-1880s onwards, as a dissociation of
the ideal and the real, and can be connected to the famous
pronouncement in the *Life* that, 'My art is to intensify the expression of
things' (*Life*, p. 177). The tragic aspect of the dissociation emerges in
another image of caged birds, in a further note from 1885 from the *Life*
where Hardy broods cheerlessly on the superficiality of London life:

> The people in this tragedy laugh, sing, smoke, toss off wines etc.,
> make love to girls in drawing-rooms and areas; and yet are
> playing their parts in the tragedy just the same. Some wear jewels

and feathers, some wear rags. All are caged birds; the only difference lies in the size of the cage. This too is part of the tragedy. (*Life*, p. 171)

This is certainly pessimistic in tone, but it is as well, in closing, to place it against a typical statement in which Hardy shows his exasperation with the image of him as a merely dejected sceptic. In the 'Apology' to 'Late Lyrics and Earlier' he affirms the 'questionings' which he sees as distinctive, even formative, of his poems. He links such an emphasis on unknowing with an ethical attitude which values 'the soul's betterment, and the body's also':

Heine observed nearly a hundred years ago that the soul has her eternal rights; that she will not be darkened by statutes, nor lullabied by the music of bells. And what is to-day, in allusions to the present author's pages, alleged to be 'pessimism' is, in truth, only such 'questionings' in the exploration of reality, and is the first step towards the soul's betterment, and the body's also [...] (*Complete Poems*, p. 557)

Notes

¹ John Bayley, *An Essay on Hardy* (Cambridge: Cambridge University Press, 1978), p. 40.

² Thomas Hardy, *The Complete Poems* (edited by James Gibson, London: Macmillan, 1976), p. 150.

³ So there will be many points in the discussions which follow where I acknowledge the influential work of the many critics (Grundy, Pinion, Gatrell, Shelman, Mitchell, and Jackson-Houlston among them) who have offered this direct kind of engagement with music in Hardy's work.

⁴ Bayley distinguishes Hardy from writers such as Powys, Lawrence and Faulkner for whose readers:

> [d]isappointment, if it comes, is thus a complete thing: a boredom with, or alienation from, the text. In Hardy, disappointment is a reaction much more intimate and intermingled, which may turn out to present itself as an actual asset, a greater clarity in the experience of the pleasure. (*An Essay on Hardy*, p. 4)

⁵ One could rehearse here all the commonplaces about Hardy's unlikeable personal costiveness, his creepy, snobbish ardours, his pessimism, his coldness to Emma, and so on...; as well as a suspicion of all the accompanying critical prejudices about his stylistic or poetic unevennesses. To these images, we could add other unflattering biographical images which often reinforce obstructive critical prejudices - Hardy the self-educated vulgarian parading his learning; Hardy the Ambitious, concealing his humble origins; Hardy the village-idiot philosopher, in G. K. Chesterton's phrase ('Thomas Hardy', *Illustrated London News*, Vol. clxxii [21 January 1928], p. 94). In Chapter 3 I discuss the critical opprobrium which has attached itself to the poetry, but the formal and expressive aspects of the fiction have attracted their equal share of influential disparagements, often in the work of otherwise appreciative critics. Katherine Anne Porter wrote of how his 'prose lumbers along, it jogs, it creaks' ('Notes on a Criticism of Thomas Hardy', *Southern Review*, Vol. 6 [Autumn 1940], p. 161), Irving Howe lamented the autodidact's 'pretentiousness of style' (*Thomas Hardy* [London: Weidenfeld and Nicolson, 1968], p. 59), while Lord David Cecil wrote that '[n]o amount of painstaking study got him within sight of achieving that intuitive good taste, that instinctive grasp of the laws of literature, which is the native heritage of one bred from childhood in the atmosphere of a high culture' (*Hardy the Novelist* [London: Constable, 1943], p. 146). Without diminishing the partial truth of such clichés, it is productive to loosen their mesmirizing hold, so as to offer a fuller sense of Hardy's writing, its ways of working, and its subtle pleasures. In the following two chapters, I discuss more recent work by critics (like Wootton, Widdowson, Goode, and Eagleton) who have adopted a more sympathetic approach to Hardy's formal dissonances, and whose arguments are broadly compatible with Raymond Williams's earlier reassessment of Hardy's fictional modes. Williams sees Hardy's divided writing modes as an expression of 'the alienation, the frustration, the separation and isolation', of his social dislocation. (*The English Novel from Dickens to Lawrence* [London: Chatto and Windus, 1970], p. 97.) This book argues for a view of Hardy's disjunctions, and shifts in mood and tone, that is informed by these critics (as by others like Bayley). Specifically, the view is that these features are to be seen no longer as personal or aesthetic shortcomings, but a function of how his writing operates back and forth

across the division between conscious and bodily experience. In content and expression, Hardy's writing importantly both represents these experiential passages and performs them.

⁶ Thomas Hardy, *Selected Poetry and Non-Fictional Prose* (edited by Peter Widdowson, London: Macmillan, 1997), p. 215.

⁷ Florence Emily Hardy, *The Life of Thomas Hardy* (London: Macmillan, 1962), pp. 113-14.

⁸ See for instance the discussion of Hardy in *Dialogues* by Deleuze and Claire Parnet (translated by Hugh Tomlinson and Barbara Habberjam, London: Athlone, 1987), p. 40.

⁹ Michael Holquist, Introduction to Mikhail Bakhtin, *Towards a Philosophy of the Act* (translated by Vadim Liapunov, edited by Michael Holquist and Vadim Liapunov, Austin: University of Texas, 1993), p. x.

¹⁰ So a Bakhtin scholar might point out that Bakhtin's discussion of the 'aesthetic' here is only secondarily concerned with aesthetic activity as such, and bears most directly on unresolved issues in the Kantian architectonic (to do with feeling and intuition, and their relation to understanding, in the first Critique, and ethical situatedness in the second). While the analysis above centres on questions of empathy and artistic creation, one could point out the larger links between it and those aspects of it which connect up with Deleuze's work, and with this book: in his probing of Kant's work, and its formalism, Bakhtin, like Deleuze, is concerned with the singularity of actual events, and the concrete, differentiated kinds of individuality, and relatedness, which their participants reveal.

¹¹ Of course, the look could equally be read as 'her' look or as both of theirs, in each case with similar consequences for my reading here.

¹² Bayley's comments, as to the emotional effect the poem 'always' has for him, indicates clearly how inevitable and recurrent this is.

¹³ John Lucas, 'Hardy Among the Poets', *Critical Survey*, Vol. 5, no. 2 (Oxford: Oxford University Press, 1993), p. 201.

¹⁴ Michael Millgate, *Thomas Hardy* (Oxford: Oxford University Press, 1982), p. 270.

¹⁵ Deleuze saw such an empiricist practice as characteristic of Anglo-American literature in general ways. See, for instance, Chapter 1 of *Dialogues*, 'On the Superiority of Anglo-American Literature'.

¹⁶ Interestingly, Hardy cut from the published version of the poem a verse that identified the bird as possibly a jilted lover's gift:

True, a woman was found drowned the day ensuing,
    And some at times averred
The grave to be her false one's, who when wooing
    Gave her the bird. *The Complete Poetical Works of Thomas Hardy*, Vol. II (edited by Samuel Hynes, Oxford: Oxford University Press, 1984), p. 234.

¹⁷ Edward Thomas, *A Language Not to Be Betrayed: Selected Prose* (selected by Edna Longley, Manchester: Carcanet, 1981), p. 70.

¹⁸ James E. Ireby, Introduction to Jorge Luis Borges, *Other Inquisitions, 1937-1952* (translated by Ruth L. C. Simms, London: Souvenir, 1973), p. x.

¹⁹ Daniel C. Melnick, *Fullness of Dissonance* (London: Associated University Presses, 1994), p. 9.

[20] *The Literary Notebooks of Thomas Hardy, Volume 1* (edited by Lennart A Björk, New York: New York University Press, 1985), p. 164.

[21] Thomas Hardy, *Tess of the d'Urbervilles* (London: Dent, 1984), p. 80.

Chapter 1

'Souls Unreconciled to Life'

An acknowledgment of Hardy's prevalent and acute awareness of the often absurd, or crushing, conditions of life must be qualified by a recognition that his texts are always contrarily animated by a sense of the expressive needs and possibilities of individuals. In a comment recorded in the *Life*, dated November 1891, Hardy identifies the process of writing itself with this conflict between the outwardly-orientated motions of the 'soul' and the returning consciousness of life itself, a conflict now explicitly given a tragic inflection:

> The highest flights of the pen are mostly the excursions and revelations of souls unreconciled to life. (*Life*, p. 240)

Dispirited, withdrawn, though the tone of the remark is, the clear implication is still that the truth of the soul is revealed through such 'flights'. This is so, although such passages are fated to fall back into a scheme of things more adapted to depressive, objective, and customary kinds of thinking.

In this chapter, musical experience provides a key for unlocking how fundamental such 'excursions and revelations' were for Hardy the novelist. Throughout his fictional career, music was associated by him with a mode of self-expression that is both physical and ideal: physical in that it relies on accidents of sensation and feeling, but also ideal in that it reveals these essential qualities of the 'soul'. This idea of individuality, and the notions of affective relatedness and involuntary response that it presupposes, provides the chapter with its central thread. In the second half of the chapter the oscillation between exhilaration and grim, hopeless, introspection is considered not only as a feature of Hardy's own way of seeing, but also as marking the fundamental shift in mode and temper within his novel-writing career, and the closing sections develop, through their differing treatment of musical experience, how the early and late novels contrast in terms of Hardy's darkening consciousness of the possibilities of self-expression.

I

The ratio between the ideal and the real can be detected in Hardy's recurrent identification of music with a vocabulary, evident in 'The Darkling Thrush', in which music is written about in terms of joy, hope and the soul. 'Soul' is a favourite word of Hardy's in these and connected contexts, one which refers to a quality of individuality that he was always concerned to observe and convey:

> You may regard a throng of people as containing a certain small minority who have sensitive souls; these, and the aspects of these, being what is worth observing. So you divide them into the mentally unquickened, mechanical, soulless; and the living, throbbing, suffering, vital. In other words, into souls and machines, ether and clay. (*Life*, pp. 185-186)

The interest in the soul is identified with a susceptibility or sensitivity that provokes the same qualities in the observer, as in the observation about the sympathetic (and sympathizing) trumpet-major, that 'gallant musician' whose 'soul was so much disturbed by tender vibrations'.[1] Some such criterion is evident also in a remark such as the following, in which the operations of literary language are identified as addressed to those who can adequately respond to its fleeting resonances and intimations:

> I must trust for right note-catching to those finely-touched spirits who can divine without half a whisper, whose intuitiveness is proof against all the accidents of inconsequence.[2]

A useful point of access into these areas of Hardy's work is provided by an enigmatic note in the *Life*, dated 25 June 1887. Writes Hardy:

> At a concert at Prince's Hall I saw Souls outside Bodies. (*Life*, p. 201)

As with many such interpolations in the *Life*, the remark intrigues the reader by its brevity and oddity of expression. It seems imbued with personal significances which are, nonetheless, withheld, and to which the reader must attempt to attune himself, herself. If we pause to reflect on this initially bemusing note, the first thought would be that the souls and bodies which fascinated Hardy were, we might suspect, predominantly female. At that moment the reader begins to enter imaginatively into the incident, and Hardy's response to it, and to glean, too, something of the motive behind Hardy's wanting to remember the incident by writing it down, as well as of his adopting a cryptic expression. Cannily oblique, even voyeuristic, as the note is, it seems to have a whole poem wrapped up potentially within it, and something of Hardy's own remembered intentness at the incident begins eerily to pass into the reader.

More generally, as in this note, Hardy often identifies music with a power to induce movements of the soul outside of the body. In 'The Fiddler of the Reels', the narrator writes of Mop's power to move sensitive children to tears, and of the way in which '[o]ccasionally Mop could produce the aforesaid moving effect upon the souls of grown-up persons',[3] playing the fiddle so 'as to draw your soul out of your body like a spider's thread' (*Stories*, Vol. 2, p. 127). Again, we have seen a similar emphasis, when the narrator comments on Tess in terms of how:

> That innate love of melody, which she had inherited from her ballad-singing mother, gave the simplest music a power over her which could well-nigh drag her heart out of her bosom at times. (*Tess*, p. 80)

The word 'soul' is used again of another encounter in the *Life*, one which passed into poetry, an encounter with a salvation army girl whom he met at midnight on February 4, 1894, 'beating a tambourine and dancing. She looked like one of the "angelic quire", who had tumbled down out of the sky, and', he continues rather disingenuously (as if the oddity of the incident were the reason for recalling it), 'I could hardly believe my eyes', before adding, tellingly, 'Not a soul was there but her and myself' (*Life*, p. 262).

Such musical incidents appear especially memorable for Hardy. It does not seem possible as yet to be more precise about the meaning of the word 'soul' for him, other than to reiterate that in listening to music, the soul is said somehow to leave the body. My main point in describing Hardy's uses of music, however, is that music, in ways obviously reminiscent of his description above of literary language, is itself described as something that passes between your soul and that of another person, catching up both in a common movement or accord that surprises our sense of purely physical and subjective separation.[4] It involves an expression of relatedness whose transports involve a certain absent-mindedness and indefinite duration, as during the concert at Sturminster in 1878, where he reported in the *Life* that:

> [a] 'Miss Marsh [...] sang "Should he upbraid", to Bishop's old
> tune. She is the sweetest of singers - thrush-like in the descending
> scale, and lark-like in the ascending - drawing out the soul of
> listeners in a gradual thread of excruciating attenuation like silk
> from a cocoon'. (*Life*, p. 118)

So too, even for Jude music can seem like a signal, of expressions of the
soul, of community and the future:

> Suddenly there came along this wind something towards him - a
> message from the place - from some soul residing there, it seemed.
> Surely it was the sound of bells, the voice of the city, faint and
> musical, calling to him, 'We are happy here!'
>   He had become entirely lost to his bodily situation during this
> mental leap, and only got back to it by a rough recalling.[5]

Of course, within the ironic world of this novel, such effects of music in
fact merely encourage a fated and forlorn hope or projection of
relatedness, as when Jude visits the composer of the hymn that moved
him so much, intending to confide in him only to discover that the man
is moving into the more lucrative intoxications of the wine trade:

> It took Jude more than by surprise that the man with the soul was
> thus and thus; and he felt he could not open up his confidences.
> (*Jude*, p. 216)

And, similarly, when Jude's soul can be said finally to leave his body,
it is to the ironic sounds of music, the bells and organ concert and
waltzes which punctuate his dying remarks. The piano which no-one
can play on the novel's opening page, and about which the characters
all gather in static and perplexed attitudes, in a scene framed in the
foursquare blocks of the syntax and paragraphs, seems an appropriate
image of the novel's sardonic intensification of the experience of lost
community and relatedness, as well as of its insistence on attendant and
ironically construed problems of movement. However, the wrenching
black humour in these episodes has as its background also a belief in
the ineradicability of the hopes to which music appears to testify. The
more repeatedly Hardy piles on the satire, the more the ghastly
hollowness of the laughter has as its condition the pathos of an affective
inclination now increasingly dissociated from any belief in its
realization, yet which must repeat itself. Again, one could cite the
following example from *The Well-Beloved*, as Pierston talks to Nicola

Pine-Avon, conscious both of his feeling for her, and a sense of his own ridiculousness:

> They talked over the day's news, and then an organ began to grind outside. The tune was a rollicking air he had heard at some music-hall; and, by way of a diversion, he asked her if she knew the composition.
> 'No, I don't!' she replied.
> 'Now, I'll tell you all about it,' said he gravely. 'It is based on a sound old melody called "The Jilt's Hornpipe". Just as they turn Madeira into port in the space of a single night, so this old air has been taken and doctored, and twisted about and brought out as a new popular ditty.'[6]

The mechanical organ, grinding a hollowed-out version of an old tune, appropriately called 'The Jilt's Hornpipe', appears as a pitiless and crude musical metaphor for the way in which Pierston's particular form of idealism is subject to increasing kinds of mockery in the text. He becomes a shell of his former self, compelled by merely repetitive affective promptings in whose realization he no longer believes. These have long been a torment to him, as is evident in his conscious employment of the image of the well-beloved's departures from '[E]ach mournful empty shape' which 'stands ever after like the nest of some beautiful bird from which the inhabitant has departed and left it to fill with snow' (*The Well-Beloved*, p. 40).

An apparent contrast would be with the fullness and centrality and romance of the representation of music in *Tess*, as in the important example of this noted also by Caroline Jackson-Houlston in her article on Hardy's use of traditional songs and ballads in Hardy's work.[7] This is the scene where Angel first becomes aware of Tess, and selects her from the others as the object of his attentions. Looking over a music score, Clare is oblivious to the 'particulars' of the outward scene which 'did not strike him as possessing a new note'. Then, as it were, he begins to pass into this outward scene, hearing the domestic objects that surround him as musical instruments: 'the half-empty kettle whining an accompaniment' and so on. Next we read:

> The conversation at the table mixed in with his phantasmal orchestra till he thought: 'What a fluty voice one of those milkmaids has! I suppose it is the new one.'
> Clare looked round upon her, seated with the others.
> She was not looking towards him. Indeed, owing to his long silence, his presence in the room was almost forgotten.

'I don't know about ghosts,' she was saying; 'but I do know that
our souls can be made to go outside our bodies when we are alive'.
(*Tess*, p. 115)

The example Tess gives is of staring at the stars until you are 'hundreds
and hundreds o' miles away from your body'. This characteristic speech
of Tess's appears as the decisive moment in the context in which
Angel's attention is fixed upon her, and so the chapter ends:

And then he seemed to discern in her something that was familiar,
something which carried him back into a joyous and unforeseeing
past, before the necessity of taking thought had made the heavens
gray. (*Tess*, p. 116)

At this moment, tellingly, the narrator's attitude appears to overlay the
narrative's representation of Angel's perceptions somewhat, since the as
yet unremembered episode of his having not danced with her scarcely
seems adequate to justify the mysterious sense of familiarity and joy
that Tess evokes in him.

II

There are, then, many facets in the representation of music in Hardy's
fiction. Music is the occasion of effects of transport in which the
individual's powers of relatedness, seen as potentially joyous, are
evoked, but as being no longer identifiable with the spatial position of
the body, or the reflective or volitional conditions of subjectivity. In this
section I want to look in more detail at how music is described in
Hardy's writing as inducing these involuntary, unconscious activities of
thought and body, and at how these can be related to the modes of
writings that he employs. My main points are that such unconscious
activities are always at once physical, mental and social, since they are
effects of conjunctions or accords of various types (through sensation
and feeling); and that they are represented as at odds with the belated
awareness of separation and loss associated with the reflective
interiority of self-consciousness, 'the necessity of taking thought'.
    To try and put a more explicit analytical gloss on these points,
one could begin by citing Joan Grundy's fascinating account of Hardy's
uses of music in *Hardy and the Sister Arts*. Grundy describes Hardy's
writing, in line with his own remarks, in terms of an aesthetic of
sensations, impressions, in which individuality is expressed through its

finding correspondences with the world outside. For Grundy, the music inside answers the music outside, both natural and man-made, converting the body into a musical instrument of sorts, at once expressive and pliable. Noting how Hardy uses musical metaphors for the descriptions of the characters' emotional capacities, and adumbrating a whole Hardyan vocabulary of the vital passion for sound and the ability to resound and respond, she comes to the following suggestive formulation:

> Vitality and vibrancy: these are the qualities Hardy celebrates in his characters and in human life generally. Both are sustained by and expressed in the beating, throbbing, pulsing of the heart, which itself finds expression and correspondence in the beating, throbbing, pulsing of music and the dance.[8]

The phrase, 'expression and correspondence', is intriguing, since for Hardy the self is only fully expressed through correspondences, associations - through vibrations in which the material is raised for an indefinite interval to the condition of the spiritual. If this is so, it is because the physical is always spiritual also for Hardy, as the means of individuality and relatedness, of 'expression and correspondence'. The expression of the soul through the body in its associations, though, has little to do with everyday consciousness, as a reflective interior understanding. Music as sensation involves the body in indeterminate areas, introducing it into the events of passages outside its purely spatial situation and organic form, in movements where the soul can be expressed in the extraction of ideal qualities of rhythm and resonance from material elements. The determinate difference between my body and that of other bodies is suspended for an open-ended moment in the activities of sensation and of music.

In this emphasis, I am provoked by Gilles Deleuze's comment about Hardy that he had an 'extraordinary respect for the individual', conceived as a collection or 'a bloc of variable sensations'.[9] Individuals are less than personalities than, as the narrator in *Tess* puts it, 'sheafs of susceptibilities' (*Tess*, p. 170). The individual or soul, on this conception, is not identifiable with the pregiven form of personality, but is actualized according to a process of individuation that takes effect between bodies, and for which music provides us with a clearly observable means. Further, Deleuze often employs the distinction of soul and consciousness in the way in which I am using the former term. For Deleuze, the soul, as a virtual and reiterable ensemble of relational potentials, the ideal parallel or counterpart to the multiple potentials of the body, is expressed in different forms through the individuations into which it is drawn through particular encounters. Deleuze's comments about Hardy are useful as a way of relating this discussion of individuation, in distinction from the personality and subjectivity, to the work:

> There is a strange respect for the individual, an extraordinary respect: not because he would seize upon himself as a person, and be recognized as a person, in the French way, but on the contrary because he saw himself and saw others as so many 'unique chances' - the unique chance from which one combination or another had been drawn. Individuation without a subject. And these packets of sensation in the raw, these collections of combinations run along the lines of chance, or mischance, where their encounters take place - if need be, their bad encounters which lead to death, to murder. Hardy invokes a sort of Greek destiny for this empiricist, experimental world. (*Dialogues*, p. 40)

And in the same discussion, Deleuze comments on the soul as the body's counterpart, incorporating a quotation of Lawrence's into his remarks:

> the Soul and the Body, the soul is neither above nor inside, it is 'with', it is on the road, exposed to all contacts, encounters, in the company of those who follow the same way, 'feel with them, seize the vibrations of their soul and their body as they pass'. (*Dialogues*, p. 62)[10]

Certainly, Hardy himself responds most sympathetically to another human being when their behaviour involuntarily betrays the soul. In this connection we can consider how Knight, in *A Pair of Blue Eyes*, becomes most engaging when he is discomposed, or 'disembodied' as it is put, by the actualities of his love for Elfride. Displaying a hitherto unsuspected passivity, this feeling has gradually invaded his consciousness. It is a process facilitated by music in chapter XIX, so that at the beginning of chapter XX he ponders at length on the fact that somehow she has come to 'rule him so imperiously now':

> Knight's experience was a complete disproof of the assumption that love always comes by glances of the eye and sympathetic touches of the fingers; that, like flame, it makes itself palpable at the moment of generation. Not till they were parted, and she had become sublimated in his memory, could he be said to have even attentively regarded her.

Thus having passively gathered up images of her which his mind did not act upon till the cause of them was no longer before him, he appeared to himself to have fallen in love with her soul, which had temporarily assumed its disembodiment to accompany him on his way. (*A Pair of Blue Eyes*, p. 245)

Music brings about a similar self-forgetfulness and betrayal of underlying emotion in *The Hand of Ethelberta* when Montclere, Ethelberta, Christopher and Picotee are all brought together in the cathedral. Montclere spies on Ethelberta who has, unknown to Christopher, re-entered the Cathedral where she hears him play the organ, his music compelling her in 'an act of unconsciousness' to move like a sleep-walker towards the organ-loft:

She continued to regard feature after feature till the choristers had filed in from the south side, and peals broke forth from the organ on the black oaken mass at the junction of nave and choir, shaking every cobweb in the dusky vaults, and Ethelberta's heart no less. She knew the fingers that were pressing out those rolling sounds, and knowing them, became absorbed in tracing their progress. To go towards the organ-loft was an act of unconsciousness, and she did not pause till she stood almost beneath it. (*The Hand of Ethelberta*, p. 320)

In this novel, though, Ethelberta is unable to act on such impulses and is compelled to subdue her heart for the greater good. Thus, she is said here to be 'awakened from vague imaginings' by the approach of Lord Montclere. Together they spy the lovesick Picotee lingering and 'looking up at the organ as Ethelberta had done' (*The Hand of Ethelberta*, p. 321). Accordingly, she agrees to marry Montclere soon, so that they can bring about a wedding between Picotee and Christopher.

There are, then, several features of Hardy's use of music which are emerging here. Passages of music become the means of relatedness between characters, a means in which the concerted operations of subjectivity are surprised for an interval as the individual is expressed as an open multiplicity of different ways of relating outside the recognisable forms of self-relation in subjectivity. Music involves a forgetting or absent-mindedness, through which the individual enters into larger affective ensembles. More than this, music invokes a different, and more dynamic, form of temporality from the merely chronological which it interrupts and holds in abeyance.

The following example from *Tess* allows for a closer description of some of the complex ways in which music can affirm and express individuality. It is the often discussed passage in which she is drawn to Angel's harp notes:

> Tess was conscious of neither time nor space. The exaltation which she had described as being producible at will by gazing at a star, came now without any determination of hers; she undulated upon the thin notes of the second-hand harp, and their harmonies passed like breezes through her, bringing tears into her eyes. The floating pollen seemed to be his notes made visible, and the dampness of the garden the weeping of the garden's sensibility. Though near nightfall, the rank-smelling weed-flowers glowed as if they would not close for intentness, and the waves of colour mixed with the waves of sound. (*Tess*, p. 118)

Tess's response here may be involuntary, yet in her exaltation the most essential feature of her nature is manifested, we are led to believe. Her impressibility, and sensitiveness to Angel's harp notes, have all the immediate pathos that such unguarded rapture always has for Hardy. As this implies, her response sets up the characteristically empathetic counter-responses of narrator and reader. To describe this more closely involves one in paradoxical formulations, since the reader's engagement is itself a kind of mobile orchestration of diverse elements, a compound relay of sympathy, romantic and sexual interest, as well as empathy. This is to talk of a typically Hardyan dimension of independent elements, as in Bayley's use of the term 'separations', but it is worth teasing out this diversity here. It is indeed remarkable in this passage how the reader's response becomes indeterminate, passing into Tess's sense of things, and outside again, so that we move between solicitude for her and absorption in her perceptions and feelings. The distinction between bodies seems suspended by the process of music, and this extends to the other elements of the scene. The flowers that 'would not close for intentness' convey a breathless raptness that is both Tess's and the reader's, but that visits even the vegetation as well. Again, '[t]he floating pollen seemed to be his notes made visible, and the dampness of the garden the weeping of the garden's sensibility'. The mixing of waves of colour and the waves of sound is merely one more example here of how music for Hardy overcomes the distinctions of things, creating paradoxical effects of indetermination, in whose passages, there is no diminishment of individuality, but on the contrary, a fuller expression of it.

    One could ponder further the complex focusing on the central figure in *Tess*, by examining the discordance between the larger determinations of narrative, and the romantic possibilities revealed by music. This could lead into a development of some of the points above, about Hardy's use of tragedy and satire, as the fictional forms most adequate to the incompatibility. However, in the context of the writing of the Hardy of the 1880s and 1890s, the important feature of his treatment would seem to be the pronounced and determined sense that overhangs this novel, as in the other writings of the period, of the transient nature of human joy and hope. The prolonged intensity of the episode at the dairy in *Tess*, for instance, seems merely set up for an ironic fall, a complement at the level of plot to the way kinds of narrative intentness often prolong and postpone the closures of sentences when Hardy's narrator is writing about Tess herself. Characteristically, the poetic intensity of such scenes is at one with the way the narrator fluently mingles his external representation of her, with his imagined sense of bodily sensation and feeling. To take a further example, within the following sentences, the narrator moves from depicting the scene to registering, as it were from the inside, Angel's sensations. Further, as the extract closes, the narrative appears both to observe and to inhabit Tess's own excited confusion, as Angel kisses her arm:

> Although the early September weather was sultry, her arm, from her dabbling in the curds, was as cold and damp to his mouth as a new-gathered mushroom, and tasted of the whey. But she was such a sheaf of susceptibilities that her pulse was accelerated by the touch, her blood driven to her finger-ends, and the cool arms flushed hot. (*Tess*, p. 170)

For John Bayley, such divisions between romance and its eclipse have a determination in Hardy's fiction of the 1890s which he sees as marking a shift from earlier characteristic uses of fictional form. While it is difficult to disagree with Bayley's description of the more rigid and concerted modes which, to paraphrase his position, convert more unconsciously produced effects of separation into more consciously controlling kinds of opposition, it is obviously possible, as so many critics have done (John Goode, Terry Eagleton, and Peter Widdowson among them), to emphasize rather differently the political powers of the parodic or satiric modes which Hardy adopts in the last novels.[11] However, this is not to deny that there is an alteration of the kind that Bayley remarks in Hardy's fictional art by the 1880s and 1890s, and this can be seen clearly in its employment of music. Plot becomes a means of expressing this, as so often in the stories. In 'On the Western Circuit', Raye, the barrister hero, comes across his unsuitable bride-to-be at the fair. Among the sounds of barrel-organs and hand bells, he selects her, as she moves round and round on the roundabout or 'steam circus':

> She was absolutely unconscious of everything save the act of riding: her features were rapt in an ecstatic dreaminess; for the moment she did not know her age or her history or her lineaments, much less her troubles. He himself was full of vague latter-day glooms and popular melancholies, and it was a refreshing sensation to behold this young thing then and there, absolutely as happy as if she were in a Paradise. (*Stories*, Vol. 2, *Stories*, p. 87)

Such an unconscious joy, revealing as it does the girl's nature, is once again the condition of reawakening in Raye, as in Angel, his capacity for love, but it is a merely temporary interval, bound to yield to the sardonic ending, as also in 'The Fiddler of the Reels' where Car'line's relish for music is fatally subject to a narrative treatment which insists on its ultimate recklessness. To take one more example: Hardy's appending of the unhappy revised ending to 'The Distracted Preacher' seems similarly concerned to snuff out the hope of the earlier moment where:

> The birds began to get lively, and a single thrush came just before sunset each evening, and sang hopefully on the large elm-tree which stood nearest to Mrs Newberry's house.[12]

There is certainly, in these examples, a centripetal thematic collectedness which differs from the interruptive centrifugal movements of Hardy's early language and imagination. Where his early writing was characterized by truant movements away from story into marginal and fleeting emotions and impressions, in his later work there is a greater aspiration to narrative unity. The more unreflective disunity of the early books is transformed into a greater overseeing narrative preoccupation with the ironic notation of disunity as the structure of experience. This contrast in mode, technique and tone between the early and late books, becomes the topic proper of the next two sections. However, it is important here to stress simply that one can construe this differently from Bayley, in that these characteristics of over determination, as in *Jude* or *The Well-Beloved*, produce complicated intensities of feeling whose ultimate after-effect, to put it most crudely, is that life is impossible without hope. This is a way of saying that the author's conscious vision is not as conclusive as Bayley's evaluation suggests. Hope is, after all, *the* main emotion that is engendered by the narratives of *Tess* and *Jude*. And if the deaths in the novels are so wrenching, it is precisely because this intensification of disappointment has the effect of testifying to its opposite, as dissonance evokes a counter-image of harmony perhaps, and so invokes our need for it. This is so in the stories, too, as with the character in 'Fellow-Townsmen', for whom the 'few minutes of hope, between the reading of the first and second letters, had carried him to extraordinary heights of rapture' (*Stories*, Vol. 1, p. 114). The sense of lost hope as markedly expressed through a preoccupation with music can be seen also in the plot of 'The Fiddler of the Reels' which tinges and displaces Car'line's real rapture by turning it into at best a repeatable experience that becomes increasingly ridiculous with the onward press of time. Nevertheless, the effect of the story is that the value of the experience of music survives all the designs upon it of plot and characterization, and stands outside the story's conclusion, inescapable though the ironies are.

III

It is interesting, in connection with the early fiction, to remember Virginia Woolf's amused and slightly perplexed fascination with the involuntary imaginative processes of the author himself. Of *Desperate Remedies*, she wrote, 'Here is a young man [...] who can create characters but cannot control them'.[13] This is true, but we need to add that these characters are also little able to control themselves. For instance, there is a passage towards the beginning of *Desperate Remedies*, when Cytherea and Edward's eyes meet for the first time, as the music begins on the boat deck:

> Their eyes having met, became, as it were, mutually locked together, and the single instant only which good breeding allows as the length of such a look became trebled: a clear penetrating ray of intelligence had shot from each into each, giving birth to one of those unaccountable sensations which carry home to the heart before the hand has been touched or the merest compliment passed, by something stronger than mathematical proof, the conviction, 'A tie has begun to unite us'.
> Both faces also unconsciously stated that their owners had been much in each other's thoughts of late [...] Then the band of harps and violins struck a lively melody, and the deck was cleared for dancing.[14]

As Woolf might say, Hardy's narrator certainly surrenders narrative control of the scene, but this becomes his way of maximizing his and our participation within its play of sensation and feeling. What is most remarkable about the writing, though, is not simply its unfolding adjustment to unconscious experience, but the way it places itself, as it were, between the two individuals concerned, like the narrow river which weaves its way between them in a later scene. In this way, the narrative becomes a sympathetic and resonating medium. It is concerned with unconscious dynamics of feeling and intelligence that cannot be understood in terms of one character alone, but which criss-cross from one to the other. For instance, it seems impossible here to say how, or by whose intentions, this eye contact passed into something more, or to track the logic of the electric sequence of glances which double and treble the well-bred duration of a look until each acknowledges, 'stronger than mathematical proof, the conviction that "A tie has begun to unite us."' With a comic dismissiveness, the whirling speed and sureness of response and counter-response eludes logical comprehension and certainty, as it sweeps along characters, narrator and reader.

And indeed, few readers of the novel will have escaped Woolf's sense of the paradox here: that there appears to be a direct correlation in *Desperate Remedies* between the vivacity with which the writer's gifts revealed themselves, and the novel's lapses in construction. Hardy does not seem the text's controlling subject, so much as a means of conduction for the feelings, thoughts, and impressions that just spring up and circulate within such scenes. Comprehensible pattern is the price paid for a language which works so inimitably on the senses and the emotions. In this connection, consider the celebrated scene between Manston and Cytherea, and the former's machinations as the self-taught musician plies the organ he has made, bringing out its overwhelming seductive tones and chromatic spells, and 'extemporizing a harmony which meandered through every variety of expression of which the instrument was capable' (*Desperate Remedies*, p. 153). In this most meandering, extemporized and sonic of scenes (in this most meandering, extemporized and sonic of novels), Manston's pursuit of momentary musical effects and nuances has a comic correspondence with the text's own principles: its own interruptive absorptions in the circumambient world of impressions, in the pleasures of sensation. The scene plays out Manston's 'wonderful indifference to all external circumstances [...] now evinced by his complete absorption in the music before him' (*Desperate Remedies*, p. 154):

He now played more powerfully. Cytherea had never heard music in the completeness of full orchestral power, and the tones of the organ, which reverberated with considerable effect in the comparatively small space of the room, heightened by the elemental strife of light and sound outside, moved her to a degree out of proportion to the actual power of the mere notes, practised as was the hand that produced them. The varying strains - now loud, now soft; simple, complicated, weird, touching, grand, boisterous, subdued; each phrase distinct, yet modulating into the next with a graceful and easy flow - shook and bent her to themselves, as a gushing brook shakes and bends a shadow cast across its surface. The power of the music did not show itself so much by attracting her attention to the subject of the piece, as by taking up and developing as its libretto the poem of her life and soul, shifting her deeds and intentions from the hands of judgement and holding them in its own.

She was swayed into emotional opinions concerning the strange man before her; new impulses of thought came with new harmonies, and entered into her with a gnawing thrill. A dreadful flash of lightening then, and the thunder close upon it. She found herself involuntarily shrinking up beside him, and looking with parted lips at his face.

He turned his eyes and saw her emotion, which greatly increased the ideal element in her expressive face. She was in the state in which woman's instinct to conceal has lost its power over the impulse to tell; and he saw it. (*Desperate Remedies*, p. 155)

Hardy's writing, itself all eyes and all ears, is expansively sensitive to the nature, varieties and extent of Cytherea's 'involuntarily' responses, as she is alternately moved, shaken, thrilled, swayed by the dynamic changes, and immense reverberations of these notes which 'greatly increased the ideal element in her expressive face'. The modulations of erotic delirium and delicate beauty in the music suspend her power of self-control and judgment, and her sense of the everyday, 'taking up and developing as its libretto the poem of her life and soul', and bringing forth 'new impulses of thought'. The improvisatory virtuosity of which Manston is master here, displacing convention, and the self-forgetfulness which Cytherea displays, so that it is the music which controls her, are inward with the formal and stylistic qualities of the novel itself:

The varying strains - now loud, now soft; simple, complicated, weird, touching, grand, boisterous, subdued; each phrase distinct, yet modulating into the next with a graceful and easy flow - shook

and bent her to themselves, as a gushing brook shakes and bends
a shadow cast across its surface.

Manston's art, like Hardy's, accommodates its diverse and singular
elements into an unformed and open texture within the continuous
tense of the present. As the organist adapts his music to the variable
inspirations of his musical sense and the presentiments of the sounds
themselves, so sentence and paragraph dilate and diversify in phrasing
the fugitive loose-ends of perception and desire. In the process, the
language conveys the power of the music to hold and move Cytherea,
and to channel all the natural power of the storm into its own intense
effects.

Involuntariness in such a scene is a feature both of drama and of
language. This characteristic marked Hardy out for Woolf as one of
those 'unconscious writers [...] like Dickens and Scott' whose greatest
resource is that they are continually 'taken by surprise' as they write. In
such scenes, authors like these:

> seem suddenly and without their own consent to be lifted up and
> swept onwards. The wave sinks and they cannot say what has
> happened or why [... Hardy's] own word, 'moments of vision',
> exactly describes those passages of astonishing beauty and force
> which are to be found in every book he wrote. With a sudden
> quickening of power which we cannot foretell, nor he, it seems,
> control, a single scene breaks off from the rest [...][15]

Her comments emphasize how distinctively and remarkably Hardy's
narrative is attentive to events of unconsidered responsiveness, and to
capturing the extraordinary complexity of embodied thought. Above
all, Woolf suggests how individuality for Hardy's narrator, as for his
characters, is a matter of self-differentiation. In this connection, we can
compare the first scene from *Desperate Remedies* with one from *The Hand
of Ethelberta*, where Christopher and Ethelberta's romance is rekindled
by the mute signallings of eye contact. Although the scenes are similar,
and indicate the self-modifications of the characters brought about by
music, there are important differences, too, which indicate the formal
differences between the novels. In this case too, music works as a
catalyst, drawing together Christopher and Ethelberta as their eyes
meet at the dance where he is playing, towards the beginning of the
novel:

> It was only a look, and yet what a look it was! One may say of a
> look that it is capable of division into as many species, genera,

orders and classes, as the animal world itself. Christopher saw
Ethelberta Petherwin's performance in this kind - the well-known
spark of light upon the well-known depths of mystery - and felt
something going out of him which had gone out of him once
before.[16]

For Christopher, the 'well-known spark of light' in Ethelberta's eloquent
look is a self-revelation to which he finds that he has already
responded, with a disconcerting sense of emotional and spiritual
transit. Indisputable as this ocular communiqué is, however, its
meaning remains also obscure and mysterious. In one sense, it is
enigmatic in a generic way, as in any such scene, since how do we
explain what takes place, and changes, between two people when they
look at each other in an emotionally charged situation like this? In
another sense, there is a specifically enigmatic quality to this scene
which has to do with this relationship, and this novel. The look which
Ethelberta gives Christopher is full of that sense of mysterious
motivation and unresolved possibility which she always possesses for
him. Ethelberta's withholding of the verbal expression of feeling here is
not, as with Cytherea, linked to naiveté, or to circumstances outside her
control, but to that very excess of control over self and circumstances
that has made her prematurely a guardian of her own destiny and that
of her family.

Within these scenes, then, effects of involuntary transport have
an inwardness with the imaginative processes of the writing, as well as
with the specific formal and thematic configurations of a particular text.
Like that of one of his characters, Hardy's own individuality as a writer
involves recurrent lapses of responsibility, and unfolds differently at
different times, presenting the most subtle, often idiosyncratic,
variations and modulations. In both cases, individuality appears to
operate in an importantly unwilled way, as a power of self-difference.
Certainly, these earlier novels are the product of a mind overtaken by,
immersed in, the events it narrates, and which struggles, often
somewhat belatedly, to get outside these scenes, and to graft them onto
a narrative structure.

These points bring to mind D. H. Lawrence's memorable
observation about Hardy that the 'chiefest factor' in the characters'
process of becoming or individuation (what he calls their 'struggle into
being'), is 'the struggle with love':

The *via media* to being, for man or woman, is love, and love
alone.[17]

While the spontaneous selfhood which Woolf commented on in Hardy's work can often seem comparatively forced or lacking in Lawrence's own characters, the comment does indicate the terms in which Lawrence conceived of his connection to Hardy. In respect of the particular treatment of love in Hardy's texts, music has a particular status. As already seen, it is often instrumental in producing new arrangements of feeling between individuals. At the same time, as a stimulus to self-differentiation, it also produces new arrangements of feeling *within* individuals. That is to say, music both brings people together and helps produce the changes which take place within them. For instance, Dick Dewy falls in love with Fancy as the band sings beneath her window. The next morning in the church he feels, comically and all too pronouncedly, both a new sense of himself and a new sense of connection with her, as he:

> saw the vision of the past night enter the porch-door as methodically as if she had never been a vision at all. A new atmosphere seemed suddenly to be puffed into the ancient edifice by her movement, which made Dick's body and soul tingle with novel sensations.[18]

For Dick, reason is pushed aside by the overwhelming and embarrassing physicality of the moment, by his enhanced awareness, when he:

> began to breathe more freely the warm new air she had brought with her; to feel rushings of blood, and to have impressions that there was a tie between her and himself visible to all the congregation. (*Under the Greenwood Tree*, p. 64)

Similarly, in *A Pair of Blue Eyes*, the narrator describes how, for Stephen, falling in love with Elfride is a new departure for him. It is her singing which is the crucial incident, and it provides him with a mental recording, an internal video, he can replay endlessly in his day-dreams. More importantly, this 'particular scene' brings out new qualities in both himself and in Elfride, who is now seen in 'her special form of manifestation':

> Every woman who makes a permanent impression on a man is usually recalled to his mind's eye as she appeared in one particular scene, which seems ordained to be her special form of manifestation throughout the pages of his memory [...]

> Miss Elfride's image chose the form in which she was beheld
> during these minutes of singing, for her permanent attitude of
> visitation to Stephen's eyes during his sleeping and waking hours
> in after days [...] Her head is forward a little, and her eyes directed
> keenly upward to the top of the page of music confronting her.
> Then comes a rapid look into Stephen's face, and a still more rapid
> look back again to her business, her face having dropped its
> sadness, and acquired a certain expression of mischievous
> archness the while; which lingered there for some time, but was
> never developed into a positive smile of flirtation. (*A Pair of Blue
> Eyes*, pp. 67-68)

For Elfride, too, the expression of her 'impressionable soul' is identified
with the 'accidents' and 'touches' of aesthetic experience (*A Pair of Blue
Eyes*, p. 278):

> Elfride's emotion was cumulative, and after a while would assert
> itself on a sudden. A slight touch was enough to set it free - a
> poem, a sunset, a cunningly contrived chord of music, a vague
> imagining, being the usual accidents of its exhibition. (*A Pair of
> Blue Eyes*, p. 237)

We can contrast the control she exercises over Stephen with the
different feeling produced in her by Knight. Her 'longing for Knight's
respect' is translated into a positive 'yearning for his love' by the
qualified tone of his remarks about her organ-playing. He says that she
plays 'excellently' and 'correctly': that is, without sufficient taste,
individuality and feeling.

To take another example, at the end of *Far from the Madding
Crowd*, Bathsheba's somewhat surprised recognition of her need for Oak
is precipitated by music. Passing the church where Troy and Fanny are
buried, she hears the children in the choir singing, and 'was stirred by
emotions which latterly she had assumed to be altogether dead within
her' (*Far from the Madding Crowd*, p. 412). In the following pages, her
feeling for Oak crystallizes out of her sense of his independence of her,
an impression given not least by the manner of his singing:

> Coming out of church that day she looked round in hope that Oak,
> whose bass voice she had heard rolling out from the gallery
> overhead in a most unconcerned manner, might chance to linger
> in her path in the old way. (*Far from the Madding Crowd*, p. 415)

In *The Mayor of Casterbridge*, too, Elizabeth-Jane is drawn to Farfrae by
his singing:

> Elizabeth-Jane was fond of music; she could not help pausing to
> listen; and the longer she listened the more she was enraptured.
> She had never heard any singing like this.[19]

The novels abound with these sorts of episode, where music acts as a
lightening rod for feeling. Often accidental, such scenes of music
transform or illuminate the relationships of the characters. In *A
Laodicean*, Somerset follows the singing of a favourite psalm-tune, until,
after some dithering, he ends up in the chapel where Paula is refusing
to be baptized:

> Somerset could for the first time see her face. Though humanly
> imperfect, as is every face we see, it was one which made him
> think that the best in woman-kind no less than the best of psalm-
> tunes had gone over to the Dissenters.[20]

Music and a woman's face are fatally associated, as in a similar, though
crushingly ironic passage in *Jude* where the hero listens to the 'great
waves of pedal music' which 'tumbled round the choir', as the 119th
Psalm ('Wherewithal shall a young man cleanse his way?') is sung. Jude
naively regards it as a propitious sign of a new beginning after
Arabella, as if 'Providence' were ratifying his feeling for Sue. He passes
the service carried away by this promise of 'both social and spiritual
possibilities', buoyed up by a 'sustaining atmosphere of ecstasy':

> The girl for whom he was beginning to nourish an extraordinary
> tenderness was at this time ensphered by the same harmonies as
> those which floated into his ears; and the thought was a delight to
> him. She was probably a frequenter of this place, and, steeped
> body and soul in church sentiment as she must be by occupation
> and habit, had, no doubt, much in common with him. (*Jude*, p.
> 112)

Ominously self-deluding though Jude's pleasure is represented as
being, the use of church music in itself here is not substantially different
from Hardy's use of it in the passage from *A Laodicean*, or elsewhere, as
a sort of comically incongruous Trojan Horse for amorous feelings. In
Under the Greenwood Tree, Maybold glories in Fancy's playing in church,
and 'loved her during that sermon-time as he had never loved a woman
before' (*Under the Greenwood Tree*, pp. 178-79). Similarly, Eustacia's
raciness is indicated by the fact that she sings psalms on Saturday
nights, and in *The Trumpet-Major*, the miller suggests, to enliven their
Sunday evening, that they 'should sing psalms which, by choosing

lively tunes, and not thinking of the words, would be almost as good as ballads' (*The Trumpet-Major*, p.164). Again, in *Desperate Remedies*, Cytherea, with understandable trepidation, observes the predatory Manston as she sings the Evening Hymn 'already regarding her with some purpose in his glance' (*Desperate Remedies*, p. 259).

This peculiar power of music to facilitate the workings of romance is evident throughout Hardy's fictional career, and at its most extreme, music can work like a spell, one which binds the will and transforms things, as in the following scene from *Under The Greenwood Tree*. Dick dances with Fancy, and finds that the hitherto excruciating gap between his wishes and the facts is tantalizingly disappearing:

> Fancy was now held so closely that Dick and she were practically one person. The room became to Dick like a picture in a dream; all that he could remember of it afterwards being the look of the fiddlers going to sleep as humming-tops sleep, by increasing their motion and hum, together with the figures of grandfather James and old Simon Crumpler sitting by the chimney-corner talking and nodding in dumb-show, and beating the air to their emphatic sentences like people near a threshing machine. (*Under the Greenwood Tree*, p. 76)

A hypnotized automatism has taken over the dancers, the fiddlers, and the old men. The magical suspension of will here, affecting the fiddlers so that they seem as if turned into humming-tops, can be compared with many other scenes, such as the one in *A Laodicean* where Somerset dances with Paula. Here, it seems:

> as if those musicians had thrown a double sweetness into their notes on seeing the mistress of the castle in the dance, that a perfumed southern atmosphere had begun to pervade the marquee, and that human beings were shaking themselves free of all gravitation. (*A Laodicean*, p. 114)

The sentence describes a web of feeling which, as in the previous example, appears to affect everyone in the marquee, and which imparts a wholly new and ideal, almost enchanted, quality to the dance. The uplift which the characters feel is all but literal: it is 'as if [...] human beings were shaking themselves free of all gravitation'. Once again, this emergent power of feeling is indicated by the syntax which seems to break its bounds, in sympathy with the scene's moving aside of the bounds of duty and of physical gravity.

Finally, when one considers the qualities and vivacity of Hardy's early work, their power to cut through convention and to identify individuality and physicality, it is extraordinary how often these novels have been subject to patronization or dismissal. As with the poetry, though, it is worth stressing that creative writers have been undeterred. After all, *A Pair of Blue Eyes* was Proust's favourite novel.[21] Moreover, Virginia Woolf is certainly not excluding these less fêted texts when she refers to that 'sudden quickening of power' on which she says that Hardy's fiction depends, in its capacity to give to the 'moment' what she called 'all the bloom and beauty of life'.[22] To adopt D. H. Lawrence's terminology, these early novels themselves also could be said to be those which *most* attempt to 'struggle into being', while conveying with extraordinary originality, subtlety and lucidity the play of feeling and impression. Certainly, it is the aim of this discussion to link the open-ended compositional values of the earlier texts with the idea and value of individuality in Hardy's fiction. In so doing, the argument becomes broadly aligned with the work of those critics like Peter Widdowson, Joe Fisher, Roger Ebbatson and John Bayley, who have argued for a reconsideration of the hierarchical scheme, the developmental narrative, into which the texts are usually placed.[23] Part of the difficulty here, of course, as suggested above, is that the relative coherence of *Tess* or *Jude* in terms of effect, structure and social critique makes them more amenable to criticism, whereas the early texts can seem exasperatingly improvised and fitful in comparison. The pleasures they offer are obviously of a far more local and diffuse kind, both more immediate and more easily forgotten, but surely no less remarkable and valuable, than those offered than the later fiction, to which we now turn.

IV

Caroline Jackson-Houlston has indicated how, in *The Mayor of Casterbridge*, 'Farfrae's kind of music is set against Henchard's'.[24] The latter's 'tragic stature' is characterized through his affinity for ancient music, where Farfrae's use of Scottish songs suggests:

> the slightly superficial or *ersatz* quality of his feelings, which purport to be expressed in verse that depends on or parasitizes older and deeper traditions and that in any case is not an accurate expression of his own nature. The clientele of 'The Three Mariners' notice this. If they receive him with applause and 'a deep silence which was even more eloquent than the applause,' some of them

at least are also capable of the recognition, 'be dazed, if I love my country half as well as the young feller do, I'd live by claning my neighbour's pigsties afore I'd go away'! (*Ballads, Songs and Snatches*, p. 154)

The songs that Farfrae tends to sing, Jackson-Houlston points out, are part of a late eighteenth and nineteenth-century tradition that worked to market cultural difference, 'by adapting (and often trivializing and sentimentalizing) images and situations from the traditional songs of the Scottish countryside' (*Ballads, Songs and Snatches*, p. 153). While these songs allow Farfrae to ingratiate himself with the different levels of Casterbridge society, they ironically reveal his real cultural deracination. Musical taste points out the nature of this conflict between Henchard's fatally passionate nature, and Farfrae's more circumspect qualities, since Henchard:

> though sensitive to all types, is characterized by his feelings for psalms. The grim, dark tones of the Old Testament, particularly those parts associated with Job and Cain, with which Hardy connects Henchard in order to give him the tragic stature of a man of ancient times left stranded by the tides of the present, are reinforced by the psalm Henchard forces the choir to sing in Chapter 33. (*Ballads, Songs and Snatches*, p. 154)

The conflict between Henchard and Farfrae, is not only a conflict of personalities, but of 'cultural traditions and social aspiration' (*Ballads, Songs and Snatches*, p. 151). Key themes of the later novels - the dislocation of rural communities, modernity, and the restrictive influence of social norms - can be detected in this difference of musical taste.

This more adroit use of music - to define the conflicts and themes of the novel, and the characters themselves - indicates the divergence between the deliberately 'tragic' focus and organization of a novel like *The Mayor of Casterbridge*, and the qualities of the early texts. Certainly, the socializing, or romantically seductive, use of music in this novel is identified with what the narrator unsympathetically represents as the slightly specious qualities of Farfrae, and his tendency to self-advancement. Against this, the deepest courses of narrative sympathy run firmly with Henchard whose tastes tend, as Jackson-Houlston suggests, to a very different kind of musical expression - the large emotions, the tragic declamations, of the Old Testament outcast. Involuntariness, one can say, appears in the world of *The Mayor of Casterbridge* (as in *The Woodlanders, Tess*, or *Jude*) less as a feature of spontaneous events of romantic or social association, than an effect of the inescapable and tragic predicament in which the character finds him or herself enmeshed. Where musical scenes in those novels dramatized individuality as a function of the soul's involuntary susceptibility, in these novels music reveals individuality as a matter of socially fatal patterns of desire.

Music brings out this more tragic and systematic conception of the possibilities of individuality in *The Mayor of Casterbridge* in many other moments where Hardy uses it to reinforce the main conflicts and themes which govern the novel. After wrestling Farfrae, Henchard is torn by the memory of 'that time when the curious mixture of romance and thrift in the young man's composition so commanded his heart that Farfrae could play on him as an instrument' (*The Mayor of Casterbridge*, p. 297). This musical image indicates the strength of the hold which his emotions have over Henchard, and his passivity before them. However, the image also encapsulates their destructive changeability - Henchard's capacity first to embrace Farfrae as like his own brother; then to be betrayed by imperious impulses of anger towards him; and then to be regretfully amazed at what he has done. This unconscious cycle of love, hatred and regret is a recurrent and defining one in the novel, as when Henchard breaks off from killing Farfrae. The latter sings again an old song, from the time when 'he had arrived years before at the Three Mariners':

a poor young man, adventuring for life and fortune, and scarcely knowing witherward: -

'And here's a hand, my trusty fiere,
And gie's a hand o' thine,'

Nothing moved Henchard like an old melody. He sank back. 'No; I can't do it!' he gasped. (*The Mayor of Casterbridge*, p. 294)

An even more obvious case of this emotional loop arises with the sale of Susan at the beginning. Music is associated with the emotional intensities of these early scenes. There is Henchard's wilful 'resentment' as he reads, or pretends 'to read, a ballad sheet', so preserving his taciturnity from any conversation with his wife which might dispel it (*The Mayor of Casterbridge*, p. 47). In the ensuing emotional explosion, musical tokens convey Henchard's negative and obsessive state of mind. Full of feelings of boredom, entrapment and self-loathing, as he approaches the tent, he hears 'the voice of a weak bird singing a trite old evening song' (*The Mayor of Casterbridge*, p. 37) - the bird's voice and song corresponding to what strikes him as impossible about living with Susan. In the marquee, the morning after, unable to liberate his mind and emotions from what he has done, we hear of how 'a single big blue fly buzzed musically round and round' (*The Mayor of Casterbridge*, p. 47). In this case once more the musical incident conveys Henchard's isolating emotion, the inescapable state of mortification and confusion in which he is caught up.

In such ways, music works within the tragic world of the novel to accompany and symbolize the unconscious turmoil, the disastrous passions, of the central character. The diabolic aspect of Henchard's negativity surfaces when he cannot resist tricking the choir to sing the vengeful 'Hundred-and-Ninth' psalm 'to the tune of Wiltshire' in the Three Mariners (*The Mayor of Casterbridge*, p. 257). Conversely, consumed once more by remorse and 'defiant endurance' after Susan's death, he himself notices in the sounds of the river near the site for hangings '[t]he lugubrious harmony of the spot with his domestic situation' (*The Mayor of Casterbridge*, p. 155). Likewise, an appropriate music accompanies the humiliations of the skimmity ride. In other cases, music provokes Henchard towards some ruinous act of rage, as with 'the bell-ringing and the band-playing, loud as Tamerlane's trumpet' (associated with Farfrae the new mayor), which 'goaded the downfallen Henchard indescribably,' and which brought to the surface his wish to destroy Farfrae's relationship with Lucetta (*The Mayor of Casterbridge*, p. 294).

At the same time, Henchard's inability to control the fluctuations of generosity and hatred that subject him is the main quality that secures our automatic sympathy with him. He is ultimately as defenceless to the emotions which sweep him along as is the effigy 'lying stiff and stark upon the surface of the stream' (*The Mayor of Casterbridge*, p. 318), which he contemplates at Ten Hatches, that supremely musical spot where, under cover of night, he contemplates suicide:

> The wanderer in this direction who should stand still for a few moments on a quiet night, might hear singular symphonies from these waters, as from a lampless orchestra, all playing in their sundry tones from near and far parts of the moor [...] The spot at which their instrumentation rose loudest was a place called Ten Hatches, whence during high springs there proceeded a very fugue of sounds. (*The Mayor of Casterbridge*, p. 318)

As the narrative provokes in us a round of sympathy, repulsion, indulgence and horror in relation to Henchard, so it makes us confused counterparts of the man himself as he suffers his own immediate and changeable emotions towards himself and others. We respond in kind to his own responses, sharing the depth and range of his feelings, a fact which accounts for the otherwise perhaps unaccountable affective inwardness which binds us to him, for the most part, even at his most monstrous.

Conversely, this involuntary intimacy tends to divide us from the relatively lukewarm, measured affections of Farfrae or Elizabeth-Jane. In contrast to the reader's mobile sense of connection with Henchard, Farfrae is far less sympathetic because he is less likely to be carried away.[25] Further, because he is a more consistent and calculating character he is himself far more subject to defining and limiting judgments, as when the narrator comments on Farfrae's singing. Having placed Henchard outside Elizabeth-Jane's wedding feast, he describes the Scotsman's notes with a rare and often quoted acidity: Farfrae is said to be singing a song of 'his dear native country that he loved so well as never to have revisited it' (*The Mayor of Casterbridge*, p. 344). This passage clinches for the reader an impression throughout the novel of that strand of opportunism in Farfrae's personality, that facility in somewhat factitious self-projection, which recurrently manifests itself in his adeptness at using music to charm and ease his way into the good graces of others. Even Henchard cannot help responding positively (though he will shortly sack him in jealous rage) as he observes Farfrae dancing at his improvised pavilion under the trees:

> A reel or fling of some sort was in progress; and the usually sedate Farfrae was in the midst of the other dancers in the costume of a wild Highlander, flinging himself about and spinning to the tune. For a moment Henchard could not help laughing. Then he perceived the immense admiration for the Scotchman that revealed itself in the women's faces. (*The Mayor of Casterbridge*, p. 135)

At this moment, though, the reader responds less to Farfrae, than to Henchard, and Henchard alone. We enter positively into Henchard's own involuntary generosity, as we are always triggered by Henchard's display of similar emotions, but this is assuredly not a scene of individuation of the more inclusive, kind discussed in the previous section. We see and judge Farfrae, but we feel with and as Henchard.

The Woodlanders provides a further interesting case of Hardy's tragic use of music. One of the few instances of music in the book comes as old South broods on the threat of the tall elm swaying outside his window:

> Whenever the wind blew, as it did now, the tree rocked, naturally enough; and the sight of its motion, and sound of its sighs, had gradually bred the terrifying illusion in the woodman's mind. Thus he would sit all day, in spite of persuasion, watching its every sway, and listening to the melancholy Gregorian melodies which the air wrung out if it [...].[26]

The music of the tree is associated with melancholy and the threat of death, and in such ways it reflects the solitary, fearful and impotent obsessiveness of the old man. Like the narrator, he occupies a painful temporal interval in which he can merely spectate, anticipating the destruction of his way of life. As this suggests, the relative lack of explicit references to music in the novel seems linked to the intensity of its mournfully contemplative concentration on the passing of the woods and the community of the woodlanders. Human obsessions, longings and infatuations provide an anti-image of community, signs of a cultural dislocation which is evident in the novel's syntax and form, its awkward transitions.

Against the happy chances, the meetings of glances, of the early fiction discussed above, we can note the prevalence in this novel of scenes of dissociation. Characters are endlessly spying on, or catching glimpses of one another, powerless to connect, and thus to respond.[27] The enduring images of the novel, of Giles standing with his uprooted apple-trees in the town, or of Marty mourning him alone, indicate the sense of static and vulnerable disconnection, of blighted hopes, which distinguishes the particular tonality of the novel, its elegaic mood and air.[28] The narrator appears deliberately to adopt specific technical means which complement this emphasis:[29] the novel's abiding sense of dislocation is inseparable from what Margaret Elvy has described as its 'continually shifting viewpoints and mediations'.[30] Within the world of *The Woodlanders*, then, there appear few of the conditions of reciprocity, or even of hope, which would in the earlier fiction have been associated with music.

Phillip Mallett has linked the comparative bleakness of the social world represented in *The Woodlanders* with Hardy's rigour to the facts of history as he saw them. The novel is seen as offering a corrective to those stylizations and omissions which marked the idyllic treatment of rural life in the novels of the early 1870s, in particular *Under the Greenwood Tree*. Making a similar point, Peter Conrad writes of how music in this earlier novel:

> is an ancient remedy for harmonising the world and soothing its grumbles. The choir laboriously goes the rounds of the large parish, taking care to bestow a carol on every family. They are the creators of social adhesion, and [...] their music describes generously all-embracing, reliably repetitive circles.[31]

Mallett points out how Hardy's representation in *Under the Greenwood Tree* of 'the unchanging aspects of rural life' was untrue to 'strikes, arson' and 'Joseph Arch'.[32] The relative absence of music in *The Woodlanders* might then be part of this desire to contradict the falsely ameliorating politics of the earlier novel, employing music as it did so extensively as a vehicle and image of locatedness and relatedness.[33] In the later novel, the adherence to the truth of the social situation requires from Hardy a guardedness towards the ways in which the social aspects of music can lend themselves to a sentimentalizing retrospection, and in which the ideal can become merely the idealized. *The Woodlanders* is a novel that seeks to dramatize the real violence of social forces, and music's place in this is a largely sad one, as when Giles's guests put paid to his courtship of Grace by singing a cheery folk song of lost virginity:

> "A maid again I shall never be,
> Till apples grow on an orange tree!" (*The Woodlanders*, p. 105)

As Caroline Jackson-Houlston puts it, at this moment:

> Melbury's hesitations are over. He puts particular stress on the unsuitability of the song for the new type of propriety Grace represents: 'for us old folk it don't matter; but for Grace - Giles should have known better'. (*The Woodlanders*, p. 163)

This self-steeling, on the narrator's part, against the possible idealizations associated with music, continues in the novels which follow *The Woodlanders*. Hardy's fiction now uses music endlessly and bitterly to display the gap between life's potentials and social possibility. Music becomes a powerful tool for social critique, for that encompassing vision of lives lived according to 'shattered ideals', where tragedy comes out of 'the forced adaptation of human instincts to rusty and irksome moulds that do not fit them'.[34] At the beginning of *Tess*, the failure of Angel to dance with the heroine (as his brothers drag him off for another chapter of *A Counterblast to Agnosticism* before bed) is an obvious enough case of this contrast between Tess's instincts and these distorting social values. In *Tess*, music is used recurrently as an image of Tess's continuity with the natural order, as when, after the birth of her child, we read of nature's indifference to social prescriptions, and artificial moral guilt:

> Meanwhile the trees were just as green as before; the birds sang and the sun shone as clearly now as ever. The familiar surroundings had not darkened because of her grief, nor sickened because of her pain. (*Tess*, p. 87)

Hardy's narrator explicitly refers to the purveyors of such norms, in contrast to Tess herself, as being those 'that were out of harmony with the actual world, not she' (*Tess*, p. 82). There is, of course, music at the dairy, where it often accentuates such a natural harmony - the women sing to encourage the cows to produce milk, and Crick tells the story of William Dewy who played the fiddle to pacify a bull. We saw earlier how, as Tess and Angel fall in love, the narrative becomes charged and affected by romance, as if by an atmosphere, so that the writing becomes open to the new plane of feeling which is constituted between them. Palpable and yet also ideal, love lends to the episodes at the dairy this other-worldly enchantment, like that created by the mist or fog or candle-light in the early mornings which Tess and Angel share at the dairy. Or, as is evident here, in the early evening:

> They were so absorbed in the sense of being close to each other that they did not begin talking for a long while. (*Tess*, p. 178)

It is, though, in the nature of such unvoiced moments in *Tess* that the reader can sense their fragility, before reading of the 'dull sky' which 'soon began to tell its meaning by sending down herald-drops of rain' (*Tess*, p. 179):

> The quicksilvery glaze on the rivers and pools vanished; from broad mirrors of light they changed to lustreless sheets of lead, with a surface like a rasp. (*Tess*, p. 179)

We intuit that the moments of illumination and reciprocity, associated with this *intermezzo*, are shortly to yield to the deadening influences of the larger world, and the tragic operatic fate which will overtake Tess. From now on, music will tend to take on pathos merely, as an expression of those aspects of Tess's emotional self which are denied, in accordance with the law the narrator observes in the scheme of things:

> So the two forces were at work here as everywhere, the inherent will to enjoy, and the circumstantial will against enjoyment. (*Tess*, p. 277)

We come to see Tess continually singing to perfect the pastoral songs she associates with Angel, so that it 'would have melted the heart of a stone to hear her singing these ditties [...] the tears running down her cheeks all the while at the thought that perhaps he would not, after all, come to hear her' (*Tess*, p. 333). She continues to do this, even when she has 'scarce now a hope that Clare would ever hear them' (*Tess*, p. 338).

In *Tess*, then, the character cannot help (if only in memory) clinging on to the 'will to enjoy', and the text intensifies its effects out of the envisioned discordance of this with the cruel logic of circumstance. Music is a marker of what society denies her. In *Jude*, Hardy's narrator, in a self-scourging manner, escapes even this kind of sympathetic sensitivity or pathos. *Jude* is the only novel, Jackson-Houlston says, without 'folk song references' (*Ballads, Songs and Snatches*, p. 166). Further, what intermissions of feeling and relatedness there are in the narrative, in association with music, offer only temporary respites to the cumulative narrative of cruelty. Moreover, these respites are subject themselves to satirizing twists, and to the ironic boomerang effects which define increasingly in this novel the recoil of pitiless fact upon hope. Music is tied in *Jude* to the predicament of solitude and illusion in which the character is caught. Jude, with his 'dark harmonizing eyes' (*Jude*, p. 96), has a fatal tendency selectively to abstract and idealize. The negative association of this with music was evident in the example given earlier at the morning service in Cardinal College where, in his loneliness, Jude conjoins Sue and religion. We read of Jude that '[w]here he passed objects out of harmony with its general expression he allowed his eyes to slip over them as if he did not see them' (*Jude*, p. 98).

Contrary to *Tess*, then, where music was employed as a device to accentuate and secure our sense of the romance and tragedy of the novel, in *Jude* it is used to undermine straightforward feeling. Music is a compositional element in *Jude*'s satiric focus on the delusions which persistently betray the central figure. As Jude is constantly alienated, on the outside of the relationships and institutions with which he identifies, this entails that the narrator put us outside him, dislocating our recurrent immediate response of sympathy, so that our feelings for the central figure return with a tragically intensified, and/or parodic, ironic twist. Hardy highlights Jude's delusions by tortuously subjecting the reader to a complementary demystification in relation to Jude himself. It is possible to see how music is repeatedly used in this effect. For instance, just prior to the deaths of the children, Arabella observes Sue and Jude at the Great Wessex Agricultural Show, wrapped up in each other, in Jude's models of Christminster, and in 'the music of the military performers'. Hence they are 'too deeply absorbed in their own lives, as translated into emotion by the military band to perceive her'. Arabella's sardonic commentary punctuates the scene, as at the end, when she observes Jude and Sue's 'mutual responsiveness' brought about by the band's music, and their tentative hand-holding:

> 'Silly fools - like two children!' Arabella whispered to herself.
> (*Jude*, p. 314)

Arabella's view has a reductive validity, and echoes the ambivalent tone of Hardy's projected title for the novel, *The Simpletons*. Most importantly, her comments are the surrogate expression, even at this most tender moment of the book, of the excoriating emotional logic of the novel. Constantly in *Jude*, Hardy's narrator reacts (with an equal and opposite force, so to speak) against the novel's moments of feeling, so that the reader is propelled back and forth, between the narrative's moments of intense sympathy and its moments of bizarre, satiric, debunking, over-determination.

Unsurprisingly, Hardy's treatment of music becomes drawn into the bitterness and intensity of the novel. Consider the scene where Jude visits the town hall, having moments before been impressed by the egalitarian sentiment and revelation that the 'town life was a book of humanity infinitely more palpitating, varied, and compendious than the gown life' (*Jude*, p. 137):

> He looked at his watch, and in pursuit of this idea, he went on till he came to a public hall, where a promenade concert was in progress. Jude entered, and found the room full of shop youths and girls, soldiers, apprentices, boys of eleven smoking cigarettes, and light women of the more respectable and amateur class. A band was playing, and the crowd walked about and jostled each other, and every now and then a man got upon a platform and sang a comic song. The spirit of Sue seemed to hover round him and prevent his flirting and drinking with the frolicsome girls who made advances - wistful to gain a little joy. (*Jude*, p. 138)

The 'spirit of Sue' apart, the narrator suggests indirectly that this is not Jude's world, so that we see round Jude's illusions to the unsavoury aspects of the scene. This divergence of the narrator's perceptions from Jude's is, though, rather unpleasantly mocking. The narrator's humour is at Jude's expense, rebounding against his naiveté, in a way which inverts Hardy's instinctive sensitivities towards his characters, as much as Hardy's own lyrical and musical tendencies would be turned inside out by association with the mass-manufactured, ephemeral, music of such concerts. The ribald and comic songs we imagine being sung in this scene by the men who get up on stage were precisely those which Hardy most despised, since he associated them with the decline of the very rural songs he loved most, as in the list he made towards the very end of his life, entitled:

> Country Songs of 1820 onwards
> Killed by the Comic Song of the Music Hall [35]

It is Jude's inevitable disappointment and exile, then, that are repeated by what Peter Widdowson has argued is the satirical method of *Jude*.[36] The bathetic hopelessness of the hero's hopes are time and again worked out through music:

> He hired a harmonium, set it up in his lodging, and practised chants thereon, single and double. (*Jude*, p. 155)

To take one final example, when Jude plays 'The Foot of the Cross' for Sue on the old piano, he brings about a collective emotional impression and impulse which overcomes, for a time, their estrangement, such that 'by an unpremeditated instinct each clasped the other's hand again' (*Jude*, p. 223). However, at this moment in the text, we feel the narrator allows only as much incipient joy as is compatible with the eventual maximizing of the pain of disappointment. Hardy's Shelleyan vision of the pair as twin souls is inevitably accompanied by the annihilating narrative sense of a prosaic modern world crushingly opposed to such eternal truths. Even within the scene, ironic effects strike this jarring note, as Sue puts on the kettle, which we hear was a wedding present from him to her:

> The kettle of his gift sang with some satire in its note to his mind.
> (*Jude*, p. 224)

At the end of the book, Jude is enclosed by this sense of self-satire, dying as a result of a chill caught from 'putting up some stone work of a music hall' (*Jude*, p. 331).

In their differing ways, these later tragic novels, social critiques as Hardy conceived them, designedly convert into problematic theme and drama that division of involuntary responsiveness and reflective self-consciousness which is always evident in the different aspects of his narratives. In this respect, *The Well-Beloved* remains the last word in Hardy's fiction. It self-consciously and unsparingly diagnoses the expressive, differentiating structure of unconscious desire that I have been tracing in this chapter through the theme of music. However, in so doing it stages and analyzes desire as a function of the solitary individual, rather than as a function of transpersonal individuation. Accordingly, the novel is a profound study of the idealizing component in Pierston's mind, rather than a study any longer of the ideal elements of physicality. Hardy himself observed the ways in which the novel's analyses of the mechanics of passion made him a precursor of Proust's similar 'theory of the transmigration of the ideal beloved one, who only exists in the lover, from material woman to material woman' (*Life*, p. 286). This exclusivity is replicated in the narrator's own intense focus on Pierston, and his ironic series of loves, 'vexed from his soul' (*The Well-Beloved*, p. 13) as he is by his sense of:

> the migratory, elusive idealization he called his Love who, ever since his boyhoodom had flitted from human shell to human shell an indefinite number of times. (*The Well-Beloved*, p. 16)

The unconscious in *The Well-Beloved* is conceived as an interior theatre of sublime fiction and fantasy, but a theatre where, ultimately, tragic farce is the only show in town. Pierston does not fall in love with the various Avices so much as fall in love *at* them, and, in its unremitting focus on the disappointments, idealizations, and impositions of solitary desire, the novel is a profound summation of the logic of the later fiction.

Predictably enough, perhaps, in *The Well-Beloved* music is associated with the chimerical incarnations of desire in the various Avices, and with the movement from one to another. Within the novel, music is always associated with the sounds of their voices, as in the 'cadences' of the second Avice's 'voice', whose:

> charm lay in the intervals [...] She would say a few syllables in one note, and end her sentence in a soft modulation upwards, then

downwards, then into her own note again. The curve of sound was as satisfying as any line of beauty ever struck by his pencil. He took special pains that in catching her voice he might not comprehend her words. (*The Well-Beloved*, p. 95)

Again, it is associated with the playing of the third Avice:

'She plays that instrument, I suppose?' said Pierston, regarding the piano.
'Yes, she plays beautifully; she had the best instruction that masters could give her'. (*The Well-Beloved*, p. 149)

V

This chapter has explored some of the ways in which questions and values of individuality emerge in Hardy's fiction. In following the linked topics of music and the soul, it has argued that both share and involve temporal dimensions and qualities which do not correspond to those relatively stable identities given by subjectivity, and the spatial limits of the body. Hardy's fiction fundamentally reveals an evaluation of human life as existing not in such effects of identity, but in involuntary, materially mediated, kinds of relatedness. Further, the chapter has argued that it is possible to see Hardy's fiction as increasingly dominated by a critique which, in the later novels, directs against society's norms a despairing anger. In *Jude* and *The Well-Beloved*, this anger turns also against the self produced by such a society, which becomes increasingly scrutinized as a site of mystification and fantasy. One can point here to a similarity between Hardy at the end of his novel-writing career, and Sue Bridehead at the end of *Jude*, as she becomes defensively enthralled by self-persecuting High Anglican religiosity. There is a masochism in both cases which appears, paradoxically, as a highly emotional attempt to overcome painful emotion. Both Sue and Hardy (like Jude or Pierston or Henchard), are brought by events to a sense that their kinds of emotional responsiveness have no function in the world, and so turn their emotions against themselves, precipitating themselves into a contradictory vortex of self-irony. In this respect, the turning against emotion itself is an extension of that turning against society, because of the ways it defeats the possibilities of joy associated with nature. We can cite Sue again here:

'We said - do you remember? - that we would make a virtue of joy. I said it was Nature's intention, Nature's law and raison d'être that we should be joyful in what instincts she afforded us - instincts which civilization had taken upon itself to thwart'. (*Jude*, p. 358)

Notes

[1]   Thomas Hardy, *The Trumpet-Major* (London: Macmillan, 1974), pp. 117-18.

[2]   Thomas Hardy, *Preface* to 'Late Lyrics and Earlier' (*Complete Poems*, p. 359).
The passage continues by unfolding into a more explicitly musical reference:

> In respect of the less alert, however, should any one's train of thought be
> thrown out of gear by a consecutive piping of vocal reeds in jarring
> tonics, without a semi-quaver's rest in between, and be led thereby to
> miss the writer's aim and meaning in one out of two contiguous
> compositions, I shall deeply regret it. (*Complete Poems*, pp. 359-60)

[3]   Thomas Hardy, 'The Fiddler of the Reels', Vol. 2 of *The Stories of Thomas
Hardy* (edited by F. B. Pinion, London: Macmillan, 1977), p. 125.

[4]   It is interesting to compare Hardy here with Proust's Marcel whose
meditations on music often elucidate a similar image of its powerful status as a 'proof
of the irreducibly individual existence of the soul' (Marcel Proust, *Remembrance of
Things Past*, Vol. 2 [translated by C. K. Scott Moncrieff and Terence Kilmartin; and by
Andreas Mayor, London: Penguin, 1989], p. 258). So, Marcel reflects, at the concert on
the night of the Baron de Charlus's great humiliation, as the andante dies away and
conversation begins again:

> I was truly like an angel who, fallen from the inebriating bliss of paradise,
> subsides into the most humdrum reality. And, just as certain creatures are
> the last surviving testimony to a form of life which nature has discarded,
> I wondered whether music might not be the unique example of what
> might have been - if the invention of language, the formation of words,
> the analysis of ideas had not intervened - the means of communication
> between souls. (*Remembrance of Things Past*, Vol. 2, p. 260)

[5]   Thomas Hardy, *Jude the Obscure* (London: Macmillan, 1974), p. 43.

[6]   Thomas Hardy, *The Well-Beloved* (Oxford: Oxford World's Classics, 1986), p.
66.

[7]   Caroline Jackson-Houlston, 'Thomas Hardy's Use of Traditional Song',
Nineteenth-Century Literature (December 1989), pp. 301-34.

[8]   Joan Grundy, *Hardy and the Sister Arts* (London: Macmillan, 1979), p. 139.

[9]   Gilles Deleuze and Claire Parnet, *Dialogues* (translated by Hugh Tomlinson
and Barbara Habberjam, London: Athlone, 1987), pp. 39-40.

[10]   Deleuze's conception of mind and body as parallel (and more or less
autonomous, more or less passive) manifestations of individuality draws on the
metaphysics of Spinoza. Hardy was aware of Spinoza, though perhaps the most
explicit trace of such a conception comes from a formulation by Spencer, which he
noted down and underlined in his notebooks:

> 'One substance with two sets of properties, two sides, the physical & the
> mental - a <u>double-faced unity</u>.' (*Literary Notebooks*, Vol. 2, p. 108)

For a fuller discussion of the relevant connections between Deleuze and Spinoza, see
Gilles Deleuze, *Spinoza: Practical Philosophy*, translated by Robert Hurley (San
Francisco: City Lights, 1988); or, for a gloss on these ideas in relation to literature,

there is my book *Lines of Flight* (Sheffield: Sheffield Academic Press, 1997).

[11] Indeed, even more to the point, John Goode's analysis of *Tess* has an interesting page or two on the use of music in the novel that link with this discussion. Goode sees music as tied to the novel's emphasis on nature, and thereby to 'a lost potential of womanhood [...] in Tess's case'. This potential is at odds with the society which destroys her, and with '[t]he whole Victorian fictional discourse of the fallen woman'. For Goode, society's influences and its value system are put aside at 'the moment of musical response to the external world'. (John Goode, *Thomas Hardy: The Offensive Truth* [Oxford: Blackwell, 1988], p. 116).

[12] Thomas Hardy, 'The Distracted Preacher', Vol. 1 of *The Stories of Thomas Hardy* (edited by F. B. Pinion, London: Macmillan, 1977), p. 171.

[13] Virginia Woolf, 'Thomas Hardy's Novels', *Times Literary Supplement*, Vol. 19 (January 1928), p. 33.

[14] Thomas Hardy, *Desperate Remedies* (London: Penguin, 1995), p. 31.

[15] Virginia Woolf, 'Thomas Hardy's Novels', *The Common Reader* (London: Hogarth, 1959), p. 247.

[16] Thomas Hardy, *The Hand of Ethelberta* (London: Macmillan, 1975), p. 64.

[17] D. H. Lawrence, 'Study of Thomas Hardy', *Selected Literary Criticism* (London: Heinemann, 1973), p. 167.

[18] Thomas Hardy, *Under the Greenwood Tree* (London: Macmillan, 1974), p. 63.

[19] Thomas Hardy, *The Mayor of Casterbridge* (London: Macmillan, 1974), p. 82.

[20] Thomas Hardy, *A Laodicean* (London: Macmillan, 1975), p. 46.

[21] Rosemary Sumner, 'Discoveries of Dissonance; Hardy's Late Fiction', *The Thomas Hardy Journal*, Vol. XI, no. 3 (October 1995), pp. 79-88. She cites Curtis's edition of *Proust's Letters* (London: Chatto, 1950) and points out that he wrote in a letter also that *The Well-Beloved* was 'a thousand times better' than *Remembrance of Things Past* (p. 84).

[22] Virginia Woolf, 'The Novels of Thomas Hardy', *Collected Essays*, Vol. 1 (edited by Leonard Woolf, London: Hogarth, 1966), p. 250.

[23] For discussions of this issue, and the factors involved in the formation of a canon of 'major' novels, see Widdowson's *Hardy in History*, and Ebbatson's, *The Margin of the Unexpressed*.

[24] Caroline Jackson-Houlston, *Ballads, Songs and Snatches* (Aldershot: Ashgate, 1999), p. 154.

[25] As Jackson-Houlston, Ian Gregor and others have indicated.

[26] Thomas Hardy, *The Woodlanders* (London: Macmillan, 1974), p. 123.

[27] It is interesting in discussing such aspects of the novel, and the narrative's attitude of regretful and meditative clarity, to consider how Hardy's own attention remained fixed on this novel. The poem, 'In a Wood', of 1896, offers an interesting coda here, because subtitled, *"See 'The Woodlanders'"*, it thus provides a reading on the novel, with its image of the wood as a place whose '[g]reat growths and small' are 'Combatants all!', a site of poisoning, choking, stingings, prickings, cankerings, against which the world of the city, in a musical image, offers some solace:

There at least smiles abound,
There discourse trills around,
There, now and then, are found
Life-loyalties. (*Complete Poems*, p. 65)

[28] J. B. Bullen's discussion of *The Woodlanders*, in his book on Hardy and the

visual arts (*The Expressive Eye*) has interesting points of intersection with this discussion. Bullen takes such features of the novel - its melancholy charting of the dissolution of an old community under the invasive influences of a new; its equally melancholy sense of the powerlessness and isolation of individuals, and of the competitive destructiveness of nature - and relates them, in the first instance, to the anthropological and evolutionary reading which Hardy was undertaking at the time. Further, Bullen relates to Impressionist art the removed and painedly quiescent solipsism which seems to mark the narrative values of the text, and which manifests a dispirited and dislocated attitude to the natural world. For Bullen, Giles and Marty ultimately 'can be distinguished from the other characters in the novel, and even from the narrator himself, in possessing the capacity to read the more arcane signs and the hidden meanings of nature [...] Their view is neither that of the Impressionist with his selective eye, nor that of the Darwinian with his eye for conflict and struggle.' (J. B. Bullen, *The Expressive Eye* [Oxford: Clarendon, 1986], p. 186).

29 In terms of plot, to begin with, this can be seen in the novel's beginning with Barber Percombe, the first chapter ending with him outside Marty's door; the third chapter then enters Marty's house, and takes Marty to Melbury's house where she overhears Melbury and his wife talking; the fifth chapter introduces us to Mrs Charmond who is inside the carriage which passes Marty on the road; Grace thinks of Fitzpiers as the light from his house shines into her bedroom; Giles, as on several occasions in the novel, sees Grace at her window at the close of Chapter Seven, and then Chapter Eight begins inside with her. Examples could be multiplied of this technique of shifting the narrator's immediate centre of interest, by taking up an, as it were, accidental element of a scene, which then, or eventually, provides access to another self-sufficient narrative. The various carriages, houses, windows, entangled tree branches, crossing paths, and the man-trap, are of special interest in this text in so far as they function as spatializations or vehicles of this web-like technique in the narrative. These things mediate the successive centres of interest for the reader, but without harmonizing them. The effect produced is one of tenuous and uncomfortable connection, rather like that of the prepositional phrases in a sentence such as this:

> Over the roof of the house could be seen the orchard on yet higher ground, and behind the orchard the forest trees, reaching up to the crest of the hill. (*The Woodlanders*, p. 142)

Further, similar formal characteristics can be seen in the love stories of the text. *The Woodlanders* begins with the barber who has designs of a sort on Marty; moves to Marty who loves Giles; takes up Giles who loves Grace; takes up Grace who marries Fitzpiers; takes up Fitzpiers who turns to Suke and Mrs Charmond. The novel's progression uncovers a network of people in hopeful isolation, and the sadness involved seems to go along with a subliminal feeling of sadness on the part of the narrator - at the cultural and historical removal involved for the narrator in this contemporaneous tale of rural life. Nor does family offer a locus of harmonic integration, since even within the Melbury household there is a lack of mutual understanding productive of all sorts of disastrous displacement and interference. In terms of the novel as a whole, at the centre of this paradoxically unreciprocal social web there is Grace, who is caught, like the narrator, between the values of the woodlands and education, between Giles and Fitzpiers, between the rural and the rootless. As might be expected the narrator enters most firmly and extensively into her viewpoint.

[30] Margaret Elvy, *Sexing Hardy: Thomas Hardy and Feminism* (London: Crescent Moon, 1998), p. 85.

[31] Peter Conrad, *The Everyman History of English Literature* (London: Dent, 1985), p. 510.

[32] Phillip Mallett, '*Jude the Obscure*: A Farewell to Wessex', *The Thomas Hardy Journal*, Vol. XI, no. 2 (October 1995), p. 50.

[33] However, it is also a truism to point out how even in this text, and certainly in *Far from the Madding Crowd*, the writing incorporates tragic elements or potentials - erotic complications, obsessive compulsions, economic conflicts and divisions - that impart a continuing tension to the text. For instance, when Bathsheba and Boldwood sing in harmony to Oak's accompaniment, the words of the song ironically prefigure the fatal conflict to which the song also offers a respite:

> For his bride a soldier sought her,
>   And a winning tongue had he:
> On the banks of Allan Water
>   None was gay as she! (*Far from the Madding Crowd*, p. 188)

[34] Thomas Hardy, 'Postscript' to *Jude* (London: Macmillan, 1974), pp. 24-25.

[35] See Appendix 2 to Jackson-Houlston's *Ballads, Songs and Snatches*, pp. 182-193.

[36] See 'Arabella and the Satirical Discourse in *Jude the Obscure*' in *Late Essays and Earlier*, pp. 168-87.

Chapter 2

'Those Unaccountable Sensations'

Hardy's fascination with the paradoxical effects of music is evident in the notes he took from the first volume of John Addington Symonds's *Essays Speculative and Suggestive* in 1891. Of the following remarks, Hardy wrote down the second and third, among others:

> Music transports us to a different region.[1]

> [...] all that musical sounds convey remains within the region of emotion which has not been intellectualized.[2]

> Art is bound to introduce an equivalent for what it cannot represent. (*Literary Notebooks*, Vol. 2, p. 36)

In his essay, 'The Profitable Reading of Fiction', he describes how comparable effects take place in reading fiction, referring to the 'sudden shifting of the mental perspective into a fictitious world':

> If we speak of deriving good from a story, we usually mean something more than the gain of pleasure during the hours of its perusal. Nevertheless, to get pleasure out of a book is a beneficial and profitable thing, if the pleasure be of a kind which, while doing no moral injury, affords relaxation and relief when the mind is overstrained or sick of itself. The prime remedy in such cases is change of scene, by which change of the material scene is not necessarily implied. A sudden shifting of the mental perspective into a fictitious world, combined with rest, is well known to be as efficacious for renovation as a corporeal journey afar.
> In such a case the shifting of scene should manifestly be as complete as if the reader had taken the hind seat on a witch's broomstick.[3]

This chapter analyzes, in relation to music, further cognate aspects and implications of the individuating events that underlie Hardy's fiction, beginning with an exposition of the transpersonal nature of such events. Developing an account of the recreational, unconscious and participatory features of Hardy's musical scenes, the focus then falls on the essentially artistic and affective attributes involved: such moments entail a logic of sensory transmission and emotional transport that Hardy's writing stages and enacts. There follows an examination of the constitutive temporality of such moments, as moments of becoming, and focuses on related ideas of movement and duration in Hardy's work. This reiterated concentration on episodes of non-subjective intensity, and on the types of indetermination involved, leads into a discussion about the representation of gender and love within the novels, before the chapter closes with a discussion of those transitional texts, the short stories.

I

Music, it has been suggested, offers Hardy both a metaphor and a dramatic, scenic means for the moments of inclusive relatedness that motivate his fiction in fundamental ways. It is one of the main benefits of individuation, as the concept underlying this book, that it allows one to describe the various aspects of such passages, passages where there often appear to be less an organizing subject as such, than uncontained and individuating states and waves of feeling that take up narrator, character, reader. Vibration often appears to provide a better model than communication for this thought that surfaces within singular scenes, drawing the reader into participation.

Donald Davie remarked this physical basis of Hardy's art when he observed that Hardy as a poet is liable to be captivated by the sensory qualities of a scene, by what Davie calls his 'capacity to occupy a particular scene or situation with all his senses alert'.[4] Taking a more or less random example of this from the fiction, one can consider the scene in *Two on a Tower* where Swithin leaves Lady Constantine alone on the tower at night. The prose is intent and attentive as it is worked over by light, sound, wind:

> At first all was obscurity; but when he had gone about ten minutes lights began to move to and fro in the hollow where the house stood, and occasionally shouts mingled with the wind, which retained some violence yet, playing over the trees beneath her as on the strings of a lyre.[5]

Situating itself initially in 'obscurity', Hardy's narrative becomes itself a conductive medium, taken over as it describes how the wind works on the branches of the trees, 'as on the strings of a lyre'. The transmissions of the wind pass, with a poetic augmentation, into the cadence which closes the sentence:

> occasionally shouts mingled with the wind, which retained some violence yet, playing over the trees beneath her as on the strings of a lyre [...]

To say that the 'shifting of scene' is clearly here 'complete', is another way of saying that Hardy's scene is totally established for the reader, who finds, in a familiar way, that narrative distance has been abolished, and that he or she comes to exist for a time with Lady Constantine, and the narrator, on a common level of perception and musing. The scene, heterogeneous in its parts, has, in these ways, a consistency of its own. Effects of commutability and mobility go between its elements and *personae*, as with the anonymous 'violence' of the wind, which plays over the different trees like lyre strings. In the reader, too, the different faculties of mind, are variously stimulated and engaged, as the writing passes from sight to sound.

In *Desperate Remedies*, there is a comparable moment, where Manston pauses in the fir-plantation to listen to the musical effects of the wind in the trees:

> However, as the wood was not large, he experienced no alarm about finding the path again, and with some sense of pleasure halted awhile against the rails, to listen to the intensely melancholy yet musical wail of the fir-tops, and as the wind passed on, the prompt moan of an adjacent plantation in reply. (*Desperate Remedies*, p. 164)

The language itself vibrates like an aeolian harp, the syntax dividing to convey the varied subliminal texture, the melancholy and pleasurable intensities, aroused by the scene. Between the fir trees, the wind sets up an exchange of responses which the narrator associates with music. It is this agency of movement and sound which again gives the moment a unity of its own, as in the nocturnal responses of the forest in *Far from the Madding Crowd*, where 'the trees on the right and the trees on the left wailed or chaunted to each other in the regular antiphonies of a cathedral choir' (p. 47). In each case, music suggests if not harmony, then a rapport or commerce of sound which effectively binds together the divergent elements of the scene, and draws the reader, character and narrator together within the intent physicality of the moment. The scene as an event goes beyond and between the various individuals and elements within it, taking shape as a larger, open envelope of experience. As a further aspect of this unformed inclusiveness in these scenes, there are interwoven in each suggestions not only of pleasure and comedy, but also of pain, melancholy, loss and violence. In this way also the uncertainties of the moment reflect the disjunctive possibilities of romance and tragedy evident in each narrative as a whole.

This Hardyan sense of contingency, of the registration of an absolute and singular moment like no other, out of which the narrative unfolds, can be elucidated by a further nuance of Deleuze's use of the notion of individuation. He takes the word so that it can refer to the unique individuality of an event itself:

> In fact no individuation takes place in the manner of a subject or even of a thing. An hour, a day, a season [...] have a perfect individuality which should not be confused with that of a thing or of a formed subject. (*Dialogues*, p. 92)

Such an 'individuation without a subject' (*Dialogues* p. 40) depends on the compounding of the multiple forces of the bodies concerned, according to processes that make up new multiplicities, that:

> refer only to an 'it' of the event (it is raining) and are themselves attributed to states of things which are compounds or collectives, assemblages, even at the peak of their singularity [...] (*Dialogues*, p. 64)

The result is of an overall event with its own 'singularity' or 'perfect individuality'. The wind, or a wave, or a piece of music, would be appropriate metaphors for this metaphysic of individuation that resists the logic of the integral identities formed by its material elements. Instead, for the individuals concerned there is an exteriorization and multiplication of the self through the senses, as observed in the previous chapter, whereby the accidents of bodily encounters express powers of unconscious desire, processes of the body and mind 'not reducible to the organism' or 'to consciousness' (*Dialogues*, p. 62).[6] These features of Hardy's writing demonstrate the important element of truth in Deleuze's identification of him as a novelist whose practice operates in terms of sensations and intensities:

> Take the example of Thomas Hardy: his characters are not people or subjects, they are collections of intensive sensations. (*Dialogues*, pp. 39-40)

The important emphasis here is that these interrelated ideas of the event, individuation and desire offer useful ways of thinking of the constitutive role played by the intensities of sensory and affective experience in Hardy's fiction. Individuation as a concept allows for a conceptualization both of the multiplicities, the 'collections', which events, music and individuals are, and for the larger multiplicities that they make up moment by moment. Further, like a musical performance, an event retains a synthetic quality that transcends the material elements it happens to combine, and the distinct intelligible potentials with which it is imbued. Like a performance, it preserves a mysterious integrity of its own, while providing the conditions for individual expression.

The analogies and continuities between these various multiplicities can be traced in a final example referring to an aeolian effect in nature: this time of the actual aeolian harp which Bob makes for Anne in *The Trumpet-Major*. Water, wind and strings combine, and the materials of nature find in musical sound a correspondence with her soul, amplifying her feelings for Bob, and redirecting them to him:

> Every night after this, during the mournful gales of autumn, the strange mixed music of water, wind and strings met her ear, swelling and sinking with an almost supernatural cadence. The character of the instrument was far enough removed from anything that she had hitherto seen of Bob's hobbies; so that she marvelled pleasantly at the new depths of poetry this contrivance revealed as existent in that young seaman's nature, and allowed her emotions to flow out yet a little further in the old direction, notwithstanding her severe resolve to bar them back. (*The Trumpet-Major*, p. 194)

The 'strange mixed music of water, wind and strings' has the effect of converting Anne's emotions into hydraulic form, as they swell and overflow the sea-wall of conscious restraint, and 'flow out yet a little further in the old direction'. The emergent phrases of the harp solicit the re-emergence of the old Anne. Her recently rather inchoate emotions are reconfigured by the aeolian music that she takes as a decisive signal of Bob's lyrical nature. At the same time, the narrator appears to take such aeolian effects as a signal of a lyricism intrinsic to nature itself, a lyricism which is at once 'strange', and yet which palpably works on Anne at an unconscious level.

To describe the unconscious affective processes of this passage, then, involves one in describing Anne's participation within a kind of scenic and sonic force-field, in which physical accidents provoke a qualitative shift in her emotional world. The aeolian harp is the instrument for this affective alteration, materially drawing together and converting into a new arrangement her potentials of feeling. As Anne's fascination and self-expression are elicited by the wind-blown harp, so too the narrator appears at an important level to be mesmirized by the harp's figural potential, as it offers itself to him as a metaphor for the revelatory, individualizing powers of the seemingly random, and so as a metaphor for the processes of his own writing that often depend on an apparent surrender to contingency.

In fact, one can even generalize that it is on such physical terms, in the middle of such scenes, that Hardy's imagination, like Anne's feeling, comes into its own. It is a writing whose pleasurable and painful effects are fundamentally linked to this openness to independent events where becomings sweep over the characters and the narrator and reader too. Such events possess, for Deleuze, an 'incorporeal' aspect (as well as a corporeal one) where the characters are opened up by the new set of relations and expressions which emerge.[7] Which is to say that for Hardy the scene has its own unique quality, while existing as the medium in which the uniqueness of the characters can take on a new form. So, for example, when Troy and Bathsheba meet in the fir plantation, or when Henchard enters the tent with Susan and his daughter, the narrative is possessed by the physical minutiae, the incalculable chances, of the scene, yet the critical significance, the accumulated intensity, of the meeting is not to do simply with what is seen or heard, but with the different question of what the scene means, as an overall encounter: what forces of change and individuality will be released by it? In what unpredictable way will it bind together or divide the fates of the characters? What are the memorable qualities and details of this event which make it both contingent and *sui generis*? Time and again, as we have seen, music is implicated in the effects of relatedness which work between the characters in such scenes. It facilitates those individuating accidents, those moments of exchange, in which the character is betrayed, by an unwilled response, into self-disclosure:

> He spoke to her in low tones, and she instinctively modulated her own to the same pitch, and her thought ultimately even caught the inflection of his. (*Far from the Madding Crowd*, p. 180)

> [...] the recent sight of Stephen's face and the sound of his voice for a moment had stirred a chord or two of ancient kindness [...] (*A Pair of Blue Eyes*, p. 328)

Even in modest examples like this, then, music shows the unconscious self-expression not only of the character, but of the narrator whose gifts come fully alive in recording such moments of interchange.

Further, one can say that music's association with such moments of exchange and combination allows it be a metaphor for the unconscious conceived in essentially physical terms. This last idea is close to Donzelot's account of the unconscious as 'an exchange with nature'.[8] The unconscious would here be conceived not as 'the secret receptacle of a meaning to be deciphered but the *state of co-extensiveness of man and nature*'.[9] That is to say, the unconscious is conceived not as a deeper, repressed, and remotely active mental interiority, but as an experimental activity of thought which finds itself, as Deleuze puts it, in the middle of things, called into being by the events of the body's diverse activities and passions. The mind is conceived in terms of the body, and the body in terms of its capacity for relatedness through sensibility and passion.[10]

In this context, it is interesting to notice a comment dated January 14 1888, in which Hardy speculated on the innovation of a new type of fiction, called a 'sensation novel':

> A "sensation-novel" is possible in which the sensationalism is not casualty, but evolution; not physical but psychical [....] The difference between the latter kind of novel and the novel of physical sensationalism - *i.e.* personal adventure, etc., - is this: that whereas in the physical the adventure itself is the subject of interest, the psychical results being passed over as commonplace, in the psychical the casualty or adventure is held to be of no intrinsic interest, but the effect upon the faculties is the important matter to be depicted. (*Life*, p. 204)

These comments about the 'effect upon the faculties' can be linked to Deleuze's idea of an empiricist practice of writing that fundamentally contests the philosophically privileged image of thought as 'recognition', where this latter model presupposes the 'concord of the faculties' and the transcendental unity of the thinking subject in relation to the perceived object. Against this, Deleuze proposes a thought:

> which would not be closed on recognition, but which would be open to encounters and which would always be defined as a function of the Outside. (*Dialogues*, p. 24)

One could reflect in this context on many fundamental features of Hardy's texts as they open themselves to events: for instance, the literal way in which Hardy nearly always begins his novels outside, and in doing so delays identification or recognition in various ways. An old man walking across the heath, then a figure against the sky in *The Return of the Native*; the woman on horseback and the other woman on the road whom Oak meets in *Far from the Madding Crowd*; the relay of initially unidentified figures at the beginning of *The Woodlanders*; and so on. As well as being merely a striking scenic and narrative device, such devices establish the physical values of Hardy's texts, the emergence of narrative and character from event and sensation. So, *Under the Greenwood Tree* begins in a world of anonymous sounds, in the darkness of the plantation, as the narrator directs the reader's attention to the different sounds of the trees, and then to the sounds of Dick Dewy, who is introduced by way of the audible 'spirit of his footsteps', and 'the liveliness of his voice as he sang in a rural cadence'. With a peculiar defiance, the narrator interrupts recognition, as the rural choir come by way of sounds to converge in the wood. Only then do they greet each other, and return to the customary world, a return signalled by the 'the faint sound of church-bells', and the light which 'streamed through the cracks and joints of outbuildings a little way from the cottage' (*Under the Greenwood Tree*, p. 37). The physical immediacy of the text, and its suspension of social presuppositions of identity, means that for the reader the experience of reading these pages is indeed an experience of that 'sudden shifting of the mental perspective into a fictitious world'. Further, the effect of such reading, as Hardy also put it, is 'as efficacious for renovation as a corporeal journey afar'.

II

As well as producing a sense of well-being (of 'relaxation', 'relief' and 'renovation') Hardy wrote, in 'The Profitable Reading of Fiction', of the necessity in a pleasurable fiction that:

> [t]he narrative must be of a somewhat absorbing kind, if not absolutely fascinating. To discover a book or books which shall possess, in addition to the special scenery, the special action required, may be a matter of some difficulty [...] and it may be asserted that after every variety of spiritual fatigue there is to be found refreshment, if not restoration, in some antithetic realm of ideas which lies waiting in the pages of romance.

In reading for such hygienic purposes it is, of course, of the first consequence that the reader be not too critical. ('The Profitable Reading of Fiction', pp. 242-43.)

Both Hardy's prose and his poetry appear to perpetuate and derive from such absorbed moments, where the mind is both fully engaged and yet relaxed under the spell of the 'special scenery' and 'special action' of the narrative.[11] This section ponders such captivating processes in Hardy's fiction, and relates them to Hardy's identification of the satisfactions of reading. As part of the emphasis on the primacy of unconscious experience in Hardy's art, the section closes by examining the strange effects of incipient reflexivity which often appear to emerge, as if unnoticed, from the scenes and words of Hardy's texts.[12]

I want to begin here by looking at two musical incidents described in the *Life*, before going on to pursue further the restorative functions of writing as Hardy describes them. In June of 1875, shortly before taking up lodgings in Swanage, Hardy spent some days house-hunting in Dorsetshire, moving from Shaftesbury to Blandford, and 'thence', as he describes it:

to Wimborne, where on arrival he entered the Minster at ten at night, having seen a light within, and sat in the stall listening to the organist practising, while the rays from the musician's solitary candle streamed across the arcades. This incident seems to have inclined him to Wimborne; but he did not go there yet. (*Life*, p. 107)

The episode is typically inconsequential and indefinite in all sorts of ways - it is related by a voice that both is and is not Hardy's; it is included in the *Life*, for who knows what purpose; it refers to an unknown organist whose sense of the incident, if any, is unrecorded; and it describes an incident which at this time did nothing more than incline the Hardys to live in Wimborne. For all these undisclosed and inconclusive aspects, though, we detect the charm and respite of the scene for Hardy. Attracted initially by the sounds of the organ, and by candle-light, his movement into the Minster is also a movement between the faculties, a movement from ear to eye. The scene inside is shaped by Hardy's painterly inner eye, in a way which also revives the inner eye of the reader:

while the rays from the musician's solitary candle streamed across the arcades.

The spectacle appeals because the sensations and response it provokes are momentarily and innately artistic, in a small-scale way. There is in the scene an inwardly expanding sense, for Hardy and for the reader, of how the art of another person can become the condition of a secondary creativity of one's own. Drawn in like a moth by the candle-light and the solitary organist's notes amidst the other-worldly obscurity of the Minster, Hardy is stimulated by the occasion offered for a play of sensibility and thought, as well as by the opportunity for physical rest. This is a modest example of Hardy's art, but it offers another useful illustration of how his mind produces a counterpoint between self and world, and makes this available to the reader. For Hardy, the fatiguing and dreary aspects of the day are momentarily forgotten. The music and the setting take over the imagination and the senses, bringing about effects of spiritual 'refreshment' and 'restoration'.

In such an incident, the revivifying effect of the music appears linked to the sense of being lost to oneself, which it produces. Such an effect is also essentially participatory, in the way Emmanuel Levinas wrote that music and literature are, outside of a purely representative function. They work, says Levinas, in an 'ontological dimension' where imagery and 'rhythm' ensure that:

> there is no longer a oneself, but rather a sort of passage from oneself to anonymity. This is the captivation or incantation of poetry and music.[13]

Levinas's sense of art's capacity to produce (and dramatize) kinds of captivated and anonymous participation can be taken further by looking at another musical episode from the *Life*, where Hardy describes a scene (later to become revisited rather differently in the poem, 'Music in a Snowy Street'). Hardy is both fascinated and moved by the innately poetical features of the contrast between the differing spectacles which are provided by a band of four girls on the same day. In the morning, they are characterized by a defensive and denatured worldliness. In their various personal manifestations (hardness, coquettishness, and so on), one can detect what the world has made them. However, by the evening all is alchemically transformed, the brute and brassy qualities of the morning are dissolved away, as all is 'sublimed to a wondrous charm' in the performance of a song which seems continuous with a changed moral world. Now the girls are tender, solicitous, pure, angelic, cherubic, no longer the strangers to themselves which 'civilization' had made them :

'April 26. Curious scene. A fine poem in it:

'Four girls - itinerant musicians - sisters, have been playing opposite Parmiter's in the High Street. The eldest had a fixed, old, hard face, and wore white roses in her hat. Her eyes remained on one close object, such as the buttons of her sister's dress; she played the violin. The next sister, with red roses in her hat, had rather bold dark eyes, and a coquettish smirk. She too played a violin. The next, with her hair in ringlets, beat the tambourine. The youngest, a mere child, dinged the triangle. She wore a bead necklace. All wore large brass earrings like Jews'-harps, which dangled to the time of the jig.

'I saw them again in the evening, the silvery gleams from Saunder's [silver-smith's] shop shining out upon them. They were now sublimed to a wondrous charm. The hard face of the eldest was now flooded with soft solicitous thought; the coquettish one was no longer bold but archly tender; her dirty white roses were pure as snow; her sister's red ones a fine crimson: the brass earrings were golden; the iron triangles silver; the tambourine Miriam's own; the third child's face that of an angel; the fourth that of a cherub. The pretty one smiled on the second, and began to play "In the gloaming", the little voices singing it. *Now* they were what Nature made them, before the smear of "civilization" had sullied their existences'. (*Life,* p. 165)

Both episodes from the *Life* appear memorable because they offer resources for the artist that are not only creative but also, in a more general sense recreational, in that Hardy, the girls, the reader (maybe the organist too) find themselves restored to themselves through musical or literary sensation. They merge into the suprapersonal relations which constitute and emerge from the event, as reader or narrator also lose themselves in it.

In these cases, as Hardy concentrates on these stimulating musical incidents, the raptness of his scrutiny conveys the 'captivation or incantation' of which Levinas spoke. In these two scenes from the *Life*, music sets off effects which radiate out, like the spreading ripples on a pond, collapsing the distinctions between bodies, and the spiritual distinctions between passive reception and active participation. Pleasure becomes indissociable from creativity (where experience takes on the musical attributes of resounding and rhythm) as in an observation recorded by Hardy in his Notebooks, and attributed to Comte:

> The capacity to enjoy is at bottom identical with the capacity to
> produce, the difference being merely one of degree. (*Literary
> Notebooks*, Vol. 1, p. 74)

In sensation, one can say, the unconscious intelligence reveals the
intrinsic artifice of thought itself, as the body composes a response to
the felt quality of what affects it. My emphasis here is that Hardy is a
writer who not only brings such responses to expression, but
perpetuates them at the level of language, making the reader similarly a
participant in this intensive and sensibly provoked thought.[14] His
fiction produces what can be called effects of corporeality by other
means, and through them engenders distinctive, innately aesthetic,
artistic, modes of thinking.

These features of Hardy's writing can be observed in the
following scene from *The Return of the Native* when again the
individuating qualities of Hardy's scenes and prose revive the
expressive potentials of reader, narrator and character. When Eustacia
and Wildeve meet, accidentally and unrecognized at the dance on the
heath, the charm of the dance for them both, as Hardy describes it, can
be construed according to this restorative, aesthetic, logic. Eustacia's
sense of her own expressive possibilities comes alive once more, as does
Hardy's creative intelligence, and the reader's imagination. For
Eustacia, the pale evening light and the music lent an 'enchantment' to
the scene which 'surprised her', so that her 'beginning to dance had
been like a change of atmosphere', a 'clear line of difference' dividing
'like a tangible fence her experience within this maze of motion from
her experience without it' [...] (*The Return of the Native*, p. 283). Tangible,
at this moment too, is the animated sense of multiplied and
differentiated precision in the writing. The narrator's inimitable powers
of discrimination, physical and affective, are accentuated, engendered
by the scene's spell, the variable, inclusive aspects of his sensibility
excited by the occasion as if they were the hairs on a cat's back.

Examining the scene itself more closely, we can note how the
writing captures the independent and 'perfect individuality' of the
dance (in Deleuze's phrase) as an event woven out of the coming
together of moonlight and the 'whole village-full of sensuous emotion,
scattered abroad all year long, [which] surged here in focus for an hour'
(p. 281):

> There is a certain degree and tone of light which tends to disturb
> the equilibrium of the senses, and to promote dangerously the
> tenderer moods; added to movement it drives the emotions to

rankness, the reason becoming sleepy and unperceiving in inverse
proportion [...] (*The Return of the Native*, p. 283)

The incident that transpires is of a suitably transfiguring kind,
provoking an overwhelming experience of expressive and erotic
enthusiasm for Eustacia who feels she and Wildeve are 'riding upon the
whirlwind', and suspending 'whatever sense of social order there was
in their minds':

> Wildeve by himself would have been merely an agitation; Wildeve
> added to the dance, and the moonlight and the secrecy, began to
> be a delight. Whether his personality supplied the greater part of
> this sweetly compounded feeling, or whether the dance and the
> scene weighed the more therein, was a nice point upon which
> Eustacia herself was entirely in a cloud [...]
>   Thus, for different reasons, what was to the rest an exhilarating
> movement was to these two a riding upon the whirlwind. The
> dance had come like an irresistible attack upon whatever sense of
> social order there was in their minds, to drive them back into old
> paths which were now doubly irregular. (*The Return of the Native*,
> p. 284)

The narrator's similarly unconstrained virtuosity is further evident in
the way his sense of Eustacia expands into the most subtle and flexible
accommodation of her divergent qualities. While the slightly occult
image of the two 'riding upon the whirlwind' suggests one aspect of
Eustacia's representation in the novel, the scene as a whole provokes for
the most part an unreserved sympathy for her at this moment. This is
perhaps inevitable since her aesthetic responses at the dance - as she
enjoys, imagines, and dreams of flight - become so entwined with our
own. Further, our sympathy is enhanced by the suspicion that her
readiness to enter into the dance betrays a desire for transcendence and
escape that is not only romantic, but dangerous:

> Eustacia floated round and round on Wildeve's arm, her face rapt
> and statuesque; her soul had passed away from and forgotten her
> features, which were left empty and quiescent, as they always are
> when feeling goes beyond their register. (*The Return of the Native*,
> p. 283)

Further, it is worth briefly describing in detail how nuanced,
supple, multiple, and acute is Hardy's writing at this moment, despite
the blur of this 'maze of motion' in the episode, and the intoxicating

feeling of overcoming social definitions and restraints. The image of Eustacia's face, for instance, is extraordinarily exact in its strange registration of the contradictory elements of her character ('rapt... statuesque; empty and quiescent'), and it also prefigures the paradoxical image we get of her face in death, with its expression both 'pleasant' and 'statel[y]' (*The Return of the Native*, p. 393). Once more, Hardy's physical sense of the character is both compellingly accurate in itself, and full of latent significance. The traits which direct Eustacia throughout the novel appear unobtrusively implied in the nuances of her facial expressions ('statuesque'; 'quiescent'), and to be revealed to the narrator no less than to the reader. As the reader visualizes and ponders these details, they seem the indices of a soul fatally compounded of both fervent self-idealization (which directs Eustacia away from the heath) and involuntary passivity (which binds her to it).

An obvious contrast to this practice of writing from the 'subjectless' middle of an event would be George Eliot's, where the formal constraints and syntheses of fiction offer a template for a socialized assimilation and tempering of impulse. When Maggie in *The Mill on the Floss*, under the influence of waltz music, feels the lure of physical movement with Stephen, the vocabulary is similar to that of Hardy, and the moment is richly evoked. However, the reader feels at the same time that the narrator is watchfully concerned to reassert the values of her fiction, and to conjoin this moment, with all the others that are modulated and surveyed in the overarching perspective of the narrative:

> Her eyes and cheeks were still brightened with her child-like enthusiasm in the dance; her whole frame was set to joy and tenderness:- even the coming pain could not seem bitter - she was ready to welcome it as a part of life, for life at this moment seemed a keen vibrating consciousness poised above pleasure or pain. This one, this last night, she might expand unrestrainedly in the warmth of the present, without those chill eating thoughts of the past and the future.[15]

The pursuit of such 'unrestrained expansion', whatever the narrator says, does not seem a genuine option within the formal world of *The Mill on the Floss*. However, it does seem what Hardy's texts are always subject to, tragically in Eustacia's case. She bears out Lawrence's comments about Hardy's characters:

> They are people each with a real, vital, potential self, even the apparently wishy-washy heroines of the earlier books, and this

self suddenly bursts the shell of manner and convention and commonplace opinion, and acts independently, absurdly, without mental knowledge or acquiescence.[16]

In the terms adopted here individuality is, in Eliot's novel, less a genuine function of the soul than it is a property of the subject, of moral responsibility and social identity.

This is another way of saying that Hardy's narrator, unlike Eliot's, does not have priority and precedence over his text. Instead of being a coherent narrative subject, Hardy's narrator seems often lost to himself, but also to find himself, in the process of writing. Anonymity is here another word for individuality. The recreational expansions of sympathy and imagination that govern his texts affect the narrator no less than the characters, and are dependent in each case on a loss of self-mastery through which emerge surprising effects and affects. Consider how much more controlled would be Eliot's version, for instance, of the highly-charged moment in *Far from the Madding Crowd* where we are granted a new type of access into Boldwood's inner life, as he holds the unconscious Bathsheba in his arms. This profoundly visionary nature of the moment derives from its corporeality, as we enter into the skin of the hitherto remote Boldwood, 'for those few, heavenly, golden moments' as he tries:

> to recover his senses. The experience had been too much for his consciousness to keep up with, and now that he had grasped it had gone again. (*Far from the Madding Crowd*, p. 351)

In an important aspect, then, the ideas of anonymity and participation involved in this account of Hardy's prose correspond to the reader's experience of the narrator. His transpersonal awareness hovers over the scene as if it were a cloud made up of differentiated possibilities of meaning and sensation yet to issue in definite ways. The reader is absorbed and stimulated by this alert, responsive musing, entering a fictional dimension whose fugitive suggestions resist translation into the more bathetic kinds of commentary which often succeed them, or which the critic supplies. Virginia Woolf indicated these ruminative pleasures of Hardy's prose when she commented on 'that halo of freshness and margin of the unexpressed which often produce the most profound sense of satisfaction' ('The Novels of Thomas Hardy', p. 248).

As a further aspect of this, and the affective and perceptual bases of intelligence in Hardy's texts, one can briefly consider here how the narrator's own absorption in a scene often releases, as a kind of by-product, reflexive potentials. The details of scene and language will reverberate with a strange prescience, appearing to signal back to the imaginative sources and principles of the text, while this reflexivity still remains, in Woolf's terminology, not fully expressed, and at the margins of the narrator's consciousness. The narrator's self-consciousness does not precede the text as a unifying, and predictive power, but remains dispersed, with an often comic inadvertence, in the unfolding texture and drama of the scene.[17] Unsurprisingly, given music's capacity to symbolize the values and modes of emergent thought and individuality at work in the prose, there are many musical scenes which can be seen as working in this connection.

Consider, for instance, the early passage in *Desperate Remedies* where Cytherea and Edward find themselves called to the boat by musical instruments. A change in the inner life of each seems to be announced by the music, anticipated by the imminent departure of the boat, and suggested through the alliterative and rhythmical features of the language:

> Presently the distant bell from the boat was heard, warning the passengers to embark. This was followed by a lively air from the harps and violins on board, their tones, as they arose, becoming intermingled with, though not marred by, the brush of the waves when their crests rolled over - at the point where the check of the shallows was first felt - and then thinned away up the slope of pebbles and sand. (*Desperate Remedies*, pp. 26-27)

The music, the enlivening beauty and the manifold delicacies of the scene offer complementary instances of the opening up of pleasure which is its romantic focus. The syntax becomes an expansive chain of adverbials, participating in the implicit significance of this event of lively intermingling. As the language in this way becomes taken up by the implicit resonances, by the rhythms of the event, so also there follows, in the setting off of the boat, an effect of comic reflexivity. Typical of *Desperate Remedies*, this reflexivity is, at once acute and defensive, but also accidental, uninsistent, immanent. While the detail of the sentence is itself wonderfully exact in physical terms, on this second, reflexive level, it works to offer a physical image of the interplay of confusion and resolution, the uncertain powers of movement, which affect both narrator and the characters in this novel:

Off went the plank; the paddles started, stopped, backed, pattered in confusion, then revolved decisively, and the boat passed into deep water. (*Desperate Remedies*, pp. 29-30)

The multiplied detail of the moment again crystallizes potentials of self-reading: the description of confusion, of false starts, of abrupt decisiveness, and of the passage into 'deep water', humorously reflect the traits of the narrative itself, and, perhaps, Hardy's anxiety about being out of his depth. In such ways Hardy's scenes often resonate with reflexive meanings and intimations, but without the narrator himself appearing to notice them. Reflexivity, one could say, is felt rather than lucidly comprehended, a matter of physical and affective intelligence rather than cognition or reason. As one further example of this, one can consider how in *A Pair of Blue Eyes*, when Hardy writes of Elfride's vacillating characteristics, his judgments also appear to be semi-consciously involved in a pursuit of correspondences between her nature and the values and qualities of his own modes of writing:

Perhaps there was a proneness to inconstancy in her nature - a nature, to those who contemplate it from a standpoint beyond the influence of that inconstancy, the most exquisite of all in its plasticity and ready sympathies. (*A Pair of Blue Eyes*, p. 314)

She dismissed the sense of sin in her past actions, and was automatic in the intoxication of the moment. (*A Pair of Blue Eyes*, p. 316)

III

Music, as an art of sound and time, is clearly also an art of movement as well as sensation. As has often been noted, Hardy was fascinated from earliest childhood not only with the movement which melody is, but also with the movements which it produces.[18] He described himself as 'wildly fond of dancing' (*Life*, p. 20). Time and again in the *Life* he catalogues the dances he attended at the different times of his youth, and refers to the contagious power of sound:

He was of ecstatic temperament, extraordinarily sensitive to music, and among the endless jigs, hornpipes, reels, waltzes, and country-dances that his father played of an evening in his early married years, and to which the boy danced a *pas seul* in the middle of the room, there were three or four that always moved the boy to tears, though he strenuously tried to hide them. (*Life*, p. 15)

A similar compulsion is channelled through music many times in the fiction - as in 'The Soldier's Joy' which 'possesses more stimulative properties for the heel and toe than the majority of dances at their first opening' (*Far from the Madding Crowd*, p. 269); or the 'Devil's Dream', the 'fury' of whose notes kindles a corresponding 'fury of personal movement' (in *The Return of the Native*, p. 157). For Joan Grundy, there is a vitalism at the heart of this innate connection of music and dance:

> Those who portray Hardy in terms only of gloom and withdrawal should remember that no one has re-created for us more often or more vividly the joy and the vigour, the fury and exaltation of the dance [...] The urgent sense of life that beats through the dance naturally allies it to the sexual passions, to the urge to perpetuate life, to create as it were a *perpetuum mobile*. (*Hardy and the Sister Arts*, p. 142)

In comments consonant with Grundy's discussion, Simon Gatrell, in a chapter entitled 'Hardy's Dances', writes of how in these dances:

> [n]either soul nor mind seeks any longer to tyrannise the body, for all are combined in communication through the movements of the lived body, in what might be considered an image of the unity of being, of the indivisibility of the elements of our nature, an indivisibility innate, but only made palpable in dance.[19]

Grundy and Gatrell between them give many instances of the urgent intoxications of those who participate in music and dance. Gatrell cites a passage from Sondra Fraleigh's *Dance and the Lived Body*:

> While I cannot know the body of the other as he lives his own unique rhythms and energies, I can know the body of the other as he dances it when we are dancing the same dance. Then we are a common presence, bound up together in the rhythm, space, and present time of the dance. (Quoted in 'Hardy's Dances', p. 38)

The links between movement and individuation can be seen in Hardy's use of the word 'soul', which is linked, not just to the physical capacity to move, but also to a capacity for being moved, as in Reuben Dewy's comment about his father: '[...] tunes. They do move his soul; don't em, father?' (*Under the Greenwood Tree*, p. 79). In a purely sensory sense, feeling or sensitivity *is* movement, in that it derives from physical reverberations. In emotional terms too, affects (in the sense I am using the word) are movements: positive or negative, they are transitions and modulations of the soul, responses and projections of relatedness which correspond to an expansion or a diminishment of the soul's powers.[20]

At this point one can indicate the inwardness between not only music and movement, but also between the concept of movement and many of the ideas and themes employed so far. The discussions about the event, affectivity and bodily sensation are all ways of describing a process of becoming which has importantly mobile qualities. In particular, movement is linked to the values of individuation or self-differentiation that we are considering, because it expresses openness, change and duration.[21] Deleuze attributes to Bergson the conceptual tools for thinking of the important temporal aspects of movement in this context:

> [...] movement has two aspects. On the one hand, that which happens between objects or parts; on the other hand that which expresses the duration of the whole. The result is that duration, by changing qualitatively, is divided up in objects, and objects, by gaining depth, by losing their contours, are united in duration. We can therefore say that movement relates the objects of a closed system to open duration, and duration to the objects of the system which it forces to open up.[22]

As part of this link of individuality and movement, we have seen in some of the discussions above, how Hardy's writing often explores self-differentiation, self-expression, as taking place in movements: that is in uninterrupted phases of time. Putting it more philosophically, in such scenes bodies undergo qualitative alteration as well as mere transposition in space. Bergson would say that such becomings are dependent on the fact that these bodies do not ultimately constitute closed entities, but are linked by their powers of relation to the whole:

> in comparing the living being to a whole, or to the whole of the universe, Bergson seems to be reviving the most ancient simile. However, he completely reverses its terms. For, if the living being is a whole and therefore, comparable to the whole of the universe, this is not because it is a microcosm as closed as the whole is assumed to be, but, on the contrary, because it is open upon a world, and the world, the universe, is itself the Open [...] [T]hrough relations, the whole is transformed or changes

> qualitatively. We can say of duration itself or of time, that it is the
> whole of relations. (*The Movement-Image*, p. 10)

Music, because it manages time and combines sounds in changing and
rhythmical relationships, provides, like movement, a '*mobile section* of
duration' (*The Movement-Image*, p. 11), and participates in this larger
sense of time itself. Like movement, a melody is indivisible: it can only
be interrupted, and so music naturally offers an image of that
paradoxical mixture of continuity and change which duration is.

This proximity between the values of movement and those of
music is directly evident also within Hardy's work in terms of
characterization. It can be remarked in the heroines especially, that they
always possess an individual grace, as well as being inevitably musical.
We often first observe them as involved in physical movements that
artistically take on some of the characteristics of dance or musical
performance, and that ethically take on the values of spontaneity and
expression: Ethelberta chasing the duck-hawks; Bathsheba 'dextrously'
riding the 'auburn pony', with the 'rapidity of her glide into [...] position
that of a kingfisher - its noiselessness that of a hawk' (*Far from the
Madding Crowd*, p. 53). Even at the beginning of *Tess*, Angel's not
dancing with Tess is a thwarting of her true promise, an index of the
gravitational pull of the customs which constrain him, and of the tragic
narrative pattern which similarly constrains Hardy. Again, in an early
scene in *Under the Greenwood Tree*, we see Fancy Day dancing, as the
band plays 'Triumph, or Follow my Lover'. She is one for whom
'flexibility was her first characteristic, by which she appeared to enjoy
the most easeful rest when she was in gliding motion'. She contrasts
with other girls, 'like a flower among vegetables' (*Under the Greenwood
Tree* p. 71). In *Desperate Remedies*, as we are introduced to Cytherea, it is
in terms of her mobility, and her ability to keep her balance. This is just
a page or so before her father fatally loses his own balance on the
scaffold, and in her view. Hardy comments on:

> the gracefulness of her movement, which was fascinating and
> delightful to an extreme degree.
> Indeed, motion was her speciality, whether shown on its most
> extended scale of bodily progression, or minutely, as in the
> uplifting of her eyelids, the bending of her fingers, the pouting of
> her lip. The carriage of her head - motion within motion - a glide
> upon a glide - was as delicate as that of a magnetic needle. And
> this flexibility and elasticity had never been taught her by rule, nor
> even been acquired by observation, but, *nullo cultu*, had naturally
> developed itself with her years. In infancy, a stone or stalk in the

way, which had been the inevitable occasion of a fall to her
playmates, had usually left her safe and upright on her feet after
the narrowest escape by oscillations and whirls for the
preservation of her balance. (*Desperate Remedies*, p. 7)

And so the narrator continues, multiplying aspects and glimpses of
Cytherea, while emphasizing that words are inadequate to capture her
coexisting fascinations, in a similar way as it is impossible to enjoy 'a
full chord of music by piping the notes in succession' (*Desperate
Remedies*, p. 8). She herself remains indivisible, resistant to
representation - in these respects like a chord or melody whose identity
is a function of harmony or undivided continuity, or like movement
which generates philosophical paradoxes if one tries to analyse it
purely spatially. If the death of Cytherea's father that follows
precipitates the crises of the plot, the contrast between her physical
intelligence (evident at the dance or in play), and the fatal fall which
afflicts her architect father at work, retains an inwardness with the
different tendencies of the narrative in the novel. There is the Hardy
who, in Bayley's phrase, is subject to 'falling flat' (p. 10), when working
on the text's architecture, as it were, and the other Hardy who works so
inimitably in the middle of things, and who comes into his own when
unfolding, unrehearsed, the moments and qualities of impressions,
sensations, feelings. (We can ponder here how Hardy when building
Max Gate worked, mole-like from 'the inside outwards' as Michael
Millgate remarked.[23]) Cytherea, for all her passivity within the novel's
social world, in these ways has a resourcefulness and precarious poise
akin to Hardy's own.

    Throughout *Desperate Remedies*, Cytherea's qualities of sensitivity
and mobility seem opposed to the larger demarcations of circumstance
and chronology in the novel. Certainly, Miss Aldclyffe is first attracted
by the young woman's capacity to glide (*Desperate Remedies*, p. 61): her
grace offers her ways of overcoming her impoverished social condition,
as it seems also to resist the constraints of gravity. Similarly, we read,
Elfride 'had the motions, without the motives, of a hoiden; the grace,
without the self-consciousness, of a pirouetter' (*A Pair of Blue Eyes*, p.
75); Bathsheba, 'glided' among the 'heavy yeomen' 'as a chaise among
carts' (*Far from the Madding Crowd*, p. 123); and Elizabeth-Jane's
attraction to Farfrae is consolidated as she dances with him to one of his
native tunes:

The tune had enticed her into it; being the tune of a busy, vaulting,
leaping sort - some low notes on the silver string of each fiddle,

then a skipping on the small, like running up and down ladders - 'Miss Mc'Leod of Ayr' was its name, so Mr Farfrae had said, and that it was very popular in his own country. (*The Mayor of Casterbridge*, pp. 137-38.)

IV

It is a paradox, given the association of vitality, movement, music and affectivity with the female characters in Hardy's fiction, that many critics have considered his focus on his women as tending towards a disturbing, stabilized, logic of subject and object.[24] Howard Jacobson comically depicts Hardy's attitude to women in terms of a unwholesome and objectifying voyeurism. J. Hillis Miller identifies in the fiction a pattern of anxiety about physical proximity, and an eroticizing of distance, where Gittings drops dark hints about Hardy's attitude to dead females.

This paradox tends to disappear once one considers these negative views in terms of the disjunction that runs through this book, between the 'closed' and the 'open' values of Hardy's texts. These twin modes - expansive, contractive - of Hardy's mind are at once inseparable and irreconcilable, so that the tragic death of Tess, for instance, appears as a bitterly dismissive flip-side of the entranced romantic focus elsewhere in the text. In a related way, against the broad charge of misogyny in Hardy's texts, one needs to emphasize how the local, mobile, texture of the writing lends itself to real subtleties and complexities in the treatment of identity, erotic attraction, and of gender. As every reader knows indeed, selfhood is constantly undone by love in Hardy's texts: what Jude or Boldwood or Bathsheba have been up to *this* point is off-set by a new, unpredicted, dynamic. And, further, as this implies, these values of mobility and instability govern the plots of the texts no less than their representations of men and women, and the relations between them.

Given that a Hardy narrative depends in so many ways on this affective dynamism, it is little surprise that a level of musicality seems an imaginative prerequisite for them, both male and female. Musical responsiveness is next to emotional readiness for Hardy, and although different in their musical tastes and talents, Cytherea, Fancy, Bathsheba, Lucetta, Elfride, Tabitha, and Sue, for instance, are all pianists. Recurrently, Hardy writes of these women in terms of the characteristic musicality of their voices, each of which has an individual note, as with Tess's 'fluty voice' (*Tess*, p. 115), or Fanny Robin's 'low and dulcet note'

(*Far from the Madding Crowd*, p. 86), or with Eustacia's voice, which summons up the memory of the viola (*The Return of the Native*, p. 94). Or again, there are the following examples, among many others:

> The charm lay in the intervals [...] She would say a few syllables in one note, and end her sentence in a soft modulation upwards, then downwards, then into her own note again. The curve of sound was as satisfying as any line of beauty ever struck by his pencil. (*The Well-Beloved*, p. 95)

> Her voice was a voice of low note, in quality that of a flute at the grave end of its gamut. If she sang she was a pure contralto unmistakably. (*A Laodicean*, p. 94)

> After this he asked Anne to sing: but though she had a very pretty voice in private performances of that nature, she declined to oblige him. (*The Trumpet-Major*, p. 66)

> 'The I heard it fall,' said the girl, in a soft, though not particularly low voice. (*Far from the Madding Crowd*, p. 43)

For the male characters too, musicality functions in the same ways. It is evident in the explicit gifts of the characters, and in more intimately personal ways. So, aside from Oak's flute, Dick's violin, Christopher's piano, Jude's harmonium, and so on, there are the musical qualities are often attributed to the voice, or are seen in other ways as closely linked to the character's selfhood. So, tones of voice are often described in musical terms: as with Lord Luxellian's 'musical laugh' (*A Pair of Blue Eyes*, p. 195) or Stephen's 'musical voice' (*A Pair of Blue Eyes*, p. 95), or, where we hear how Farfrae's 'voice musically undulated between two semitones, as it always did when he became earnest' (*The Mayor of Casterbridge*, p.123). Again, music is often used as a trope for the expression of individuality, as in the following example, when Christopher inadvertently makes Picotee cry, and takes on the qualities of a harp:

> Being in point of fact a complete bundle of nerves and nothing else, his thin figure shook like a harp-string in painful excitement at a contretemps which would scarcely have quickened the pulse of an ordinary man. (*The Hand of Ethelberta*, p. 172)

The important point here is that Hardy uses such musical metaphors and associations for both sexes. If Thomasin is said to seem 'rightly to belong to a madrigal - to require viewing through rhyme and harmony'

(*The Return of the Native*, p. 63), so, Somerset, is said to be 'an instrument of no narrow gamut: he had a key for other touches than the purely aesthetic' (*A Laodicean*, p. 44).

The readiness for erotic passion, then, is linked in both men and women to a responsiveness to the physical and spiritual art of music. As this might imply, sexual attraction in Hardy's fiction operates primarily through incalculable events of sympathetic connection, where the differences between the sexes are less important than what brings them together, and in which the recognizable facts of sexual difference and identity are often prey to effects of indetermination. As an aspect of this, Hardy's narrator often dramatizes the possessive, fixing, fixed, male gaze itself, only to subject it to all kinds of discomposition, and to open it up to this opposing logic of correspondence, as when Bathsheba turns the tables on her male observer, by catching Oak in the act, as his face rises like a moon from behind the hedge (*Far from the Madding Crowd*, p. 54).[25] In *Jude*, Sue constantly manipulates her image to deprive Jude of the power of knowledge and possession. Again, this is happening constantly to us as we read, as in the famous opening of *A Pair of Blue Eyes* (the novel so beloved by Tennyson and Coventry Patmore, as well as by Proust). Elfride's eyes are not primarily objects of study or comment, in relation to which the viewer's detached subjective position would be secured and rehearsed. Instead, they provoke an enveloping physical and mental event, a looking *into*:

> These eyes were blue; blue as the autumn distance - blue as the blue we see between the retreating mouldings of hills and woody slopes on a sunny September morning. A misty and shady blue, that had no beginning or surface, and was looked *into* rather than *at*. (*A Pair of Blue Eyes*, p. 81)

The language draws the reader into a continuous process, occasioned by '*these* eyes' as by the temporal activity of observing 'the *retreating* mouldings of hills and woody slopes on a sunny September morning...' (an image which, through implying movement, places one physically as well as merely visually within a scene). Corresponding in such a way to these open-ended features, Elfride's eyes at this moment promise the delights of movement *into*, as well as the risks of falling *from*, and so show the values of a text organized above all by the fallings in and out of love, of vertiginous enticements and threats.

Certainly, it is the case that Hardy texts are full of the real threats of passion, of moments - potentially joyful or dangerous - where social position appear at stake. We have seen how Eustacia undergoes a temporary estrangement from her marital identity, as she is overcome by her returning attraction to Wildeve at the dance on the heath. Similarly, *A Pair of Blue Eyes*, is a novel which also turns on the power of physical, affective episodes in which the conventional positions and values of selfhood are themselves displaced and thrown into risky oscillations. Effects of comedy, tragedy, poetry, and bathos alternate rapidly and unpredictably within the text, mirroring the unpredictable phases of the narration itself.[26]

Further, a certain suspension of the claims and coherence of gender identity is clearly an important aspect of these effects of confusion and movement. In *A Pair of Blue Eyes*, a typically unstable drama of passion, there is the obvious case of Stephen, the 'emotional side' of whose 'constitution was built rather after a feminine than a male model' (*A Pair of Blue Eyes*, p. 420). But even the masculinity of the promisingly named Knight himself is similarly subject to discomposure, as when, suspended from the cliff with no name, he is dependent, for his very life, on the rope Elfride makes from her underclothes. No rescuer on a white charger he. This is all too literally a scene of vulnerability, as well as of transport or uplift (and of connection). As such it comically inverts or parodies earlier scenes, such as that where Elfride, sunk at the organ, listens as Knight's voice masterfully 'ascended'. Aloft in the pulpit, he reads from the first book of *Kings*, of Elijah's defiance of gravity:

> Elfride at the organ regarded him with a throbbing sadness of mood which was fed by a sense of being far removed from his sphere. As he went deliberately through the chapter appointed [...] his deep tones echoed past with such apparent disregard of her existence that his presence inspired her with a forlorn sense of unapproachableness, which his absence would hardly have been able to cause. (*A Pair of Blue Eyes*, p. 236)

If love between Elfride and the two men develops by such dynamic exchanges, though, it is because of the correspondences between her individuality and theirs. The dynamics of erotic affiliation depend, in Hardy's fiction, on the ways in which the individuals concerned are alter-egos: Elfride's passivity finds its answering term in Stephen, her aspiration in Knight. Typically for Hardy, Elfride's intrinsic self-difference is expressed through the men she is attracted to, and music works to indicate and facilitate the differences involved.

More generally, we can say that what is important for Hardy's lovers are these individuating points of similarity and transfer between

self and other. Likewise, Jude finds himself through, and in, Arabella
and Sue, as Tess finds herself through Angel and Alec. In musical
terms, one can consider in this last case, how Tess's predicament is
indicated by Angel's harp-playing, and by Alec's invasive advice about
whistling. Again, Christopher's disciplined and practical musicality in
The Hand of Ethelberta is a correlative of the emotional fortitude and
necessary worldliness, as well as the lyrical gifts, which Ethelberta also
possesses. Bathsheba's emotional education in *Far from the Madding
Crowd* can similarly be construed in terms of the contrast between Oak's
singing bass in the choir, and Troy's courting of disaster on the stormy
night of the harvest-home-cum-wedding-feast, as he encourages
everyone to dance to 'The Soldier's Joy'. Troy's self-celebrating, self-
serving and shallow behaviour corresponds to one aspect of Bathsheba,
as her enjoyment of Oak's communal and cheering flute playing does to
another:

> He drew out his flute and began to play 'Jockey to the Fair' in the
> style of a man who had never known a moment's sorrow. Oak
> could pipe with Arcadian sweetness, and the sound of the well-
> known notes cheered his own heart as well as those of the
> loungers. (*Far from the Madding Crowd*, p. 77)

Contrastingly, in *The Return of the Native*, Eustacia's contradictory
desires are tragic, though similarly betrayed through musical incidents,
as in her fantasies about Paris or Budmouth, or, as in the scene
previously mentioned, where amid the blur of a 'maze of motion', social
restraints are overcome for her and Wildeve.

Because love for Hardy is essentially a process rather than a
state, there is much romance and seduction for his protagonists, but
little domesticity, and virtually no mutuality that is not open to
disequilibrium, as with the marriages of Grace and Fitzpiers, Clym and
Eustacia, Jude and Arabella. Like the dance in *The Hand of Ethelberta*,
with the characters who 'knot themselves like house-flies and part
again' (*The Hand of Ethelberta*, p. 64), 'threading and spinning about the
floor' (*The Hand of Ethelberta*, p. 62), Hardy's texts dramatize
predominantly shifts and patterns of attraction, the perpetual coming
together, parting, and alternation of partners. The scene between
Eustacia and Wildeve at the dance on the heath does not only expresses
that fatal principle of unconscious self-abandonment, and the fervent
desire for escape, which always underlie Eustacia's actions. It also
shows how such erotic imperatives have a dangerous contagion within

The Return of the Native, so that the plot becomes shaped, under her abiding influence, as a ceaseless erotic dance and exchange of partners.

Similarly, in terms of the dramatic content of the novels, one can note how narrative is generated time and again out of such a conflict between accountability and desire, between a conscious sense of identity, as consolidated through social position and obligation, and these animating elements of momentary affinity, betrayal and enticement. To begin with, the plots often depend on episodes where desire finds its opposing term in the character's responsibility to an earlier undisclosed relationship: against the individuating event, the singular and compelling scene of romance, there is the bond of a relationship that is (for now at least) more or less undesired. Elfride resists telling Knight about Stephen, or Stephen about young Jethway, Fancy resists telling anyone else about Dick, or Dick about anyone else. Similarly, Troy withholds from Bashsheba his relations with Fanny, Eustacia keeps secret from Clym her ties with Wildeve, Tess keeps from Angel her past, Fitzpiers keeps Grace in the dark about his past and present dalliances, and so on. Hardy's plots are mobile enactments of these mutations and investments of desire. In another variation on the principle, one can note how such a conflict, between process and stasis, becomes repeated in the ironic failures of Hardy's characters to settle down. The compelling moment of erotic or amorous magnetism refuses to translate into an enduring happiness, as in the marriages or relations of Troy and Bathsheba, Jude and Sue, Angel and Tess and others.

Technically also, a similar conflict surfaces for Hardy the novelist in his own obligation to provide closure. This imperative works against his instinct for the open, the provisional, and the indeterminate, as Patricia Ingham and Gillian Beer have pointed out.[27] Given this, it is unsurprising that Hardy's novels end so often by appearing to simplify and objectify the female characters who have been their animating spirits, as at the end of *The Hand of Ethelberta*, where Ethelberta agrees to marry Montclere so that they can bring about a wedding between Picotee and Christopher. As with Elfride's marriage to Luxellian, or Grace's staying with Fitzpiers, or Sue's returning to Phillotson, the novel's ending appears unsatisfying, arbitrary, and stuck on.

It would be possible to explore further such issues of gender, and love or desire in the texts, in the terms which have been advanced variously by Patricia Ingham, Elaine Showalter, and Sarah Davies, the latter commenting on how Hardy's work results in a certain 'degendering' of 'previously gendered roles and characteristics'.[28] Certainly, one could expect their emphases on the deconstitution of the gender code in Hardy's fiction to coincide at important points with a development of this account of Hardy's dramatization of love as process, becoming, and correspondence.

V

In the short stories, because of constraints of convention and brevity, the twin aspects of Hardy's sensibility - irony and amorousness - appear to be yoked together into a kind of enforced proximity. Unlike the fiction, these imaginative components are constantly rubbing each other up the wrong way, so that we can never forget the often denaturing, derisive, mechanism of plot, any more than Barbara of the House of Grebe can free herself from the grotesque apparition of Willowes which Uplandtowers yanks up time and again by his system of wires and pulleys, as his husbandly *aide-memoire* against her tender nocturnal imaginings of the other man. Certainly, it befits their status as a half-way house between the novels and the poetry, that the short stories are more immediately driven, like many of the poems, by pressing necessities of design and moral.

This raises the question, as to the use of music within the tales. Generally, Hardy associates music in them with illicit and fated romance, so that music becomes more determinedly a device in the intensifying critique of social restrictions that marks the closing phase of his fiction writing career. Desire within the stories is pointedly conceived of as essentially *unappeased* desire, and there is often within them, as in 'Barbara of the House of Grebe', a sardonic recoil against the potentials of feelings they set up, so that local effects of pathos, or romance, or sympathy, alternate with other moments where the narrator, orientated towards the themes and design of the whole narrative, steels himself into pitiless irony. Infamously, as has just been mentioned, 'Barbara of the House of Grebe' turns on the heroine's yearning desire for her first husband, Willowes, as he had been before his despairing death, which was brought on by his disfigurement by fire and her rejection of him. Her second husband overcomes this retrospective and idealizing habit by disfiguring in turn the statue of him which she had privately used to preserve her passion, before confronting her with it time and again in the way described.

Although this controlling use of the grotesque in 'Barbara of the House of Grebe' is in fact untypically extreme, the story is an illuminating indicator of what appears the inescapable ironic loop, of erotic longing and marital frustration, that repeats itself over and over again in the fiction of the late 1880s and onwards.[29] As a sign, perhaps, of this story's particularly grim nature we notice that music scarcely figures within it, and when it does, it is in a context overshadowed by solitude and negativity. At the beginning, music plays at the ball, but Barbara is solitary and 'preoccupied', before absconding to meet Willowes. This inversion of Hardy's characteristic use of music surfaces, also, with the birds which live near Barbara's first marital home, on:

> a slope so solitary, and surrounded by trees so dense, that the birds who inhabited the boughs sang at strange hours, as if they could hardly distinguish night from day. (*Stories*, Vol. 1, p. 256)

These moments are suggestive of the darker emotional themes and conflicts of the story, and of the narrator's apparently self-punishing treatment of the type of amatory susceptibilities (romantic hope, and later for Barbara, retrospective and regretful ardour) which nearly always provide the tales, like the novels, with their sympathetic pretexts.

So, in 'The History of the Hardcomes', music kindles the encounters and reversals that govern the narrative. The fatal exchange of partners begins at a dance, and then comes to a tragic turn as the two former intendeds, Stephen and Olive, reunited for a fatal interval, set out to sea in a boat to the sounds of the band, only to be drowned. A comparable logic of disappointment and regret governs 'The Waiting Supper', where music points up once again the tale's specific thematic essence. This story revolves around the circumstances that have kept the lovers apart throughout, from the failed marriage service of their youth, to the inconsequential neighbourliness of their mature years when Christine and Nicholas are free to associate but not to marry, owing to her husband's prolonged absence. Against this frustrating play of events, there is the dance of their youth where the couple's innate suitability for each other is clearly revealed:

> She turned to the band. ' "The Honeymoon", ' she said.
> And then they trod the delightful last-century measure of that name, which if it had ever been danced better, was never danced with more zest. The perfect responsiveness which their tender acquaintance threw into the motions of Nicholas and his partner lent their gyrations the fine adjustment of two interacting parts of a single machine. The excitement of the movement carried Christine back to the time - the unreflecting passionate time, about two years before - when she and Nic had been incipient lovers only; and it made her forget the carking anxieties, the vision of

social breakers ahead, that had begun to take the gilding off her position now. (*Stories*, Vol. 2, pp. 227-28)

At the end of the story, the couple discover that they could have married years ago since the body of her absent husband has lain long undiscovered beneath the waterfall. However, now familiarity and age are too much for them:

> Their wills were somewhat enfeebled now, their hearts sickened of tender enterprise by hope too long deferred. (*Stories*, Vol. 2, p. 257)

If 'The Waiting Supper' is about how convention can make a non-event of love, 'The Son's Veto' traces, through two generations, the negative consequences of flouting it. In this story, the narrator's focus on the unnatural influences and oppressive rigidities of social forms is for a moment pushed aside as Mr Twycott, knowing 'perfectly well that he had committed social suicide', marries Sophy, his maid, in the village of Gaymead:

> Thus it happened that one fine morning, when the doors of the church were naturally open for ventilation, and the singing birds fluttered in and alighted on the tie-beams of the roof, there was a marriage-service at the communion-rails, which hardly a soul knew of. (*Stories*, Vol. 2, p. 37)

This scene finds its contrary image, though, in the closing of the story, where the couple's son, tirelessly and inhumanely insistent on family status, glares from the funeral cortège at the grocer, Sam, whose marriage to his widowed, and now dead, mother he had successfully opposed for years:

> The man, whose eyes were wet, held his hat in his hand as the vehicles moved by; while from the mourning-coach a young smooth-shaven priest in a high waistcoat looked black as a cloud at the shopkeeper standing there. (*Stories*, Vol. 2, p. 46)

At this moment the son bitterly embodies the implacable rigours of class that his parents' obscure marriage had sought to elude.

Marriage across class divides, and not being able to marry the beloved, are also the ingredients of 'On the Western Circuit', though in this case they are differently combined. Nevertheless, this is another tale of doomed love, where convention and law offer adamantine opposition to sentiment. Love in this tale, is once again generated by a passage of notes, though this time of an epistolary rather than musical kind. Raye comes to mourn, after his mismarriage to the real Anna, the ideal version who had so poetically written to him during their courtship, when he had then been unwitting that the words were in fact supplied by her mistress, Edith. This ironic distance between ideal aspiration and jarring fact is strikingly announced at the beginning by the sounds, later identified as those of the fair, which distract Raye from his intended 'glimpse of the most homogeneous pile of medieval architecture in England':

> He postponed till the morrow his attempt to examine the deserted edifice, and turned his attention to the noise. It was compounded of steam barrel-organs, the clanging of gongs, the ringing of hand-bells, the clack of rattles, and the indistinguishable shouts of men. A lurid light hung in the air in the direction of the tumult. (*Stories*, Vol. 2, p. 85)

The constricting sense of mocking fate in the story appears to be announced here by the clanging sounds, and the 'lurid light', where one might expect or hope for bells and stained glass. Interestingly, in the story Hardy is fascinated by the possibility of a compensatory (if also tormenting) telepathic union between Raye and Edith. This prefigures the way he would insinuate (a couple of years or so later) his feelings for Mrs Florence Henniker, that 'charming, *intuitive* woman' (*Life*, p. 270). In 'On the Western Circuit', Raye's attraction for Edith is described in free indirect mode as 'a species of telepathy' which 'had exercised such an influence on her' (p. 102); and later Raye tells her that whereas '[l]egally I have married her - God help us both! - in soul and spirit I have married you...' (p. 105). Once again, marriage to the wrong person becomes the black joke played upon desire, and ratified by society.

Similarly, in 'An Imaginative Woman', the woman of the title falls in love outside marriage, and the story provides a remarkable, enactment of the power of love to escape the limits of the body and of society. The telepathic communion of 'On The Western Circuit' becomes revisited in this story by Ella's falling in love with a poet she has come to love by way of his work. Mysteriously, her child then comes, as if by some ideal suggestion, to take on the physical attributes of the poet whom she has never met. Accordingly, the story ends with her husband rejecting his son, in the mistaken belief that he is the son of the poet:

> By a known but inexplicable trick of Nature there were undoubtedly strong traces of resemblance to the man Ella

had never seen; the dreamy and peculiar expression of the poet's face sat, as the transmitted idea upon the child's, and the hair was of the same hue.

'I'm damned if I don't think so!' murmured Marchmill. 'Then she did play me false with that fellow at the lodgings! Let me see: the dates - the second week in August... the third week in May... Yes... yes... Get away, you poor little brat! You are nothing to me!' (*Stories*, Vol. 2, p. 32)

As in these examples, so throughout the tales, their most striking given is their determination to point out that experience is an unresolved discordance between social constraints and the magnetic forces of desire. Music often takes on an extraordinary intensity in this context, bringing to the surface the deepest desires and socially transgressive feelings of the characters. Musical experience encapsulates the forces and aspirations of individuality which society denies, as in 'For Conscience' Sake', where the abandoned unmarried mother is a music teacher; or, as in 'An Indiscretion in the Life of an Heiress', where Geraldine agrees to a meeting with Egbert before - mindful again of her social position - she overturns her decision once again, writing:

> It was when under the influence of much emotion, kindled in me by the power of music, that I half assented to a meeting with you tonight.[30]

Again, to take a more obviously comic example, in 'Absentmindedness in a Parish Choir', the dozing band in the Church occasion their replacement by a barrel organ as they suddenly and forgetfully burst, as one, into 'The Devil Among the Tailors'.

Typical of Hardy though such forgetful moments of expression are, then, in the world of the stories they are persistently frustrated, bursting forth like the stream in 'Our Exploits in West Poley' only to be dammed up time and again. Even in another apparently benign story, 'The Romantic Adventures of a Milkmaid', the plot blocks the longings it releases. In the middle, Margery's secret adventures with the Baron take on the aspect of a fairy story, although the sense of transfiguration involved is conjoined with the story's open sense of physicality. So, when she goes to the ball, we read of how:

> The bewildered Margery was led by the Baron up the steps to the interior of the house, whence the sounds of music and dancing were already proceeding. The tones were strange. At every fourth

beat a deep and mighty note throbbed through the air, reaching Margery's soul with all the force of a blow. (*Stories*, Vol. 2, p. 427)

In the imagination of reader and narrator, the interworking or mingling of erotic fantasy and observation is remarkably brought off by Hardy, at this moment, as he describes Margery's bewilderment, surprise, and excitement. The reader's sympathy with the guileless Margery is total, a function of the wholesale absorption of the narrator's attention within the enchanted interval of the dance and the blows and throbs of sound. Almost inevitably, though, given Hardy's use of the story genre, this interval is merely transitory, a postponement of disappointment.

The socially transgressive power of music is again evident, though with contrasting outcomes, in two further stories, 'The Three Strangers' and 'The Melancholy Hussar of the German Legion'. In the first of these, the hangman and his potential victim, the sheep-stealer, sing alongside each other as they shelter from the storm. Musical activity helps to keep the former of the two men oblivious to the true social nature of their relationship, and so provides an important contributory factor in the latter's flight. Indeed music not only brings about the sheep-stealer's actual escape, but it provokes the admiration and protection that keeps him safe. Responding to his boldness, and reacting against the cruel disproportion of his sentence, the country-folk offer the 'bass-voiced man' 'sympathetic assistance' (*Stories*, Vol. 1, p. 32). In 'The Melancholy Hussar of the German Legion', Hardy narrates, contrastingly, the tragedy of the hussar's thwarted attempt at engineering a love-lorn flight from his situation. The story begins with the anonymous narrator's sense of how the downs, 'high and breezy and green', are at night visited by the ghosts of the legion who camped there ninety years ago:

> At night, when I walk across the lonely place, it is impossible to avoid hearing, amid the scourings of the wind over the grass-bents and thistles the old trumpet and bugle calls, the rattle of the halters; to help seeing rows of spectral tents and the *impedimenta* of the soldiery. From within the canvases come guttural syllables of foreign tongues, and broken songs of the fatherland; for they were mainly regiments of the King's German Legion that slept round the tent-poles hereabout at that time. (*Stories*, Vol. 1, p. 40)

The evocation of the sounds of the past offers the narrator a way of banishing the present, and moving into the earlier time of the romance between the hussar and Phyllis:

> It all began with the arrival of the York Hussars [...] Before that
> day scarcely a soul had been seen near her father's house for
> weeks. When a noise like the brushing skirt of a visitor was heard
> on the doorstep, it proved to be a scudding leaf; when a carriage
> seemed to be nearing the door, it was her father grinding his sickle
> on the stone in the garden [...] A sound like luggage thrown down
> from the coach was a gun far away at sea. (*Stories*, Vol. 1, p. 41)

Sound becomes the way in which the remote past is recaptured as the
imagined present of the tale. But so too, the hussar's fateful
homesickness is associated at the beginning of the story with the
nostalgia served by music. As we read the narrator's imagined sense of
how the soldiers' camp would have been filled with 'broken songs of
the fatherland', we can imagine how this might have stirred up his fatal
desire for his absent betrothed.[31]

Two final examples are of tales which Hardy never completed.
The first of these, Hardy sketched out in different versions, giving it
various titles (including 'The Sparrow' and 'For want of a word') and
different endings (of tragic misunderstanding or happy resolution).
Further, in one conception, the story was to be narrated by a sparrow,
and in the other by the young man within it. For all the technical and
circumstantial uncertainty of the project, however, there recurs in the
different versions a particular scene, in which the two lovers, meeting
in church each week share the same hymn book. They are in love yet
unable to broach the topic openly. The exactitude of detail is a very
literal instance of how the tender content of a scene can take precedence
over the plot in the narrator's imagination:

> The mutual shyness of the two made their situation a painfully
> attractive one. Their furthest stage of recognition so far was her
> offering him her hymn book to look over one day when he had
> come without his own. This grew into a habit. Every week they
> sang from the same book, her lemon-gloved thumb and finger
> nipping one bottom corner of the volume, and his brown gloved
> ones the other - and their elbows nearly touching. (*Stories*, Vol. 3,
> p. 122)

Save for differences between the third- and the first-person the passages
describing this moment are almost identical. In the same way, the
sketches for the other projected tale (variously entitled 'The
fiddler/player/bandsman at the dancing-rooms', 'The Vauxhall
Fiddler', 'The Morning Hymn', 'An Incident in the Life of Barthélémon')
centre on a pivotal moment, that in which Barthélémon has the

inspiration for the morning hymn as he crosses the bridge from Vauxhall, where he had been playing the fiddle the night before. It was a story, of course, that Hardy was to revisit in verse, and it seems that the circumstances of the scene, with its suggestions of the contrasts and continuities between dissipation and inspiration, fascinated him. In both these cases, though, our acquaintance with Hardy's tales ensures that we await the springing closed of the plot, and the abolition of the promise of such tender or inspired moments.

VII

At this point, before leaving the fiction, it is worthwhile briefly to draw together some of the threads of these two chapters, to summarize their account of how music acts on the soul for Hardy in these fictional texts. In the first place, music works as a sort of binding agent, providing a means of relatedness and individuation at the bodily level. In the second place, to alter the metaphor, it can be said to be a revealing agent, since through music the soul is acted upon to develop, or express, hitherto unnoticed or forgotten qualities. In short, the soul discloses its spiritual qualities by way of primarily physical means of association. Both these features can be seen in comic form in the following anecdote from *The Return of the Native*, describing how Thomasin's father plays Andrey's clarinet in a way that inspires his audience with a new collective access of religious sentiment:

> 'No sooner was Andrey asleep and the first whiff of neighbour Yeobright's wind had got inside Andrey's clarinet than every one in church felt in a moment there was a great soul among 'em'.
> (*The Return of the Native*, p. 75)

Further, it has been argued that the equation of music with this type of social cohesion becomes increasingly impossible as the later texts intensify their social critique. In this second chapter, nonetheless, the central emphasis has been on the animating values in Hardy's texts of those provisional moments where individual expression appears coextensive with the whole unfolding, scattered and provisional texture of the writing. Music retains a peculiar privilege in expressing the returning susceptibility which marks the corporeal modes of these novels and tales, and by which the narrator becomes taken up by, and introduces the reader into, events of indetermination which function outside of the identity logic of subjectivity.

Notes

¹ John Addington Symonds, *Essays Speculative and Suggestive*, Vol. 1 (London: Chapman and Hall, 1890), p. 138.

² *The Literary Notebooks of Thomas Hardy*, edited by Lennart A. Björk, Vol. 2 (New York: New York University Press, 1985), p. 34.

³ Thomas Hardy, 'The Profitable Reading of Fiction', in *Thomas Hardy: Selected Poetry and Prose* (edited by Peter Widdowson, London: Macmillan, 1997), p. 242.

⁴ Donald Davie, *Thomas Hardy and British Poetry* (London: Routledge and Kegan Paul, 1973), p. 117.

⁵ Thomas Hardy, *Two on a Tower* (London: Macmillan, 1975), p. 82.

⁶ Writes Deleuze:

> What we tried to show [...] was how desire was beyond [...]
> personological or objectal co-ordinates. It seemed to us that desire was a
> process, and that it unrolled a *plane of consistence*, a field of immanence
> [...] criss-crossed by particles and fluxes which break free from objects
> and subjects... Desire is therefore not internal to a subject any more than it
> tends towards an object: it is strictly immanent to a plane which it does
> not pre-exist, to a plane which must be constructed, where particles are
> emitted and fluxes combine [...] Far from presupposing a subject, desire
> cannot be attained except at the point where someone is deprived of the
> power of saying 'I'. (*Dialogues*, p. 89)

Colin Gordon cites another formulation close to this discussion which usefully
suggests music:

> A theory of desire, Deleuze writes, has to do with "the ensemble of affects
> which circulate and transform themselves within a symbiotic assemblage,
> defined by the co-functioning of its heterogeneous parts". (Colin Gordon, 'The
> Subtracting Machine', *I & C* [Spring 1981], p. 30)

⁷ Deleuze had many ways of describing this distinction between the logic of
the purely physical and the unifying logic of the event, but he attributed the insight to
the Stoic philosophers, whose 'strength' he said, 'lay in making a line of separation
pass [...] between physical depth and metaphysical surface. Between things and
events':

> But see how, from all these bodily struggles, there arises a sort of
> incorporeal vapour, which no longer consists in qualities, in actions and
> passions, in causes acting upon one another, but in results of these actions
> and passions, in effects which result from all these causes together.
> (*Dialogues*, p. 63)

⁸ Quoted by Colin Gordon, 'The Subtracting Machine', p. 31.

⁹ Gordon's words, 'The Subtracting Machine', p. 31.

¹⁰ Such a thought, we have seen, affirms 'immanent modes of existence' at the
same time as it critiques, more or less implicitly, the socially prescribed fiction of a
unified and recognisable, self-coherent, moral and cognitive subject. Deleuze traces
such a philosophy of immanence back to Spinoza:

Ethics, which is to say, a typology of immanent modes of existence, replaces Morality, which always refers existence to transcendent values. (*Spinoza: Practical Philosophy*, p. 23)

All individuals are in Nature as on a plane of consistence whose entire figure, variable at each moment. they go to compose. They affect one another in so far as the relation that constitutes each individual forms a degree of *puissance*, a power of being affected. Everything in the universe is encounters, happy or unhappy encounters [...] Hence Spinoza's question: *what is a body capable of*? of what affects is it capable? (I have retained here Colin Gordon's translation from *Dialogues* since its vocabulary is more musically suggestive in this passage. ('The Subtracting Machine', p. 30)

As this musical terminology (figures, variation, composition) suggests, music provides an exemplary image of this physical condition of thought.

11   Similarly, Chapter Three begins by exploring how a Hardy poem often crystallizes out around the seed of a distracting impression, and the often paradoxical senses which it conveys.

12   To describe this briefly, a scene appears to take on significance as an analogue of the narrative's own formal principles or processes, but without the narrator appearing overly concerned to pursue these latent potentials of self-reading. Such reflexive significances appear to remain at the margin of his apparent awareness and concerns, though they are made available for the reader in interesting ways.

13   The essay referred to is 'Reality and its Shadow', reproduced in *The Levinas Reader* (edited by Seán Hand, Oxford: Blackwell, 1989). The quotation is from page 133. Levinas published the essay in 1948 as a polemical piece. Within it, he draws from the cases of music and poetry an idea of participation which then is used to describe all the arts. Levinas argues that criticism and philosophy are dominated by the form of objectivity which seizes and makes the world intelligible according to the conceptual resources of the conscious subject. 'Art', on the other hand, 'contrasts with knowledge', and elementarily 'substitutes for the object its image. Its image and not its concept'. As has been suggested in earlier passages of this book, this foregoing of subjectivity is the foregoing of the assumption of mastery involved in both knowledge and volition. Instead, for Levinas, the image 'marks a hold over us rather than an initiative, a fundamental passivity' ('Reality and its Shadow', p. 132). For my purposes, the central insight of Levinas's essay is the contention that the 'image is interesting', in the etymological sense (of *inter-esse* as Seán Hand points out ['Reality and its Shadow', p. 131]). It involves us with things, beings, according to the immanent principles of sensibility and not the categories of a transcendental subject. Artistic experience, involves a 'commerce with the obscure, as a totally independent ontological event', operating according to 'categories irreducible to those of cognition'.

14   Daniel W. Smith offers a lucid exposition of Deleuze's thinking in this area:

If Deleuze's many writings on art constitute an integral part of his philosophy, it is because works of art are themselves explorations of his transcendental realm of sensibility. The most general aim of art, according to Deleuze, is to produce a sensation, to create a 'pure being of sensation', a sign. The work of art is, as it were, a 'machine' or 'apparatus' that utilizes these passive syntheses of sensation to produce effects of its own. The genetic principles of sensation are thus at the same time the principles of composition of the work of art; and conversely, it is the structure of the work of art that reveals these conditions [...] Great artists are [...] great thinkers, but they think in terms of sensations rather than concepts. (Daniel W. Smith, 'Deleuze's Theory of Sensation: Overcoming the Kantian Duality', in *Deleuze: A Critical Reader* [edited by Paul Patton, Oxford: Basil Blackwell, 1996], pp. 39-40)

[15] George Eliot, *The Mill on the Floss* (London: Penguin, 1979), p. 560.

[16] D. H. Lawrence, *Study of Thomas Hardy, Selected Literary Criticism* (London: Heinemann, 1973), p. 167.

[17] I have written at length about this aspect of Hardy's writing in my discussion of *Jude the Obscure* in an earlier book, *Lines of Flight* (Sheffield: Sheffield Academic Press, 1997).

[18] See for instance, the biographies by Millgate and Gittings, and Pinion's companion to Hardy.

[19] Simon Gatrell, 'Hardy's Dances', *Thomas Hardy and the Proper Study of Mankind* (London: Macmillan, 1993), p. 34.

[20] With reference to the point about the material basis of sensation, I have in mind Deleuze's discussion in *Bergsonism*, that:

> When we perceive, we contract millions of vibrations or elementary shocks into a felt quality. (*Bergsonism* [translated by Hugh Tomlinson and Barbara Habberjam, New York: Zone, 1988], p. 87)

Similarly, with reference to the point about the affect, I have in mind comments such as that affects have to do with 'transitions, passages that are experienced, durations through which we pass' (Deleuze, *Spinoza: Practical Philosophy*, p. 48), and the following:

> Whence the force of Spinoza's question: 'What can a body do?', of what affects is it capable? Affects are becomings: sometimes they weaken us in so far as they diminish our power to act and decompose our relationships (sadness), sometimes they make us stronger in so far as they increase our power and make us enter into a more vast or superior individual (joy). (*Dialogues*, p. 60)

[21] To draw together some of the philosophical threads here: ethically, becoming actualizes the virtual powers of the soul through a process of self-differentiation which intrinsically affirms both the unchanging necessity of these abiding and ideal powers of relation, and the accidents and changes, the events, of these singular actualizations of selfhood. Ontologically, becoming in this way affirms the eternal in the set of ideal relations which composes an individual. It expresses this set as variations in time, through the unfolding of a personal history. Temporally, becoming operates in duration, in fluent movements of time which resist the measurable, representable logic of chronology. These points of time correspond to the upheavals of duration like volcanic rock corresponds to the eruptions of the volcano itself.

[22] Gilles Deleuze, *Cinema 1: The Movement-Image* (translated by Hugh Tomlinson and Barbara Habberjam, London: Athlone, 1992), p. 11.

[23] Millgate's remarks intriguingly suggest how Hardy's tendency to

improvisation in matters of style and form was reproduced in the building of the house, as he mixed styles so that there was 'a failure of the various elements of the front elevation to balance with one another'. More fully, Millgate wrote of how Hardy seemed:

> to have designed the house from the inside outwards, first deciding upon the number, function, and size of the rooms and then contriving to fit those requirements within a reasonably coherent over-all structure, at whatever cost in terms of external symmetry. (*Thomas Hardy*, p. 259)

This is obviously comparable to the way in which Hardy's narrative writing in general unfolds from the middle of its scenes, and appears only reluctantly and belatedly concerned with matters of stylistic consistency or the larger design.

24 See Eliot's *After Strange Gods* (London: Faber and Faber, 1934), Hillis Miller's *Distance and Desire* (Oxford: Oxford University Press, 1970), Gittings's biography of Hardy (London: Penguin, 1980), Jacobson's *Peeping Tom* (London: Chatto & Windus, 1984), and Fisher's *The Hidden Hardy* (London: Macmillan, 1992).

25 So, in a more general way, the fiction is full of this sense of being observed. The passage in *Desperate Remedies*, where Cytherea feels Manston's eyes going through her, needs little glossing, though it corresponds to the less threatening, though similarly comic moment in *Far From the Madding Crowd* where Joseph Poorgrass's complains that 'Twere blush, blush, blush with me every minute of the time, when she was speaking to me' (*Far from the Madding Crowd*, p. 93). At times, of course, this embodied sense of oneself as taken up as the object of another's perception is extraordinarily acute, and inimitably conveyed. In the first case, Bathsheba is being stalked by Boldwood, where in the second one, she is being observed by Oak:

> She heard footsteps brushing the grass, and had a consciousness that love was encircling her like a perfume. (*Far from the Madding Crowd*, p. 158)

> Rays of male vision seem to have a tickling effect upon virgin faces in rural districts; she brushed her with her hand, as if Gabriel had been irritating its pink surface by actual touch, and the free air of her previous movements was reduced at the same time to a chastened phase of itself. (*Far from the Madding Crowd*, p. 55)

For Sue Bridehead, contrarily, as she addresses Jude, the indifference of the observer would constitute a terrible abandonment:

> 'Don't turn away from me! I can't bear the loneliness of being out of your looks!'

Again differently, Harold Bloom has commented on how for 'Henchard "the humiliation of exposure" becomes a terrible passion, until at last he makes an exhibition of himself during a royal visit. Perhaps he can revert to what Frye calls "the horror of being watched" only when he knows that the gesture involved will be his last [...]' (*Modern Critical Interpretations: Thomas Hardy's The Mayor of Casterbridge* [edited by Harold Bloom, New York: Chelsea House, 1988], p. 4).

26 At this point, it is relevant to mention Marjorie Garson's Lacanian discussion of Hardy's novels in terms of what she sees as their underlying and

gendered drama of corporeality (*Hardy's Fables of Integrity* [Oxford: Clarendon Press, 1991]). For Garson, Hardy is a writer whose texts betray a persistent male anxiety of downfall and dissolution, a 'concern about integrity and wholeness - both psychic and bodily' (*Hardy's Fables of Integrity*, p. 1), in the face of women who are conceived as emasculating in their self-sufficiency. While acknowledging the shrewdness of many of Garson's individual perceptions, her wholesale reading of Hardy's texts in terms of a phenomenology of castration-anxiety is open to criticism, and certainly runs wholly counter to this chapter's discussion of the more mobile modes of individuality which are attributable to Hardy's female characters. So too, obviously, it has been argued that it is precisely in terms of a dissolve of bodily distinctions, and through moments of linguistic indetermination, that Hardy's writing establishes the characters' sense of inter-relatedness, on the one hand, and, on the other, the narrative's most essential kinds of comic, erotic, and affective rapport with the reader.

    27 In describing the 'provisionality' of plotting in Hardy's novels, Patricia Ingham has emphasized how he resisted and deferred the final composition of plot. (Where Ingham talks about the 'subjunctive' in Hardy's plotting, Gillian Beer has discussed in a similar vein the 'optative' [Gillian Beer, *Darwin's Plots* (London: Routledge, 1983), pp. 239-40]). In Ingham's argument, the texts remain unresolved in their use of 'ghost' plots, and various alternative lines of possibility which the narrator suggests or explores. She stresses how the 'what if' and the 'if only' function in Hardy as both plot devices and the indices of a recurrent structure of feeling:

> Concentration on openness of endings has meant a failure to recognise an equally important aspect of the final trilogy: provisionality of plot. Hillis Miller's suggested alternative endings, for instance, are rather to be construed as alternative plots frustrated before the novel ends, not left open. They are two of many, openness goes further back into the texts than a stress on endings suggests. It makes evident the fact that all accounts are interim and it reveals the potential of all events to take another course or courses. (Patricia Ingham, 'Provisional Narratives: Hardy's Final Trilogy', in *Alternative Hardy* [edited and introduced by Lance St John Butler, London: Macmillan, 1989], p. 61)

    28 Sarah Davies, '*The Hand of Ethelberta*: de-mythologising "woman"', *Critical Survey*, Vol. 5, no. 2, (1993), p. 126.
    29 More specifically, one can remember, too, his disclaimer that *A Group of Noble Dames* was rather 'a frivolous piece of work which I took in hand in a sort of desperation during a fit of low spirits' (*Collected Letters*, Vol. 1, p. 239). Paul Turner cites an intriguing passage from the time about the effects of a 'rheumatic attack' in London:

> if there is any way of getting a melancholic satisfaction out of life it lies in dying, so to speak, before one is out of the flesh, by which I mean putting on the manners of ghosts, wandering in their haunts, and taking their views of surrounding things. To think of life as passing away is a sadness; to think of it as past is at least tolerable. (Paul Turner, *The Life of Thomas Hardy* [Oxford: Blackwell, 1998], p. 116)

Circumstances can be seen as bringing into sharp conflict here tender feeling (with all its risks of rejection and foolishness) and the petrified state (fearful, rigid, postmortem) which attempts to find a stable position beyond these intensities. In terms of the story itself, also, it is possible to see the conflict between Lord Uplandtowers and Barbara as reflecting and dramatizing such a conflict: the desire to reach a state coldly and inanimately removed from feeling has its origin in an excessive vulnerability to the pull of sentiment. For all the mockery and determination of the tale, the final ironic twist is that this satirical and despoiling activity can itself be read in this respect, in relation to Hardy himself, as a testament to the recurrent desire which it attempts to overcome and extinguish.

   30   Thomas Hardy, 'An Indiscretion in the Life of an Heiress', Vol. 3 of *The Stories of Thomas Hardy* (edited by F. B. Pinion, London: Macmillan, 1977), p. 93.

   31   One can consider here also, the ways in which Hardy introduces us into the era of *The Trumpet-Major*, through evoking the customary and unregarded sounds of the mill:

> In this dwelling Mrs Garland's and Anne's ears were soothed morning, noon, and night by the music of the mill, the wheels and cogs of which, being of wood, produced notes that might have borne in their minds a resemblance to the wooden tones of the stopped diapason in an organ...
> (*The Trumpet-Major*, p. 54)

Again, Anne will wake to the sounds of the soldiers' industry which announce their arrival (*The Trumpet-Major*, p. 54), as she will a little later chafe at the sounds of the miller's party on the other side of the wall (*The Trumpet-Major*, p. 58). Recurrently in this novel too, the sounds of music (like the sounds of the heath at the beginning of *The Return of the Native*, or of the sound of the trees in *Under the Greenwood Tree* - both themselves associated with music) becomes a way in which Hardy's narrator overcomes the barriers that divide us and him from the time of the novel, a time which has intimate associations for Hardy. We can cite here two further cases: the songs of the sailors that Anne and Bob hear as 'they strayed upon the velvet sands' between the King's departure from the beach, and the opening of the theatre (*The Trumpet-Major*, p. 255); 'the musical tinkle from the hollow sides of the arch' as Anne and Matilda hide under the bridge with the unconscious Bob from the press-gang (*The Trumpet-Major*, p. 272). Music specifically, and sound generally, work in such cases as privileged means of access or introduction for Hardy to a different culture or time.

Chapter 3

'The Beats of Being'

In an essay of 1925, R. W. King suggested that the lyrical functions of Hardy's poetry principally involved the registering of a 'momentary sensation' or 'a brief incident', so that it becomes shaped as:

> a *significant anecdote*, chosen, or invented, not merely for its own sake, but for its value as a symbol, as a 'moment of vision', which gathers up the emotional experience of years. 'Beeny Cliff', for instance, not only renders the radiance of that March day in 1870, but suggests the whole course of the poet's life since then.

Likewise, he wrote:

> To Hardy the commonest object - a garden seat, a 'little old table', a signpost or an almanack - may have tremendous significance, may carry memories and associations of a lifetime's love, with all its joys and sorrows. He says truly of himself: 'I only need the homeliest of heartstirrings.'[1]

Today King's emphasis may seem overly biographical, but it indicates the familiar way in which Hardy's poems often turn on his receptivity to 'seemings', 'impressions', to phenomena which telegraph a kind of message to his 'idiosyncratic mode of regard' (*Life*, p. 225), like the coffin lid of William Barnes in 'The Last Signal', as it catches the light of the setting sun:

> Thus a farewell to me he signalled on his grave-way,
>   As with a wave of his hand. (*Complete Poems*, p. 473)

What is important and characteristic is the way in which the poem unpacks its dimension of meaning from such an accidental effect. The reflection from a coffin lid becomes a kind of hieroglyph, expanding in Hardy's mind into an intimate and many-sided meditation on his relation to Barnes. In another poem, the Roman coin shown to Hardy by a little girl in Fiesole is identical to 'coins of like impress' buried at home, and consequently:

her act flashed home
In that mute moment to my opened mind
The power, the pride, the reach of perished Rome. (*Complete Poems*, p. 102)

These cases usefully show how Hardy's creativity is fundamentally not a matter of free invention, but of his capacity for finding an adequate language for such 'moments of vision'. A humble phenomenon, perceived or imagined, will act like a genie's lamp, releasing a cloud of significant emotion which gradually takes on definition and intelligibility as the poet translates it into poetry. This chapter explores the role of music in this context, since countless poems originate with moments of musical inspiration. Inspiration, in fact, is the key idea throughout the chapter, chosen since it preserves obvious links with the concept of individuation, as well as because it has specific applications to the affirmative aspects of Hardy's poetry. Like individuation, inspiration is a way of describing enhancements and renewals of self-expression that depend on extra-subjective modes of relatedness or transmission.

The more one contemplates Hardy's 'moments of vision', indeed, the more musical experience appear to have an exemplary status for Hardy as he focuses on the happiness and pleasure, and the experiences of transcendence, that it carries with it. In many such scenes in poems, music creates incidental and surprising effects of concordance and significance, within an otherwise discordant, prosaic *mise-en-scène*. Music's 'insistent calls of joy' produce a real rapture, even though such magical effects tend to be transient and inconsequential, ironically encroached upon by loss, betrayal, forgetfulness, and death. The phrase is from the closing lines of 'After the Burial', where Hardy writes of the joyful peals of the church bells, as heard by the mourners:

Nor window did they close, to numb
   The bells' insistent calls
Of joy; but suffered the harassing din to come
And penetrate their souls. (*Complete Poems*, p. 876)

Beyond the scenic and dramatic effects of these musical interludes, an invasive musicality will manifest itself for the reader in complementary ways at the level of hearing, as unpredictable, intensive features of metre or sound off-set the otherwise disharmonious texture of the verse. So, it is a typical experience (and a tantalizing and pleasurable one) when reading Hardy's poetry, to find for an ephemeral, virtual instant that an evocative power of sound has abolished one's distance from the scene, turning the poem inside out, so that the reader is introduced into its world of perception and feeling before the effect vanishes again. The ecstatic responsiveness which a poem plays out as a major element of its drama is thus effected in a similar way in this corresponding transfer - rush - between the forms of content and expression.   These lines, from 'The Fiddler', are a clear example of this:

> 'There's many a heart now mangled,
> And waiting its time to go,
> Whose tendrils were first entangled
> By my sweet viol and bow!' (*Complete Poems*, p. 248)

The seductive arabesques of sound entangle the reader, inspiring an instantaneous sense of immediate connection to the scene as surely as the 'blaze' of Barnes's coffin-lid did for Hardy in the other poem.

In such ways, the 'Lyric Ecstasy inspired by music', in Hardy's phrase, can be importantly referred both to the musical transports of the *dramatis personae* of the poems, and to their formal correlates for the reader in effects of sound. This phrase, from a note in the *Life*, records a collection projected in 1892 as a set of songs (as the furore over *Tess* broke out):

> Title: - "Songs of Five-and-Twenty Years". Arrangement of the songs: Lyric Ecstasy inspired by music to have precedence. (*Life* p. 243)

'Lyric ecstasy' here is a power of transformative expression, occasioned by music, that the poems as songs explicitly aspire to reproduce in their own lyricism. At the same time, the concentration on music also implies how musical experience offers Hardy himself both an important source for his own poetic inspiration, and also, as in the fiction, a template or analogue for his thinking about it. In this respect, the poems can be read as auto-meditations - through music as metaphor - on the mysterious processes of inspiration that provoke them, as well as expressions and dramatizations of these processes.

So far as the poet's own experiences and reflections on lyrical composition are concerned, Hardy is himself often explicit about its involuntary and inspirational features, as in his description of the writing of *The Dynasts*:

> Lyrical activity was essential for my existence - and *The Dynasts*
> was crying for materialization, crying to be born, for many years. I
> wrote it because I had to, because of orders from within. (*Life*, p.
> 334)

For Hardy, *qua* poet, the art of writing is always a form of automatic
writing, however much it entails conscious challenges and satisfactions
of its own (as in Davie's notion that Hardy as a poet be considered
primarily as an engineer of words, metres and verse forms).[2] The
technical emphasis on control, that is, cannot account for the poet's own
experience of yielding to the incalculable imperatives, the strange
transpositions of mind, associated with inspiration. On Christmas Day
1890, Hardy records:

> While thinking of resuming "the viewless wings of poesy" before
> dawn this morning, new horizons seemed to open, and worrying
> pettinesses to disappear. (*Life*, p. 230)

In terms of Hardy's own life, such effects of imaginative and
spiritual enlargement can be seen as evidence of the 'developing sense
of a liberated subjectivity' that Tim Armstrong identifies in Hardy's
turning to poetry.[3] Implicit also in this, and in these associations of
ecstasy, lyricism and inspiration, is the affirmative ethical strain in
Hardy's work, his desire to celebrate life. An early critic, Arthur S.
Macdowall, referred to such an innate vitality, as Hardy's 'immediate
response to life',[4] and Armstrong writes of how 'Life calls him to song',
and of 'the moments of revivification' which are central to Hardy's
work.[5] Musical experience is implicitly ethical, as well as aesthetic, for
Hardy because for him goodness and joy are inseparable from the
reanimating events and processes of self-expression through which
'new horizons' seem 'to open, and worrying pettinesses to disappear'.
Further, ethics is inseparable from the social, even the ecological,
because self-expression is always a function of relations with other
people and nature. For this reason, this study puts what is seen as a
corrective emphasis on the side of the evaluation of life that Hardy's
poetry implicitly affirms.[6]

Further, it is one of the fascinations of music for Hardy that its
experiences of joy are undeniably physical and mundane, even as they
appear also to have metaphysical import. But to stress physicality is not
to deny transcendence, although it makes it essential to understand in
what sense the idea of transcendence is being used. John Lucas links the

question to the more specific issue of what Hardy's relation to Romanticism might be. He writes:

> Hardy is too intelligent to indulge in a timeless, idyllic past, a golden world from which he has been thrust out into the cold hillside.[7]

One could even identify Hardy in these terms as a great poet of 'the cold hillside'. However, in his lyricism he remains a residual romantic, and his work can be seen as carrying on a subtle dialogue with these more remote forebears, as well as with Browning, Barnes, or Swinburne. Lucas in fact more than any critic indicates how Hardy's poetry is written around - out of - 'moments of vision'. The apparent paradox - on which Lucas insists - is that Hardy's world-view refuses any notion of a transcendent 'golden world' from which one is exiled, while his poetic work remains fascinated by, shot through with, glimmers of the ideal. My account of this paradox is that Hardy's work depends not on a secondary transcendent domain, but on transcendent moments. In these the limits of chronology and identity are opened up to ecstatic affirmations of those subsistent, virtual powers of relatedness and self-differentiation which define the 'soul' for Hardy. Transcendence is a function of the immanent, of mobile sensory and affective moments, of significant events that introduce the respondent into a momentarily expanded and real (however temporary and unsustainable) sense of connection and expression. Hardy's apparent lack of belief in immortality, in myth or religion, or in any form of enduring happiness, did not prevent him acknowledging the reality of experience as punctuated by such events. Moreover, in these inspiring passages are repeated what Lucas also sees as 'timeless', ideal, potentials of relatedness and creativity. Music offers in this context potent and irrefutable signs of transcendence through physical connection. The captivating effects oi rhythm and melody may be impermanent, but they return, and in doing so, repeat these inexhaustible possibilities.

So, the desires and pleasures associated with music off-set the reality principle operative in the poems. A poem seeks to capture this intensity and promise of longing, and to make it endlessly repeatable within its own substance. Often, of course, the circumstances are unpropitious, as in 'On Stinsford Hill at Midnight', where, the speaker feels compelled, with mounting desperation, to call out to the singing woman, though she remains oblivious or unheeding:

Her voice swam on; nor did she show
   Thought of me anyhow.

I called again: 'Come nearer; much
   That kind of note I need!'
The song kept softening, loudening on
   In placid calm unheed.

'What home is yours now?' then I said;
   'You seem to have no care.'
But the wild wavering tune went forth
   As if I had not been there.

'This world is dark, and where you are,'
   I said, 'I cannot be!'
But still the happy one sang on,
   And had no heed of me. (*Complete Poems*, p. 597)

At the end of the poem, the poet registers his mortification, as the 'wild wavering tune' torments him in his compulsive desire to connect. However, as the language recurrently and teasingly evokes her song ('softening, loudening on'), so thereby this disappointment is turned into an endlessly renewable erotic drama of possibility: poetry, like music or desire in this case, exploits the flirtatious time of the continuous present. Although the poem results in disappointment and frustration for the poetic figure who narrates it, it is still constitutively organized around music as innately a sign of longed-for ecstasy.

These preliminary remarks make it possible now to describe the main ways in which the topic of inspiration organizes the following sections. Firstly, musical incidents in Hardy's poetry set up scenes of identification, whereby the distinction of self and other is suspended, and through these the poetry investigates ethical and political possibilities obscured by custom: music provides a powerful way of feeling with or as another person. Secondly, such inspiring augmentations of identity are constantly evident in erotic terms too in the *Complete Poems*, and the chapter explores the links between music and love, and the loss of love. Thirdly, there are many poems which involve what can be called scenes of aesthetic inspiration: of these, I shall concentrate on those which employ music to occasion and reflect on the kinds of exchanges and modulations of selfhood involved in the paradoxical processes of artistic invention. Like individuation, inspiration works by effects of contagion - for the poet in relation to his muse, certainly, but for the reader too, as in Timothy Clark's observation that it is a time-honoured characteristic of inspiration, that '[T]o be inspired is, necessarily, to inspire others.'[8] Fourthly, these productive transfers of identity - artistic, erotic, social, readerly - are linked to what is seen as the constitutive transfers in Hardy's lyric poetry of musical and poetic modes: music as topic or content is inside the framework of a poem, as it were, but the poem also becomes opened up by effects of rhythm and sound. To describe these passages between the representative and expressive functions of the poetry will involve reference to the traditionally vexed issue of Hardy's versification, as well as to the general idea of rhythm, and the chapter revisits these and the other topics in terms of Deleuze and Guattari's discussion of rhythm in *A Thousand Plateaus*. Finally, the closing sections are concerned with another kind of inspiration - the ways in which Hardy's poetry persistently inscribes within itself, and inscribes itself within, poetic tradition. This involves the poet in dialogue with other poets, so that a poem expands, goes outside itself, includes other poems, incorporates other voices, within itself and becomes readable in terms of its associations, resonances, references.[9] For instance, 'On Stinsford Hill' could clearly be seen as a response to Wordsworth's encounter with the solitary reaper. As a further aspect of this intertextual, dialogic, dimension, Armstrong has pointed out the metrical and other references to Barnes's work employed in 'The Last Signal', which thus convey Hardy's sense of indebtedness to the earlier poet (*Selected Poems*, edited Armstrong, pp. 218-19). Finally, it is true in many poems that the affirmations of inspiration are muted, and ironised at times - often qualified almost to vanishing point. However, the argument is that they are irreducibly and variously there as a condition of a poem's meaning, and as betraying its underlying associative logic of expression.

I

This section explores how musical incidents in Hardy's poetry produce effects of sympathy which in turn condition ethical and political responses and enquiries. Hardy's 'moments of vision' are in this respect often implicitly visionary. A memorable poem which allows for a more detailed development of these ideas is 'Christmastide'. The poem, 'extensively neglected' in Peter Widdowson's words, narrates the slightest kind of musical encounter (*Late Essays and Earlier*, p. 165):

> The rain-shafts splintered on me

As despondently I strode;
The twilight gloomed upon me
  And bleared the blank high-road.
Each bush gave forth, when blown on
  By gust in shower and shower,
A sigh, as it were sown on
  In handfuls by a sower.

A cheerful voice called, nigh me,
  'A merry Christmas, friend!' -
There rose a figure by me,
  Walking with townward trend,
A sodden tramp's, who, breaking
  Into thin song, bore straight
Ahead, direction taking
  Towards the Casuals' gate. (*Complete Poems*, p. 846)

In the first stanza, Hardy conveys the sense of a natural scene that is merely endured. The walker finds only his despondency returned to him by the outward aspect of what he sees ('The twilight gloomed', 'the blank high-road'. /Each bush gave forth [...] /A sigh'). The purely deadening aspect of the scene is conveyed by alliterative repetition, and by what are initially unvarying rhythmical features. Towards the end of the stanza the scene's dispiriting lack of vitality is conveyed by the effects of rhythmical fading, as in the feminine endings and half or muted stresses which take over the second halves of the last four lines:

Each bush gave forth, when blown on
  By gust in shower and shower,
A sigh, as it were sown on
  In handfuls by a sower.

Against this, in the second stanza, a spring returns to the poem's step with the advent of the cheerful voice, and the figure which 'rose by me', subsequently identified as the sodden tramp who walks undeviatingly ahead. With this surprising encounter, and the sense of contact and cheerfulness which it produces, there is a greater rhythmical intensity with the opening of the second stanza. It is as if the speaker has found fleetingly, in the example of the tramp, a counter to his own dispirited, wind-blown sense of things. Commonplace as the scene is, though, the tramp remains a figure of wonder, as well as of inspiration and pity, as different and incompatible significances of the scene multiply for the reader without resolution around him. The tramp is someone who belongs all too obviously to the everyday world, with his sodden figure and his physical frailty, evident in his 'thin song'. However, this strange apparition also suggests, as in an old Christmas tale, the appearance of Christ in disguise; or, as in the Bible, the appearance of the risen Christ to the disconsolate disciples walking on the road to Emmaus. Even if the raising of the spirit which takes place here is of a more commonplace and implicitly passing and secular kind, the encounter does offer a real inspiration. The reinvigorating effect which the man has on the language of the second stanza suggests that the speaker attunes himself to the other's mood, his sense of things and his gait. (One of the uncanny effects of the poem is the sense we get of the tramp's way of walking.) Hence, the poem gives us a dual sense of the scene: as unremarkable, ordinary and inconsequential in one respect; while being also memorable, mysterious, even profound, in another. It is one of those 'epiphanic' poems, in John Lucas's terminology, where 'a tiny incident constellates rich meanings and implications' (*Modern English Poetry*, p. 29). Lucas's use of the word 'epiphanic' suggests also something of what Hardy meant when he wrote that:

> poetry and religion touch each other, or rather modulate into each other; are, indeed, often but different names for the same thing - these, I say, the visible signs of mental and emotional life [which] must like all other things keep moving, becoming.[10]

As against an arrival at a single mode or content of meaning, the poem places any reader, like its speaker and the figure of the tramp, in a relationship which is affirmative and unforeseen, as well as unfinished and enigmatic. In fact, the subdued wonder which the man elicits in the poem is largely because of his destitute condition, and his movement towards a place that promises human meaning and contact. But more precisely, his mysterious significance goes beyond the curiosity and sympathy he provokes. It corresponds to the incontrovertible sense in the poem that at this moment he embodies innate qualities of human endurance and good will. The poem, accordingly, appears designed to render the affective power of the encounter, and its language appropriately retains a mysterious ideal power to inspire repeatedly variable kinds of reading. As we read, these possibilities of interpretation spin round, more or less subliminally, and without resolution, like the moving numbers of a roulette wheel. Or to take a more appropriate metaphor, they impinge enigmatically on the threshold of consciousness, like all the vagrant figures which the poem might lead us to imagine on this Christmas evening, as 'direction taking / Towards the Casuals' gate': that is, as in movement towards the lowering world of conventional identification. In these ways, the poem settles out as an expression of the queries and perceptions which thronged into the poet's mind.

Typically, it is part of the force of the poem that it can in this way accommodate and do justice to an endless variety of such readings and questions, while maintaining its discreet intensity of ethical and political focus. While we can imagine that an infinite number of readings could accurately be derived from the poem, it is difficult to conceive of readings which could ignore the affect of sympathy which engenders it. The poem is an example of what C. Day Lewis referred to when he remarked that sympathy was the 'seed' of Hardy's poetic imagination. Certainly, it appears here also as the seed from which his political viewpoint unfolds in its positive and negative aspects (as vision and critique). Widdowson makes the connection between sympathetic response and political viewpoint in 'Christmastide', when he comments on the way in which the poem focuses unambiguously on a moment of 'irrepressible hope' of an implicitly social kind, while leaving 'understated' or implicit its correlative elements of critique (*Late Essays and Earlier*, p. 165).[11] Brief as the human contact is in 'Christmastide', it thus results in a poem which creates the space for a series of interconnecting questions about human relatedness and society, as well as about artistic inspiration and interpretation. Art in the form of a 'thin song' provides a precarious, but genuine, connection between the individuals in the poem, and sets up connections with the speaker and the reader. Further, the Wordsworthian echoes in the incident suggests a comparable continuity between Hardy and the earlier poet.[12]

Once again, the actuality of this described occurrence is less the issue than its quality or type, as an incident which takes hold of the poet. It is one of those '[u]nadjusted impressions' referred to in the 'Preface' to *Poems of the Past and Present*. These, Hardy says, 'have their value' in so far as they are both accidental, 'forced upon us', and yet significant:

> the road to a true philosophy of life seems to lie in humbly recording diverse readings of its phenomena as they are forced upon us by chance and change. (*Complete Poems*, p. 84)

The tramp's song is valuable because it transforms things. However modestly and fleetingly, harmony occurs within the forlorn detail and momentariness of the scene. In this aspect, the tramp's own cordiality and cheer make him appear as a positive type of the human spirit. He transcends the material conditions of his life, and in so doing reawakens the ethical imagination of the reader and poet. To talk of transcendence here, once again, is not to talk of any secondary or enchanted domain which could be substituted for what Brooks refers to below as 'the here or now'. It is rather to talk of uncontrolled physical encounters, dislocating events, which raise the various capacities of the spirit - perception, memory, imagination - to autonomous expression according to the logic of individuation or becoming which Deleuze writes about. The body is taken up by a physical event and becomes an expressive instrument of the mind. Brooks describes how Hardy's work originates in incidents where the ordinary becomes altered, so that the 'here and now' takes on an ideal aspect:

> Hardy's best lyrics are moments of vision that have found their objective correlative in something close to common experience which yet evokes the underlying deeper reality that he admired in Turner's late paintings. All the unremarkable and usually unremarked aspects of routine life are brought into consciousness by Hardy's penetrating vision in search for the attainable significance that does not aspire beyond the world of here and now. ('The Homeliest of Heart-Stirrings', p. 206)

The ethical and spiritual values implicit in such 'moments of vision' are tied to this secular 'here and now'. So, for all the transience of the musical incident in 'Christmastide', it can be seen to introduce a moment of intensity in which these true capacities of the various individuals concerned are revealed. This would make it one of those incidents that Hardy had in mind when he made the citation referred to in the *Life*, following Browning's death: "Incidents in the development of a soul! little else is worth study" (*Life*, p. 233).

As in 'Christmastide', music works time and again in the poems as a genuine conduit for these abiding, if often obscured, qualities of life and mind. Even in the most modest circumstances, it can have a transformative visionary power, in its association with intermissions in life where the real becomes suffused with the ideal. This can take a predominantly social form, as in 'Christmastide', or an artistic or romantic one. In 'Architectural Masks', for instance, Hardy describes the 'poetic souls' who live in the brick villa, and who 'with book and pencil, viol and bow / Lead inner lives of dreams' (*Complete Poems*, p. 161), whereas in 'After a Romantic Day' he writes of how a charmless and weathered railway cutting becomes a backdrop for the 'visions' of the lover's mind, as 'the frail light shed by a slim young moon/ Fell like a friendly tune. /Fell like a liquid ditty' [...] (*Complete Poems*, p. 641).

The social and ethical dimensions of musical incidents can be detected again in a very different type of poem, 'On the Belgium Expatriation'. Dated 18 October 1914, Hardy narrates a dream 'that people from the Land of Chimes/Arrived one autumn morning with their bells'. This redemptive vision is in turn thrown into relief by contrary images which present the pitiful actuality of the Belgian people:

> Then I awoke; and lo, before me stood
> The visioned ones, but pale and full of fear;
> From Bruges they came, and Antwerp, and Ostend,
>
> No carillons in their train. Foes of mad mood
> Had shattered these to shards amid the gear
> Of ravaged roof, and smouldering gable-end. (*Complete Poems*, p. 541)

Nonetheless, it is a certain idealism that takes wing at the end of the poem from all the debris of destruction, since to read the poem is to feel the compelling necessity of a response which goes beyond mere quietism or cynicism. In this way, the poem's final complexity of effect preserves a connection with the hopes of the opening dream, wherein Hardy hoped that Belgian bells could be rung in Britain so as to 'solace souls of this and kindred climes'. In another war poem, 'Often When Warring' this overcoming of nationality becomes an explicit overturning of it. The soldier's instinctive kindness to a wounded enemy reveals the hollowness of war's moral rationale and 'victory's' jarring 'peal of pride':

> For natural mindsight, triumphing in the act
> Over the throes of artificial rage,
> Has thuswise muffled victory's peal of pride [...] (*Complete Poems*, p. 545)

Real indignation and fellow-feeling are the Hardyan alternatives to 'artificial rage' and military triumphalism.

In 'The Blinded Bird' or 'Julie-Jane', similarly, the reduced condition of the central figure enlivens the reader's sympathies and provokes ethical thought. The bird and Julie-Jane follow the laws of their own natures, and demonstrate, like the tramp, their powers of endurance and regeneration, even though circumstances conspire to crush them. In these cases, too, spiritual qualities are associated with music. In 'The Blinded Bird', the poet's amazement and disbelief that the bird can still sing, as if in divine forgiveness, coexists with an almost unreadably painful and careful registering of the facts of its maiming:

> So zestfully canst thou sing?
> And all this indignity,
> With God's consent, on thee!
> Blinded ere yet a-wing
> By the red-hot needle thou,
> I stand and wonder how
> So zestfully thou canst sing!
>
> Resenting not such wrong,
> Thy grievous pain forgot,
> Eternal dark thy lot,
> Groping thy whole life long,
> After that stab of fire;
> Enjailed in pitiless wire;
> Resenting not such wrong!
>
> Who hath charity? This bird.
> Who suffereth long and is kind,
> Is not provoked, though blind
> And alive ensepulchred?
> Who hopeth, endureth all things?
> Who thinketh no evil, but sings?
> Who is divine? This bird. (*Complete Poems*, p. 446)

'Julie-Jane' commends a good-time girl who infectiously remains true to herself to the end:

> Sing; how a' would sing!
> How a' would raise the tune
> When we rode in the waggon from harvesting
> By the light o' the moon! (*Complete Poems*, p. 245)

Unbroken by life, Julie-Jane ends by counselling her prospective mourners to return to their lovers, her irrepressible exuberance appearing as an indictment of society's norms.

The links of musical expression with the sympathetic and meditative responses of the reader is a key way in which Hardy's verse embeds its values in emotion, expressing his conception of a 'mental and emotional life [which] must like all other things keep moving, becoming'. The writing entwines the incommensurable worlds of fact and hope, even making the latter unfold from the former. In many poems, of course, the oscillation between the two attitudes becomes the central focus. Untypically, in 'Jubilate', 'Let Me Enjoy', or 'On a Fine Morning' celebration and optimism counter the negative counsellings, the ironic possibilities, of reason and experience:

> Whence comes Solace? - Not from seeing
> What is doing, suffering, being,
> Not from noting Life's conditions.
> Nor from heeding Time's monitions;
>   But in cleaving to the Dream,
>   And in gazing at the gleam
>   Whereby gray things golden seem.
> ('On a Fine Morning', *Complete Poems*, p. 129)

The important emphasis in these lines, though, is that human beings cannot do without 'cleaving to the Dream', as at the end of 'The Boy's Dream', where we learn that the secret longing of the provincial 'town-boy - frail, lame' was not for physical strength or agility, but to own a singing bird:

> But sometimes he would let be known
> What the wish was: - to have, next spring,
> A real green linnet - his very own -
> Like that one he had late heard sing.
>
> And as he breathed the cherished dream
> To those whose secrecy was sworn,
> His face was beautified by the theme,
>   And wore the radiance of the morn. (*Complete Poems*, p. 918)

The vocabulary of these final lines suggests a customary transfiguration, a moving, and almost literal, inspiration as the boy 'sometimes' 'breathed the cherished dream' of the singing linnet to those fellow-spirits 'whose secrecy was sworn'. The value of these moments is not diminished by our conviction that the boy's life is unlikely to be happy or fulfilled. Rather, there is an effective stand-off at the end of the poem between this poignant sense, and the final image of the 'radiance' of the boy's face, 'beautified by the theme'. While neither attitude extinguishes the other, it also seems likely that the poem itself would have been precipitated in Hardy's imagination out of a complex image such as this.

Like 'The Boy's Dream', 'In a Waiting Room' is a poem that steers a similarly effective course between ironic closure and sentimentality, offering the implacable texture of fact as a counterweight to what could otherwise seem facile or cloying about its moments of illumination. The poet, on 'a morning sick as the day of doom' in May, begins by noting all the signs of social and moral decay which abound in the room - the 'tarnished' pictures of ocean liners; the soldier and his wife parting stonily; the traveller's Bible with sordid financial sums scrawled over the gospel of St John - so that he wonders:

> if there could have been
>   Any particle of a soul
>   In that poor man at all,
>   To cypher rates of wage
>   Upon that printed page [...] (*Complete Poems*, p. 518)

The poem's climax occurs as this dismal scene is transformed by the optimism and joy of the pair of children who enter the room. Although the context inevitably suggests the dreariness in their lives, there is also the contrary sense of their exuberant faith in the quality of the time 'when the band will play, and the sun shall shine'. However partial their view of things, their faith is itself real and indispensable:

> It rained on the skylight with a din
> As we waited and still no train came in;
> But the words of the child in the squalid room
> Had spread a glory through the gloom. (*Complete Poems*, p. 519)

The children's vibrancy is moving for two contrary reasons: firstly, because it offers a necessary opposite to the cynicism and lack of community in the adult world, and secondly because we detect how powerless the children will be to resist these alienating effects as they grow up in their turn. Once again, these competing realities enter into a type of circulation that makes the poem's vision effective and inconclusive.

The emotional intensities, linked to possibilities of renewal, that are afforded by even such precarious events of inspiration can be seen by contrast with another poem, 'An East-End Curate', that contemplates a life lived without these vital qualities. The poet outlines the plight of a man wholly cut off from his world, and discreetly indicates the man's own acquiescence in the formulas and fadings that have defined his life.

Ridiculed by children, and powerless to influence his neighbours or to improve their lot, the loss of hope, individuality and society in the poem are linked, in the second stanza, to the absence of the inspiriting effects of music. The curate's piano and music are described in a language marked by enervated cadences and monotonous, routine, rhymes:

> A bleached pianoforte, with its drawn silk plaitings faded,
> Stands in his room, its keys much yellowed, cyphering, and abraded,
> 'Novello's Anthems' lies at hand, and also a few glees,
> And 'Laws of Heaven for Earth' in a frame upon the wall one sees.
> (*Complete Poems*, p. 713)

The scene, typically contrives to be both literal and allegorical at the same time, such details as the 'drawn silk' curtains and the standing 'bleached pianoforte' managing to convey the repression and colourlessness of the Curate's mental and affective life.

John Lucas is perhaps the critic who has most brought out the socially and ethically affirmative aspects of Hardy's 'moments of vision'.[13] Lucas stresses the inherent relation of these moments with the different kinds of value which become connected up, rediscovered, in the activity of writing for Hardy, regardless of his loss of faith, his scepticism, and his success in exacting 'a full look at the Worst' (*Complete Poems*, p.168). Further, Lucas's argument uses musical examples, beginning with 'The House of Silence':

> But what strikes me as powerfully suggestive about the lines from 'The House of Silence' is that music and laughter - the sounds of human voices at their most familiarly convivial - themselves achieve visionary status. They are like floods of light, are every bit as good as the visionary gleam. The visions by which Hardy's mind was lit were very often indistinguishable from, were in fact known through, sounds: of voices, music, song, laughter, murmurings. And it is as though poem after poem is a prompting of sounds from which he seeks release through the act of transcription. (I use that word in its sense of 'a representation in writing of the actual pronunciation of a speech sound'.) Such transcription repeatedly moves towards the condition of music or dance. (*Modern English Poetry*, p. 26)

Lucas points out Hardy's poetry is orientated in terms of 'glimpses', 'glows', 'gleams', 'murmurings', 'glimmerings' (favourite words for

Hardy as Lucas points out) of the transcendent.[14] Ideal values are affirmed and discovered in and through the everyday world. Hardy suggests that fiction and drama also fundamentally depend on their expressive bringing together of the ordinary and the 'eternal and the universal':

> The whole secret of fiction and drama - in the constructional part - lies in the adjustment of things unusual to things eternal and universal. The writer who knows exactly how exceptional, and how non-exceptional, his events should be made, possesses the key to the art. (*Life*, p. 252)

II

In his Oxford lecture, 'Poetry and Abstract Thought: Dancing and Walking', Paul Valéry identified the poet's function with the production in the reader of an altered state. The resulting poetic emotion is one in which:

> well-known things and beings - or rather the ideas that represent them somehow change in value. They attract one another, they become (if you will permit the expression) *musicalized*, resonant, and, as it were, harmonically related.[15]

Poetry brings about its distinctive states of mind through an '*invariably accidental shock*', by way of which, as in a concert hall, 'a quite different atmosphere' becomes created by the first musical sounds:

> a new order would arise, and you yourselves would unconsciously organize yourself to receive it. The musical universe, therefore, was within you, with all its associations and proportions - as in a saturated salt solution a crystalline universe awaits the molecular shock of a minute crystal in order to *declare itself*. ('Poetry and Abstract Thought', p. 258)

For Valéry, the poet's function is to cause 'his reader to become "inspired"' ('Poetry and Abstract Thought', p. 254), as the poet does when he 'undergoes a hidden transformation', and becomes 'an agent, a living system for producing verses' ('Poetry and Abstract Thought', p. 259). Poetic composition and the reading of poetry thus share the same characteristic, says Valéry. Agency in each essentially involves a mysterious surrender and unanalysed becoming (as also in dance, or dream):

> [...] strange discourse, as though made by someone other than the speaker and addressed to someone other than the listener. ('Poetry and Abstract Thought', p. 256)

Valéry's sense of the advent of inspiration for reader and poet has many points of contact with the logic of individuation which underpins the argument of this book. In poems such as 'Christmastide', we have seen, for example, that through an accidental encounter one finds that another person repeats to the self a different possibility of expression. This holds variously for the poet as poet, for the reader, and for the figures within the poem. In this section, the aim is to explore how Hardy often uses music in poems which meditate on artistic influence and inspiration.

Many such poems are organized around a moment in which the poet's mind is surprised into an intuitive rapport with another. From an epistemological point of view, the moment involves indetermination in various ways as can be seen in 'The Youth Who Carried a Light'. The poet begins by seeing the unnamed youth 'pass as the new day dawned,/Murmuring some musical phrase' (itself an appropriately ambiguous phase: a phrase of music, a musical piece of prose, the words of a song?). Then he is struck by a radiance of thought given out by the youth's eyes, a 'very and visible thing':

> A close light, displacing the gray of the morning air,
>   And the tokens that the dark was taking wing;
> And was it not the radiance of a purpose rare
>   That might ripe to its accomplishing? (*Complete Poems*, p. 481)

The poem ends in multiplying unanswerable questions as to what 'became of that light' (*Complete Poems*, p.481). However, what is not in question is the significance of the mental world the poet detects in the boy's inward gaze:

> Yet these were not the spectacles at all that he conned,
>   But an inner one, giving out rays.

As the poem's source is Hardy's sense of the boy's own inner world, so correspondingly we too look inward at this moment to see him in our mind's eye, in a scene irradiated by that sense of inspiration to which Hardy responded. In such relatively simple ways, the logic of transmission, and individuation, is at work in the poem. It establishes a network of the inspired that includes the reader.

In a similar poem, 'The Pedestrian', a meeting is narrated with a young man, philosopher and artist, whose talents will be denied by death and whose:

> voice was that of a man refined,
> A man, one well could feel, of mind,
> Quite winning in its musical ease;
>   But in mould maligned
>   By some disease;
> And I asked again. But he shook his head;
> Then, as if more were due, he said: -
>
> 'A student was I - of Schopenhauer.
> Kant, Hegel, - and the fountained bower
> Of the Muses, too, knew my regard:
>   But ah - I fear me
>   The grave gapes near me!...
> Would that I could this gross sheath discard,
> And rise an ethereal shape, unmarred!' (*Complete Poems*, p. 503)

The poem ends the exclamation, 'How I remember him!', so acute is Hardy's feeling of the other's artistic talent, his 'mind,/ Quite winning in its musical ease'. Similarly, the incident itself is rendered with exactitude, the language catching the play of the young man's eye and voice, and his unself-conscious individuality as it emerges in the detail of dress and gait. Once again, rhythm embodies the poet's memory of the idiosyncratic slopping and shaking of the young man's flesh as he walked:

> 'Twas as if his corpulent figure slopped
> With the shake of his walking when he stopped,
> And, though the night's pinch grew acute,
>   He wore but a thin
>   Wind-thridded suit,
> Yet well-shaped shoes for walking in,
> Artistic beaver, cane gold-topped. (*Complete Poems*, p. 502)

In these cases, the poet finds the means of poetic expression in another person, as that person finds it through the poet who remembers him. Further, the reader finds it in the poet, as his or her imagination, feelings and temperament are unconsciously worked by the poem; and the poet also requires it in the reader, since the latter's potential affinity is the condition and complement of the act of writing. In such ways, inspiration becomes a convenient figure for the events of affective becoming intrinsic to these poems. Hardy's Proustian note of December 4 1890 ruminates on the idea of how individuality is renewed through self-differentiating events of correspondence: 'I am more than ever convinced that persons are successively various persons, according as each special strand in their characters is brought uppermost by circumstances' (*Life*, p. 230). The title of 'Without, Not Within Her' clearly indicates how the soul is expressed by affective response and counter-response:

> It was what you bore with you, Woman,
>   Not inly were,
> That throned you from all else human,
>   However fair!
>
> It was that strange freshness you carried
>   Into a soul
> Whereon no thought of yours tarried
>   Two moments at all.
>
> And out from his spirit flew death,
>   And bale, and ban,
> Like the corn-chaff under the breath
>   Of the winnowing fan. (*Complete Poems*, p. 647)

In 'A Singer Asleep', Hardy's poem to Swinburne, such a chain of inspiration, troped as music, links the young Hardy to Swinburne himself, and his 'numbers freaked with musical closes'. In turn, Swinburne is linked to Sappho:

> - His singing-mistress verily was no other
> Than she the Lesbian, she the music-mother
> Of all the tribe that feel in melodies; (*Complete Poems*, p. 324)

For the reader, an animating moment in the poem comes when Hardy narrates his first encounter with Swinburne's work:

> O that far morning of a summer day
> When, down a terraced street whose pavements lay
> Glassing the sunshine into my bent eyes,
> I walked and read with a quick glad surprise
>   New words in classic guise, (*Complete Poems*, p. 323)

The 'shock' (in Valéry's terms) and delight of reading Swinburne for Hardy is that of reading a poet for whom it now appears he had been subconsciously waiting. Such paradoxical anticipations are perhaps especially characteristic of poets, but most readers have experienced this sort of immediate tuning-in to a writer, the déjà-vu of a form of surprised reading which appears equally to be a decisive event of recognition. That is to say, we cannot decide whether to describe such an event of reading in terms of its novelty, or not. We seem to be introduced into a region of thought and feeling that is overwhelmingly new and liberating, but which is exciting because of its very correspondence to the hopes of concordance which condition reading. So here, with the phrase 'quick glad surprise' the acceleration of stresses conveys the pleasurable effect of self-dissociation and self-recognition, the troubling excitement of finding a writer to be a kind of double of oneself, so that one cannot easily distinguish oneself from him. The experience of reading accordingly appears as half a process of discovery, and half a kind of overpowering reflection, like that figured in the pavements which were 'glassing the sunshine into my bent eyes'.

Beyond this vivid evocation, the poem relays in many other ways, too, the inspiring influence of Swinburne, the poet whose 'passionate pages' arrived to scandalize the public and incense the critics of 'Victoria's formal middle time':

> - It was as though a garland of red roses
> Had fallen about the hood of some smug nun
> When irresponsibly dropped as from the sun,
> In fulth of numbers freaked with musical closes,
> Upon Victoria's formal middle time
> His leaves of rhythm and rhyme. (*Complete Poems*, p. 323)

In its substance and content, too, the poem is, as Peter Sacks and Tim Armstrong have indicated, a conscious homage to Hardy's hero and friend, its variations on Swinburnian sapphics making it a celebration which also takes on a virtuoso life of its own.[16]

This incorporation of another's voice in one's own act of creativity is a paradox which could equally be one definition of poetic influence or inspiration. In terms of the poem's own commutabilities of voice in this context, Daniel Karlin has pointed out how the poem moves between talking about Swinburne in the third person, and addressing him in the second person. He sees this as an alternation for the poet between being gripped by Swinburne's presence and affected by his absence: between celebrating his survival as a poet, and mourning his death as a person. What Karlin's observations bring out, for my purposes, is that the inspirations of influence involve by turns forms of commemoration and reincarnation: Swinburne is remembered in the poem, and revived within it, as he revives Hardy, stimulating him, as Karlin says:

> to pay him homage, borrowing in multiple ways from his [Swinburne's] own elegies for other poets such as Baudelaire, Walter Savage Landor, and Victor Hugo.[17]

At the end of the poem, according to these strange transfers of poetic selfhood, Hardy and Swinburne - and Sappho - can all be identified with the inspiring 'improvisations' of the sea. The sea appears as a metaphor for the power of poetry to establish individuating possibilities which can transcend the constraints of mortality: the sea's 'reverberations' and 'everlasting strains' imply both poetry's percussive physical patternings, and the poet's lyrical and spiritual aspirations to overcome time. Of course, the sea is also literally associated with Swinburne, through his island coast burial-place, and with Sappho through her drowning, and Hardy imagines them meeting there. At the very end of the poem, Hardy's leaving of the sea is associated in the closing words with the fading of the 'gleam' 'Upon the capes and chines':

> So here, beneath the waking constellations,
> Where the waves peal their everlasting strains,
> And their dull subterrene reverberations
> Shake him when storms make mountains of their plains -
> Him once their peer in sad improvisations,
> And deft as wind to cleave their frothy manes -
> I leave him, while the daylight gleam declines
>   Upon the capes and chines. (*Complete Poems*, pp. 324-25)

Karlin writes of the 'authority and humility' of the 'gesture [...] by which Hardy, unlike Keats in "Ode to a Nightingale", leaves the singer instead of being left or abandoned' ('The Figure of the Singer', p. 24). Typically, as this suggests, Hardy acknowledges the circumscribed and temporary nature of the experience of transcendence associated with poetic inspiration.

In various ways, like the other poems about inspiration, 'A Singer Asleep' explores its ideal transfigurations and transmissions, and stages the dazzlings and the declinings of its moments of illumination. Intrinsic to these heightened moments, it has been suggested, are different kinds of relatedness (personal, aesthetic, cultural, poetic) and complex disturbances of chronology: the young Hardy's uncannily proleptic experience of reading Swinburne; the poem's invocation of past poets, and of the dead Swinburne himself. In these and other ways, the poem opens the present to the future, and the past.

In a similar fashion, John Lucas shows in his analysis of 'On a Midsummer Eve', how Hardy found inspiration in the voices of the dead or absent, becoming a medium for them. For Lucas, the poem is an enigmatic allegorical meditation on inspiration. His reading suggests, in contrast to 'A Singer Asleep' that the voice which conditions Hardy's art in this case, is a more anonymous and mysterious one. It belongs to a muse, maybe, or to someone from Hardy's own past whose tender influences still exert a powerful effect on his mind. In any case, Lucas indicates how important sound, and implicitly music, is in the strange temporal process of the poem, as inspiration arrives within it.

In the first stanza, the poetic speaker idly, and possibly unwittingly, invokes ghosts at midsummer eve as he cuts a parsley stalk; then the second stanza describes the way in which, as he drinks from a brook, he is visited by 'a faint figure' from the past; the third stanza reflects on such involuntary visitations as essential for the genesis of a poem:

> I idly cut a parsley stalk,
> And blew therein towards the moon;
> I had not thought what ghosts would walk
> With shivering footsteps to my tune.
>
> I went, and knelt, and scooped my hand
> As if to drink, into the brook,
> And a faint figure seemed to stand
> Above me, with the bygone look.
>
> I lipped rough rhymes of chance, not choice,
> I thought not what my words might be;
> There came into my ear a voice
> That turned a tenderer verse for me. (*Complete Poems*, p. 443)

The poem ends by reflecting that it is in terms of unchosen interruptions (once again, by virtue of the incorporation of chance figures of memory or inspiration) that poetry can make for 'a tenderer verse'. Lucas discusses the closing stanza of the poem:

The rhymes, Hardy says, have come to him unpremeditated. They are the kind of 'inspired' utterance suitable to a midsummer's eve when friendly if mischievous spirits of love are about; and at the very end one such spirit, or is it the ghost of a former lover, enters his ear and 'turned a tenderer verse for me'. And as that voice enters the poem, so the metre shifts from iambic to anapaestic [...] In those poems where Hardy's own voice is invaded by another, or where the isolated 'I' gives way to the collective, communal 'we' or 'they', the moment of invasion is nearly always marked by a shift from iambic to anapestic (and anapestic is the typical metre of ballad and hymn, that is, of song, shared utterance). ('Hardy Among the Poets', p. 200)

The poetic and the communal become merged and affirmed in the mysterious advent of the poem itself, depending as it does on this interweaving, this 'invasion' of Hardy's voice, ear and mind by the strange visitor, and the adoption of the balladic metre. These elements of correspondence and transposition in the closing lines are evident also in the sonic mirroring of the alliteration of the closing lines (came/voice/turned: tenderer/verse/ me):

> I lipped rough rhymes of chance, not choice,
> I thought not what my words might be;
> There came into my ear a voice
> That turned a tenderer verse for me.

As with the reverberating sea at the end of 'A Singer Asleep', inspiration is associated with an image of resounding, a moment of echo or reverberation. This is the case also in 'Barthélémon at Vauxhall', where the dawn light is identified with the inspiration of the fiddler as he paused on the bridge where it 'lit his face'. He was returning, as was his custom, in the morning from the 'adjacent gardens' where he:

>   charged his string,
> Nightly, with many a tuneful tender thing,
> Till stars were weak, and dancing hours outrun.
>
> And then were threads of matin music spun
> In trial tones as he pursued his way: (*Complete Poems*, p. 568)

The poem ends like this:

> 'This is a morn,' he murmured, 'well begun:
> This strain to Ken will count when I am clay!'

And count it did; till, caught by echoing lyres,
It spread to galleried naves and mighty quires. ((*Complete Poems*,
p. 568)

The image of the 'echoing lyres', whose music 'spread' further to
'galleried naves and mighty quires', suggests in graphic form, the
experiences of resonance and transmission, which Hardy associates
with inspiration, and with poetry and music.

In closing this section, it is important to refer to the many other
explicit poems of inspiration in which music plays a part. These are
poems of actual acknowledgment and evocation, while also being
inimitable performances in their own right: poems such as 'Shelley's
Skylark', 'At a House in Hampstead', 'George Meredith', 'To
Shakespeare' and even 'Lines to a Movement in Mozart's E-Flat
Symphony'. Though not a poem that uses music, Hardy's poem on his
mentor Leslie Stephen, 'The Schreckhorn', is a remarkable instance of
how Hardy's language is most itself when conveying another's
individuality, and the events and setting (here the mountain) which
most bring it out :

At his last change, when Life's dull coils unwind,
Will he, in old love, hitherward escape,
And the eternal essence of his mind
Enter this silent adamantine shape,
And his low voicings haunt its slipping snows
When dawn that calls the climber dyes them rose? (*Complete
Poems*, p. 322)

III

In this section, the attention shifts to the associations of music with the
particular inspirations of love and desire. 'To a Lady Playing and
Singing in the Morning', is a poem which betrays a Hardyan
concentration on the fluctuations and divisions in the speaker's
experience between pleasurable emotion and self-reproach.[18] The poem
celebrates an informal and seemingly extemporary musical event,
though one that appears to have had private, erotic or amorous,
associations for the poet:

Joyful lady, sing!
And I will lurk here listening,
Though nought be done, and nought begun,

And work-hours swift are scurrying.

Sing, O lady, still!
Aye, I will wait each note you trill,
Though duties due that press to do
This whole day long I unfulfil.

' - It is an evening tune;
One that is not designed to waste the noon,'
You say. I know: time bids me go -
For daytide passes too, too soon!

But let indulgence be,
This once, to my rash ecstasy:
When sounds nowhere that carolled air
My idled morn may comfort me! (*Complete Poems*, p. 579)

Each stanza moves between the desire to prolong the excitements of the moment, on the one hand, and, on the other, a belated consciousness of duty. In the final lines the poet guiltily registers his awareness that this 'idled morn' has been a time unfulfilled from the viewpoint of routine and work. This movement from pleasure to duty is even conveyed through a thinning out of the intensities of sound within the verses. This can be seen in the contrast between the rapidity of the opening rhymes and the more routine and predictable aspect of the final rhyme:

Joyful lady, sing!
And I will lurk here listening,
Though nought be done, and nought begun,
And work-hours swift are scurrying.

Similarly, in the imploring openings of both of the first two stanzas, there is a pleasurable physical turmoil conveyed by rhythm, particularly through the multiplication and initial positioning of stresses in the opening lines:

Joyful lady, sing!

Sing, O lady, still!

By such means, the poem moves from insistent and arresting effects of sound to lines in which, contrastingly, metrical regularity and other repetitive effects of language are indices of a dragging predictability:

Though *nought* be *done*, and *nought* be*gun*,

Though *duties due* that *press* to *do*

The reader seems to stand at these moments *outside* the language of the poem: the excitements of rhythm have been replaced by charmless repetition, and the formal features of the language have come to express a lowering and dejected sense of wasted time.

A fuller analysis of such features of the poem would indicate how masterfully, and with what nuances of sound, Hardy manages the reader's responses, taking us, back and forth between the vibrant inside and the flat outside of the experience. The language enacts and contemplates again Hardy's sense that life is made up of such divisions. As well as noting these transitions between enchantment and disenchantment, such an analysis would take in as well as the complication of them that seems wrapped up in the final two lines:

When sounds nowhere that carolled air
My idled morn may comfort me!

In line with the slightly comic overtones of these closing lines, it is appropriate that the reader should find him or herself confounded by the word 'sounds'. The syntactical position of the verb makes us take it, at first, for a noun. Like the speaker in the poem, we have been beguiled by physical features of sounds, here the word 'sounds' itself. And, like the speaker, we have to overcome this pleasurable perplexity to recover that self-possession which goes with a more consciously considered sense of meaning. For a time agitated and perplexed by postponement, we too have to return the poem's 'sounds' to its actual purpose as a verb here, and its larger context as we rewrite the sentence in our minds. In so doing we connect what the poem makes us do, with the reflection of these final lines: that the poem is committing this incident to the reworkings of memory, to the future comfort of the time when it 'sounds nowhere'.[19]

The revivifying effects of a musical event, then, are staged here once more in a poem which in itself can be said to draw intermittently on the revivifying materiality of poetic language. Music is both a means of, and a figure for, ecstasies of the commonplace, which for an 'idled time' displace the more conclusive purposes of recognition, interpretation and evaluation. The indeterminations of an erotic inspiration, in association with music, are mobilized within the poem, as it passes on the turbulence of pleasurable intervals in which the categories of the workday world do not apply.

To take one further example of these pleasurable intervals, how can we account for the intense, if transient, kind of delight which the word 'trill' produces in the second stanza:

> Sing, O lady, still!
> Aye, I will wait each note you trill,
> Though duties due that press to do
> This whole day long I unfulfil.

In part, it could perhaps be glossed in terms of the physical properties of the word itself - its alliterative, rhymed and onomatopoeic features, its rhythmical prominence ('Sing, O lady, still! / Aye, I will wait each note you *trill*'...) At the same time, one could mention the different kinds or levels of rapport which are implicit in the idea of a trill, since the word suggests various things: an accord between sounds; an accord, as music, between the materiality of sound and a cultural form of expression; an accord between past and future, as sounds are conjoined on a plane whose resonances trace each in the other; an accord between the world of the spirit and the world of nature, since pure sound finds its accord in the speaker's involuntary response; and so on. However, such paraphrases seem inadequate to the momentary effect of the word within the motion of the stanza, as it occasions a shock or surprise, enveloping within its own physical surface unformed virtualities of meaning which resonate momentarily in the reader's mind. As with a trill in music, the progression of the poem seems held for a moment by the opening-up of a counter-time which could in principle be endlessly prolonged, and which holds in itself, as if in solution, a multiplicity of nuances and possibilities. In the process, then, the word participates, at the level of expression, in the general way in which the passage stages and occasions, at the level of content, affective revitalizations of imagination and mind. The speaker is powerless to resist the stimulating notes, despite duty, but, equally, he is bound eventually to return to routine.

In these respects, 'To a Lady Singing and Playing in the Morning' all the time works against the more defining limits of chronology, of reading, of identity, as the lady sings 'an evening tune' at 'noon'. It is surely a covertly autobiographical poem, like 'On the Esplanade', one motivated by a desire on Hardy's part to encapsulate and record the intense romantic connotations of a musical moment. Both poems are poems of remembered hope, the implication being that in each case the romance effectively came to nothing. Hence, the important thing is to distil out of memory the accidental and ideal qualities, the affective commotion of the scene - its precious frisson of anticipation, the aura of romance, and so on. Another poem which uses a musical scene to condense these associations is 'Concerning Agnes':

> I am stopped from hoping what I have hoped before -
>> Yes, many a time! -
> To dance with that fair woman yet once more
>> As in the prime
> Of August, when the wide-eyed moon looked through
> The boughs at the faery lamps of the Larmer Avenue.
>
> I could not, though I should wish, have over again
>> That old romance,
> And sit apart in the shade as we sat then
>> After the dance
> The while I held her hand, and, to the boom
> Of contrabassos, feet still pulsed from the distant rooms.
> ('Concerning Agnes', *Complete Poems*, p. 878)

Written thirty years after the evening at Larmer Avenue, following Agnes Grove's death in 1926, 'Concerning Agnes' is a clear case of a poem which remains driven by the persistence, in fantasy and memory, of excitement and tender anticipation.

The dominant yearning behind these poems, to condense the excitement of flirtation and infatuation of a remembered musical scene, contrasts in tone with otherwise similar poems, in which a negative context of loss and transience is introduced as a more conclusively ironic comment on music's function as a sign of joy, of communal pleasure, erotic desire, and amorous feeling.[20] In many poems a two-part structure indicates the failure of the initial vision of happiness to endure, as in 'On the Doorstep', 'The Curtains Now Are Drawn', 'At the Piano', 'A Merrymaking in Question', 'The Voice of Things', and 'At the Entering of the New Year'. In each of these the gap between the stanzas indicates the falling away of the 'all-including joy', the conviviality or romance, associated with music (*Complete Poems*, p. 427). In 'The Chimes Play "Life's a Bumper!"', the chimes of the title providing a sweet and gleeful accompaniment in the first two stanzas to youthful adventure and marriage, while in the third stanza they inappropriately accompany the wife's burial. In 'The Difference', the speaker's lover is absent, possibly dead, and he observes the change this makes to his reception of the blackbird's tune:

Did my Heartmate but haunt here at times such as now,
The song would be joyous and cheerful the moon; (*Complete Poems*, p. 311)

One could multiply examples, musical and otherwise, where Hardy wraps pleasure into grief and heartbreak. Hardy never doubts that the sense of engagement and hope associated with music is real, but this means that he can never reconcile himself to the fact that it is temporary, as in the parable, 'You on the Tower', where one waiting for the advance of 'Enjoyment with wide wings' misses it, although as the watchman says, 'How can it be that you missed him?/ He brushed you by as he flew' (*Complete Poems*, p. 488). The 'Temporary' is indeed the 'All' for Hardy - as in the title of the first poem in 'Wessex Poems' - both in the obvious negative sense of this being all there is, but also in the affirmative sense that the poem latently affirms. There are timeless values implicit in everyday attachments:

Change and chancefulness in my flowering youthtime,
Set me sun by sun near to one unchosen;
Wrought us fellowlike, and despite divergence
    Fused us in fellowship. (*Complete Poems*, p. 7)

Similarly, music's association with the fallings in and out of love is no simple ironic device to intensify the ensuing sense of pain. Instead, the values associated with music convey the actual, if evanescent, sense of an ideal arrangement which comes over things, as in 'The Change' and 'The Young Churchwarden'. In these poems, music is literally a part of love, as well as a metaphor for it, as it is in 'The Dawn after the Dance' or, to take another example, in 'The Rift' (subtitled, *Song: Minor Mode*):

'Twas just at gnat and cobweb-time,
When yellow began to show in the leaf,
That your old gamut changed its chime
From those true tones - of span so brief! -
That met my beats of joy, of grief,
    As rhyme meets rhyme. (*Complete Poems*, p. 623)

Love may fade, but it returns, and music is connected by Hardy with its new beginnings:

I mused: 'Who sings the strain
I sang ere warmth did wane?

Who thinks its numbers spell
    His Amabel?' (*Complete Poems*, p. 8)

As well as these positive associations of music with the capacity
to love, though, it needs to be pointed out that in other poems the loss
or absence of musical pleasure is explicitly linked with an inability to
connect emotionally. Accordingly, in many poems the barriers to love
and desire are represented not as circumstantial or temporal so much as
psychological. Hardy is an amazingly acute and honest diagnostician of
the internal self-thwarting factors which can govern behaviour, and
many poems twist and turn tormentedly on timidity, or some more
obscure refusal of shared affection. 'Penance', for example, centres on
the belated remorse of the male speaker as he sits by the harpsichord,
acknowledging that he 'would not join' with the woman who 'far times
ago[...] lyred here/ In the evenfall':

> "I would not join. I would not stay,
>   But drew away,
> Though the winter fire beamed brightly.... Aye!
>   I do to-day
> What I would not then; and the chill old keys,
>   Like a skull's brown teeth
>   Loose in their sheath,
> Freeze my touch; yes, freeze." (*Complete Poems*, p. 631)

In 'The Musical Box', the speaker remembers his tardy progress home
on one occasion when the music box was playing. Now, he grieves over
his gloomy self-preoccupation at that time, as he 'descried [...] her,
white-muslined, waiting there/In the porch with high-expectant heart'.
As the poem ends, he can only lament that he did not sufficiently
respond to the meaning he now associates with the notes of that
'tuneful box':

> A spirit who sang to the indoor tune,
> 'O make the most of what is nigh!'
> I did not hear in my dull soul-swoon -
> I did not see. (*Complete Poems*, p. 483)

In 'An Upbraiding', this self-made discordance of desire and
opportunity is bitterly brought home to the speaker by the now
departed loved one:

> Now I am dead you sing to me

> The songs we used to know,
> But while I lived you had no wish
>   Or care for doing so. (*Complete Poems*, p. 532)

Beyond simple regret, the man in each case seems to be confronted by an unsparing moment of self-knowledge, his mysterious failure of feeling revealed to him in relation to music. These situations indicate not only lost opportunity, but also insights into absences or perversities of feeling. For instance, at the close of 'An Upbraiding' there is the clear-sighted suggestion that once reunited in death, the cruel *status quo* of indifference and withheld affection would reassert itself in the now grieving male figure.

Remorse and regret of simpler kinds can be observed as the main emotions in, among others, 'A Bygone Occasion' (subtitled 'Song'), 'The Harvest Supper' and 'Sitting on the Bridge' (the last subtitled 'Echo of an old song'). The singer in the first of these feels the pains of lost love:

> That night, that night,
> That song, that song;
> O drink to its recalled delight,
>   Though tears may throng! (*Complete Poems*, p. 603)

In the second poem, Nell's singing to the soldiers at the barn-dance brings to her mind's ear the voice of her newly buried lover:

> 'Nevermore will I dance and sing,'
>   Mourned Nell; 'and never wed!' (*Complete Poems*, p. 778)

In 'Sitting on the Bridge', the disappointment of the girls is brought about not by obscure psychological factors but by their father, who interrupts them as they are singing "Whilst I'm in the humour,/Take me Paddy, will you now?", 'just as a lancer drew nigh'. The poem ends with the girls remembering the song and the lancer, wondering who he is now with, whether he is alive and whether he remembers them. Disappointment in each case brings desire full circle, setting up a satiric pattern of repetition once again (*Complete Poems*, pp. 456-57). Another such musical poem of interrupted desire is 'Two Serenades' which tells of a singer's two serenades a year apart at the same spot. The first time he sings to an estranged lover, who does not respond; the second time he sings to her neighbour, but abandons the singing when 'that old Love came/To the other's name' (*Complete Poems*, p. 558).

In 'The Harvest Supper' and 'Sitting on the Bridge', the women are variously presented as victims of unfulfilled feeling. In other poems, such as 'The Seasons of Her Year', 'Tess's Lament' and 'The Supplanter', the woman in each case finds that music facilitates the fulfilment of sexual desire and love. However, the result (as in many other poems) is not joy but abandonment, disgrace, and the cares of unmarried motherhood:

> But wild and wintry is my day,
>   My song-birds moan;
> For he who vowed leaves me to pay
>   Alone - alone! ('The Seasons of Her Year', *Complete Poems*, p. 156)

Contrarily, there are poems where the disappointment is that of the male speaker who suffers 'the gloom of severance' as 'mine alone', and whose pain is associated with music. These phrases are from 'In Her Precincts'. The speaker travels to his beloved's house expecting that she is sharing his misery at their parting. As he nears though, he finds that there is, in fact, 'glee within', signified by the lights, and the sounds as the 'viols gave tone' (*Complete Poems*, p. 473).

In all these cases, then, Hardy associates music with the pleasures of desire and love, and the social, temporal and psychological factors which work against them. In July 1888, Hardy made a note that summarizes this view of things, meditating on how the 'determination to enjoy' was, nonetheless, within nature, universal and irrepressible:

> Returning to Dorchester two days later, he notes down: 'Thought of the determination to enjoy. We see it in all nature, from the leaf on the tree to the titled lady at the ball.... It is achieved, of a sort, under superhuman difficulties. Like pent-up water it will find a chink of possibility somewhere. Even the most oppressed of men and animals find it, so that out of a thousand there is hardly one who has not a sun of some sort for his soul.' (*Life*, p. 213)

IV

There can be few poets with Hardy's capacities to evoke musical transports and intensities. Indeed, his gift in this area often appears almost preternatural, and there are hundreds of poems which betray his fascination with musical moments or experiences. However, it is also true that in the most obvious sense Hardy is not a musical poet. Lytton Strachey, reviewing *Satires of Circumstance* in 1914 wrote, in a generally

favourable review, that 'he speaks; he does not sing'.[21] Lawrence Binyon
began his review of the same collection by asking the question '[w]hat is
it sets a poet singing?', before asserting of Hardy that 'he is not seduced
by sound' and lamenting that Hardy's poetic universe could not be
redeemed by 'the singing-note of a Burns, a Heine, a Poe, whose music
by its victorious energy can carry the horrible and ugly from the world
of fact into the world of idea'.[22] So again, a reviewer of *Poems of the Past
and Present* in 1902, wrote that 'his verse does not sing',[23] and T. H.
Warren, reviewing the same collection for the *Spectator* in 1902,
regretted that Hardy did not strike 'Tennyson's prevailing note':

> Mr. Hardy is a master of fiction, but not a master of music.
>   Not that he has not music, for he has at times a haunting rhythm
> and a wild, eerie, melancholy timbre and ring all of his own. But
> either he is not certain of his effects, or else he deliberately chooses
> to be harsh and rough, uncouth and uncanny, and thinks that his
> style suits his theme.[24]

It is familiar enough for a Hardy's critic to pass off his own uncertainty
and clumsiness as that of the poet himself. However, although few
today would concur with such negative judgments, it is at the least a
mark of the novelty of Hardy's uses of sound that they could so
persistently provoke critical censure and confusion. Edmund Gosse was
perhaps the first critic who offered a corrective to Hardy's early critical
reception. He emphasized the poet's metrical inventiveness, and sought
to validate his effects of dissonance by reference to what he saw as a
general world-view, a metaphysic of inharmony:

> Mr Hardy has expressed himself in a thousand ways, but has
> never altered his vision [...] To early readers of his poems, before
> the full meaning of them became evident, his voice sounded
> inharmonious, because it did not fit in with the exquisite melodies
> of the Victorian age. But Mr Hardy, with characteristic pertinacity,
> did not attempt to alter his utterance in the least, and now we can
> all perceive, if we take the trouble to do so, that what seemed
> harsh in his poetry was his peculiar and personal mode of
> interpreting his thoughts to the world.[25]

Gosse's comments can be related to John Bayley's suggestion that
Hardy's suspicion towards the purely musical is a suspicion against a
poetry which seals itself within its own enchanting domain:

Notes [...] from his diary, as well as the poems, make us realise how close Hardy's art is not to ideas but to daily impressions; and also to wonder what other poets - Rossetti say, or Swinburne - actually looked at in the streets? How much, for them, were ideas and the music of language a barrier to appearances? (*An Essay on Hardy*, p. 47)

One can relate these comments, to the earlier emphasis on the disjoined and momentary effects of music within Hardy's poetry. Hardy's awareness of what Gosse calls the 'inharmonious' in experience ensures that his poetry is too scrupulous to falsify the divide between exhilaration and dejection.

Still, in 1922 Hardy placed in his notebook an extract from an anonymous *Times Literary Supplement* review, which identified the musical effects of poetry, as against the effects of prose, with such passing features and intensities:

It is certain that the poetic form, by music as well as brevity, has conveyed you out of yourself & made its whole effect more swiftly: & this may be a sign that poetry is made out of feelings not necessarily deeper than the feelings in prose, but more intensely concentrated.[26]

There are a multitude of these cases, where Hardy took down extracts exploring the function of musical sound in poetry.[27] Nevertheless, he was also keen to maintain the distinctions between poetry and music, as in his remark of 1904 that in poetry 'rhythm and rhyme are a non-necessitous presentation of language under conditions that in strictness appertain only to music'. (*The Personal Notebooks of Thomas Hardy*, p. 143) In this latter case, Hardy was alluding primarily to those nineteenth-century theorists of metre for whom a quasi-musical notation was felt to be a suitable means of description for poetry, and hence for whom music was felt to offer a type of paradigm for poetic language. If Hardy's comment above suggests his wariness as to such a conflation, it is because it skews what to him seem more essential kinds of relation between music and poetry.

For Hardy what was important was the way in which poetry maintained itself in an indeterminate zone between language and music, playing-off against each other prosaic and musical effects. Dennis Taylor, on whose survey of Victorian metrical thought (in *Hardy's Metres and Victorian Prosody*) I am largely drawing here, traces the potentials for such a metrical practice and philosophy to contemporaneous discussions of metre with which Hardy became deeply familiar. In particular, Taylor highlights the developments, by theorists and analysts such as de Selincourt and Saintsbury, of the inaugural work of Patmore in the 1850s. For Taylor, Hardy's metrical inventiveness is connected with this enduring engagement, and he documents how, from the late 1850s onwards (but particularly in the early part of the twentieth-century), writers such as Patmore, Hopkins, Bridges, Saintsbury and Omond were to combine historical descriptions of English prosody with innovative theoretical reflections on its essential principles. As Hardy's notebooks also testify, he remained in touch at the same time with the mediation and supplementation of these debates through literary journals and reviews.

More than this, Taylor's book demonstrates the actual extent of Hardy's metrical sophistication and the variegated kinds of poetic texture that resulted from this interworking - in accordance with these attitudes of the time - of metre and speech. Indeed, Taylor summarizes the innovations of the period as turning on the conception of the ways in which the rhythmical actualizations of an ideal or virtual metrical pattern (what Hardy called a 'verse skeleton' [*Life*, p. 301]) were subject to the conflicting accents of speech:

> I would say that what the Victorian period achieved in metrical theory was an understanding of the abstract nature of metrical form and the dialectic way in which it interplayed with the spoken language.[28]

It is one of the further implications of Taylor's book that Hardy's ear was haunted not simply by a metrical form but by rhythms that preserved a proximity to music. Hardy's relations to folk song and ballad traditions have been well documented elsewhere,[29] but Taylor shows also the extent to which large numbers of Hardy's rhythmical borrowings were from texts whose verses were combined with music. Taylor concludes that most of the verse forms from which Hardy took inspiration can be identified with a few sources of this musical kind:

> The texts most often cited [...] are Palgrave's *Golden Treasury* (33 times), *Hymns Ancient and Modern* (28), Linton and Stoddard (11), Heine in English translation (11), Henley's *English Lyrics* (11), Hullah's *Song Book* (9). (*Hardy's Metres*, p. 214)

As well as this effective syncopation between the intonational rhythms of speech and those of the pure metrical framework, Taylor also identifies, then, this special link between metre and music, and he cites Siegfried Sassoon's description of hearing Hardy read. For Sassoon this was an experience in which the spoken, the rhythmical and the melodic would appear at moments mysteriously to combine. For Sassoon, this enabled the poems to transcend not only mundane speech, but the moment of their recital, as the younger poet could ever afterwards hear the voice of the elder haunting the verse with his own distinctive tones and inflection:

> When Hardy recited, the recitation sounded first perhaps like an ordinary cadence of everyday speech; as he proceeded one sensed the curious interference of the 'versifying'; then 'the beauty of the whole takes you and flows back through the whole poem.' One realises the progressive disclosure of the controlling form, and the beautiful consistency of the metrical counterpoint with Hardy's ultimate assumptions about poetry and reality. 'Out of the simplest hack phrases of conversation he seems to evolve a magical melody'.[30]

Similarly, Hardy's own comments and notes recurrently turn on the intermittent nature of lyrical effects in poetry, as in the comment he wrote down from Patmore that 'there seems to be a perpetual conflict between the law of verse and the freedom of the language, and each is incessantly, though insignificantly, violated for the purpose of giving effect to the other'.[31] In a celebrated essay of 1885, Robert Louis Stevenson construed this incessant and productive conflict in explicitly musical terms, according to the idea of counterpoint, identifying true poets as those who can give 'a rare and special pleasure by the art, comparable to that of counterpoint, with which they follow at the same time, and now contrast and now combine, the double pattern of the texture and the verse.'[32]

While there are correspondences between Hardy's metrical practice and reflections and the contemporaneous insights of Patmore and Stevenson, then, it remains true that it took writers like Gosse and Sassoon to comprehend his work in these terms, and to acknowledge how Hardy's world-view found its appropriate and effective expression in the disjunctive, intermissive, musicality of his language. Many of his own statements bear this out, as in the well-known *credo* about versification in the *Life*, a passage which begins with a stress on the analogy between verse and Gothic architecture:

> For instance, as to rhythm. Years ago he had decided that too regular a beat was bad art [...] He knew that in architecture cunning irregularity is of enormous worth, and it is obvious that

he carried on into his verse, perhaps in part unconsciously, the Gothic art-principle in which he had been trained - the principle of spontaneity, found in mouldings, tracery, and such like - resulting in the 'unforeseen' (as it has been called) character of his metres and stanzas, that of stress rather than of syllable, poetic texture rather than poetic veneer [...] (*Life*, p. 301)

The values of the 'unforeseen' and the irregular, maximizing a 'principle of spontaneity' and alternating with the expected, create 'a poetic texture rather than poetic veneer': this chapter has sought to indicate how just such expressive, inspiring values of variation are essential to both the content and expression in Hardy's verse. This is reiterated in a further comment on style in the *Life*, where Hardy writes that '[b]eing a little careless, or rather seeming to be[...] brings a wonderful life in to the writing.'[33] Shock and surprise are the effects of such an access of vitality. In his notebook, Hardy wrote down a passage from Patmore which reflected on these points *vis-à-vis* metre, and which identified these alternations with the affective powers of poetry, distinguishing them from the reflective contents of meaning:

The great diff^{ty}, as well as delight [...] is not in variety of pause, tone, & stress for its own sake. Such variety must be incessantly surprised by, & expressive of, ever-varying emotion. Every ... deviation from the strict and dull iambic rhythm must be either sense or nonsense. <u>Such change is as real a mode of expressing emotion as words themselves are of expressing thought.</u> (*Literary Notebooks*, Vol. 2, p. 192)

Hardy's experimentation with stanza form is a further manifestation of this engagement with the unforeseen. For the reader, clearly, it is the case that our adaptation to a poem is often initially a subliminal physical and visual matter. A new shape on the page testifies to, underlines, a dedication to new beginnings and departures. Philip Larkin described his own relation to Hardy in terms of this experimental creativity. He saw it as reiterating itself anew in each poem, and as surfacing in their musical features - of 'tune' and rhythm. A poem's music marks it as different, and pulls the reader into the event of the reading:

I can't imagine why people say Hardy had no ear. In almost every Hardy poem in the 800 pages, barring one or two about Edward VII and that sort of thing, there is a little spinal cord of thought and each has a little tune of its own, and this is something you can say of very few poets. Immediately you begin a Hardy poem your own inner response begins to rock in time with the poem's rhythm and I think that this is quite inimitable.[34]

Thom Gunn suggests that 'people say Hardy had no ear', as Larkin puts it, because his verse refuses wholesale effects of sound:

> though so much of his poetry is different from that of his contemporaries, he is with them in reacting against Tennysonian mellifluity - in fact he is with Hopkins and Bridges rather than with Swinburne.[35]

Both writers place the control of musical effects as being centrally important in Hardy's verse, while suggesting that this is an art that conceals itself to the unsympathetic eye or ear. For Robert Langbaum, Browning was Hardy's great precursor because of his similar refusal of simple musical effects:

> In 'The Lyrical Poetry of Thomas Hardy', Cecil Day Lewis finds that 'Browning is the only poet whose idiom is strongly echoed from Hardy's own verse.' If we consider that Browning changed the sound of English poetry by replacing Miltonic resonance and mellifluousness with the rough colloquial diction and rhythms and the fragmented difficult music of modern lyricism, then Hardy emerges as the first perpetuator of Browning's style into the twentieth century.[36]

Hardy, it might be added, is also the perpetuator of that intense thinking about music which marks so much of Browning's own poetry.

For John Lucas, as for Thom Gunn, these defining kinds of oscillation of the musical and the 'inharmonious' in Gosse's word, are central to the investigations in the poems of the possibilities of community. Lucas remarks on the ways in which:

> again and again his poems start out of speech rhythms that drift near to song, or they begin with metrical regularity and then modulate into cadences that imply speech. (John Lucas, *Modern English Poetry*, pp. 30-31)

For Thom Gunn, like Lucas, the transitions of the lyrical or musical, and the spoken, imply a social drama. Gunn traces, in the echoes of ballad form in Hardy, the fading context of time-honoured community. Gunn identifies the reticence operative in the poems with the kinds of impersonality and anonymity of statement, the elliptical and mysterious art, of the ballad tradition. For Gunn, Hardy's poetry always has a more or less submerged reference to, solidarity with, such an immemorial tradition.

In a more general way, Robert Gittings locates the emotional expressiveness of the poetry in its use of musical effects:

> This is his real strength as a lyric poet: his poems are hardly ever formal exercises on the page, but contain the most subtle modulations, stresses and changes, entirely reminiscent of musical composition. These variations, with their dramatic breaks in rhythm and emphasis, are used with almost infallible skill when they underline emotional states.[37]

Hardy expressed this in his well-known remarks in the *Life*, quoted by C. Day Lewis:

> Elsewhere he says, 'To find beauty in ugliness is the province of the poet.' He made 'quantities of notes on rhyme and metre: with outlines and experiments in innumerable original measures', his tendency being always against too regular a beat. Again, writing of his prose method, he says, 'The whole secret of a living style and the difference between it and a dead style, lies in not having too much style - being, in fact a little careless, or rather seeming to be, here and there... It is, of course, simply a carrying into prose the knowledge I have acquired in poetry - that inexact rhymes and rhythms now and then are far more pleasing than correct ones.'[38]

Effects of rhythm, one could say, are more like local effects than they are like totalizing principles. Rhythmical renewal comes and goes within the poems, as a function of their dealing in events of association.

As a further aspect of this, Taylor observes how Hardy often adapts time-honoured kinds of metre or stanza, working them anew from within to multiply incidental kinds of effect; or else grafting the original onto the traditional, he raises the form to a suitably open expressiveness:

> We have seen how 'A Singer Asleep' makes the final *ottava rima* issue from the shreds and patches of earlier original stanza forms [...] 'The Haunter', and 'The Rover Come Home' enact the emergence of a more regular hymnal form out of a rougher ballad or original form - like a rover come home [...] How such play with original and traditional form intersects with meaning is of enormous interest in Hardy. (*Hardy's Metres and Victorian Prosody*, p. 215)

In 'A Singer Asleep', Swinburne's innovative lyricism, bearing on rendering '[n]ew words, in classic guise' is reawakened by Hardy's own inventive powers of expressive variation and his use of verbal echoes from Swinburne's own work.[39]

It is, of course, one of the ironies of literary history that critics, to Hardy's continuing amazement, continually lambasted him for his uses of metre. They scorned what were seen as ham-fisted crudities of syntax and tone, banal deflations of all kinds, calamitous philosophizings, and pretentious or hair-raising strivings after effect. Is the problem for Hardy - as he saw it was for Swinburne - that certain kinds of developed critical attitude can be an obstacle to the workings of his originality?

> I still can hear the brabble and the roar
> At those thy tunes, O still one, now passed through
> That fitful fire of tongues then entered new!
> Their power is spent like spindrift on this shore;
>   Thine swells yet more and more. ('A Singer Asleep', *Complete Poems*, p. 324)

Although Hardy's reputation as a major poet is now unassailable, his work still confronts critics with a problem about what criteria to apply to the poems. Peter Widdowson has documented how uneasy Hardy continues to make critics, and demonstrated how crucial a role anthologizing has had in substituting for criticism.[40]

Finally, it is worth contrasting the long-term difficulties or hostility of the critics with the response of the many poets or writers who took Hardy as an inspiration, and who often marvelled at the range and scope of his metrical subtleties and technical accomplishment. For instance, almost every poet mentioned in the following list has written substantial appreciative pieces on Hardy, and many have written poems simply about him: Ezra Pound, Siegfried Sassoon, Edmund Blunden, D. H. Lawrence, Lascelles Abercrombie, Edward and Dylan Thomas, W. H. Auden, Cecil Day Lewis, Walter de la Mare, Robert Graves, John Crowe Ransom, Mark Van Doren, John Betjeman, Philip Larkin, Seamus Heaney, Al Alvarez, Charles Tomlinson, John Wain, Delmore Schwartz, Tom Paulin, Donald Davie, John Lucas, Mark Ford and Thom Gunn. Among poets, only Yeats and R. S. Thomas were less appreciative (and T. S. Eliot, though his strictures were directed at the fiction).[41] Many of these writers have described how important the encounter with Hardy was for them, and how necessary it was to incorporate his tricks of vision and grammar of feeling, or to develop his technical experiments. To some extent, Hardy has been a 'poet's poet' or a 'reader's poet' more than a 'critic's poet', and this is perhaps the best, and last, example here of the way in which the concept of inspiration can be applied to the poetry.[42]

This chapter has read the poems in terms of their 'unforeseen' traits of content and expression, those individuating effects which involve both a dispossession of selfhood (from the point of view of consciousness), and an enriched expression of it (from the point of view of unconscious, associative, individuality). Through involuntary response the reader's mind finds an affinity with that of the poet and the protagonists. Philip Larkin suggested, in such a vein, how Hardy demanded a type of sympathetic reading which had the effect in his case (as reading Swinburne or Browning might have done for Hardy) of liberating his own sensibility:

> But when I was about 25, I suppose, I was in some digs which faced east and the sun used to wake me very early in the morning - you know, about six. It seemed too early to get up, so I used to read, and it happened that I had Hardy's own selection of his poems, and I began to read them and was immediately struck by their tunefulness and their feeling, and the sense that here was somebody writing about things I was beginning to feel myself. ('Philip Larkin Praises the Poetry of Thomas Hardy', p. 111)

V

In *A Thousand Plateaus*, Deleuze and Guattari develop a far-reaching discussion of rhythm which provides a means of drawing together the main threads of the present chapter, since it offers another way of describing the logic of transpersonal association which surfaces in the concepts of individuation or inspiration. Deleuze and Guattari identify rhythm as creating a new plane of counterpoint between two musical phrases, passing between each and holding them together, while elevating them to a new common power. They identify such musical moments with natural processes of becoming and expression ('Nature as music'). Such processes work through types of symbiosis that for an interval elude the identity logic of the bodies involved, as closed and singular terms. In terms of music itself, this can be seen when musical notes, through their combinations, participate in duration and take on the conjunctive features of melody and rhythm:

One case of transcoding is particularly important: when a code is not content to take or receive components that are coded differently, and instead takes or receives fragments of a different code as such. The first case pertains to the leaf-water relation, the second to the spider-fly relation. It has often been noted that the spider web implies that there are sequences of the fly's own code in the spider's code; it is as though the spider had a fly in its head, a fly 'motif', a fly 'refrain'. The implication may be reciprocal, as with the wasp and the orchid, or the snapdragon and the bumblebee. Jakob von Uexhüll has elaborated an admirable theory of transcodings. He sees the components as melodies in counterpoint, each of which serves as a motif for another. Nature as music. Whenever there is transcoding, we can be sure that there is not a simple addition, but the constitution of a new plane, as of a surplus value. A melodic or rhythmical plane, surplus value of passage or bridging.[43]

Such a passage, for Deleuze and Guattari, obviously has its place in a much broader ontological discussion. If becoming is a key concept for them, it is as a natural process of experimentation when mind and body discover new powers of individuation and expression through kinds of 'transcoding'. The example of the wasp and the orchid is a favourite one for Deleuze. It refers to the way in which the wasp is involved by the orchid in the latter's reproductive work. The orchid simulates the wasp's sexual organs, a process in which the wasp feeds as it fertilizes the orchid:

The wasp and the orchid provide the example. The orchid seems to form a wasp image, but in fact there is a wasp-becoming of the orchid, an orchid-becoming of the wasp, a double capture since 'what' each becomes changes no less than 'that which' it becomes. The wasp becomes part of the orchid's reproductive apparatus at the same time as the orchid becomes the sexual organ of the wasp. (*Dialogues*, p. 2)

Each enters a liminal zone outside its organic functioning and identity, and becomes involved in the state of a body not its own. The idea of transcoding is important because it allows for a way of conceiving of the thought involved, as dependent on such events of inventive participation, and on a form of unconscious thought and creative adaptation whose adventitious artifice itself depends on sensation. The wasp and orchid's reciprocal capture - the use by each of part of the coded identity of the other - is a form of artistic creativity such as Deleuze and Guattari identify with Nature's most intrinsic processes.

This is a thought 'of the Outside', occasioned by encounters, where individuality is creatively differentiated by accident and response. Such occasions of 'change and chancefulness' (or 'chance and change'), in Hardy's words, require no reference to the categories of conscious thought (those reflective foldings of self-consciousness to which, indeed, it gives belated issue), and exceed pregiven notions of self-sameness in identity. In fact, there are many notes in Hardy's notebooks which reflect his interest in such ideas: 'Symbiogeneis, in Nature [...] Cooperation thus begins to approximate to a moral law in Nature.' (*Literary Notebooks*, Vol. 2, p. 241)

Such a description of rhythm is a useful way of drawing together and revisiting the main threads of the argument. In the first place, rhythm on this conception is inevitably a function of the individual's relations, and so is, in human terms, ineradicably collective or interpersonal. Secondly, it is an involuntary and yet necessary physical expression of that individual's inmost essence or soul, and so brings out creative powers of thought which are opposed to the mechanical and purely formulaic. Implicitly, too, such a stimulating moment involves a movement away from stale values or habits of thought, and retains implicitly an inwardness with the unformed and the indeterminate, and with the indivisiblities of movement. Thirdly, rhythm implies a generative power of self-difference, as in the mundane case when the rhythm of a poem can provide the occasion for a different reading of it. Repetition can engender new intonations, and thereby new interpretations. Fourthly, rhythm draws on the reader's own susceptibilities and sympathies, so that he or she will also find, in reflecting on his or her response to the poem, that it offers possibilities of self-reading: through reflecting on one's response, one can consider those unconscious elements of one's own sensibility which have been drawn out by the poem. Fifthly, rhythm occasions a new consistency between heterogeneous elements without reducing their differences, a point which applies to earlier descriptions of the texture of individual poems within the *Complete Poems*, as well as to the heterogeneity of the collection as a whole. Sixthly, rhythm overcomes chronology because it pulls into a new synthesis, into a larger open duration, moments no longer considered simply in punctual or successive terms. Thus, it reiterates the essential and obscured (ideal or eternal) potentials which define the bodies involved. Seventhly, in its own materiality, as a movement that incorporates its elements into an unfolding and distinctive whole, rhythm is aesthetic - a matter, for a time at least, of grace and balance. In these ways, then, the idea of rhythm allows us to revisit the central emphases of the chapter on physically conditioned processes of inspiration.

Notes

[1] R. W. King, 'The Lyrical Poems of Thomas Hardy', in *Thomas Hardy: Poems* (edited by James Gibson and Trevor Johnson, London: Macmillan, 1979), pp. 106-107.

[2] Donald Davie, *Thomas Hardy and British Poetry* (London: Routledge and Kegan Paul, 1973).

[3] Tim Armstrong, Introduction, *Thomas Hardy: Selected Poems* (edited by Tim Armstrong, London: Longman, 1993), pp. 3-4. Armstrong points out that Hardy preferred late Wagner and late Turner because, as he wrote in 1906, 'the idiosyncrasies of each master' were 'more strongly shown in these strains'. This is close to the view of Hardy's creativity which underlies this discussion: the artistic career is an arduous apprenticeship in individuality, and language is the expressive instrument which it is necessary to master. These points can be usefully linked with two notebook citations which Armstrong quotes: the one on how Victor Hugo's 'supreme enjoyment was the exercise of his own brain', and the other an extract from *The Nation* in 1908:

> An artist's *self* - The most difficult thing in the word for any artist to achieve ... is to express himself, to strike out a style of writing, which shall be as natural to him as the character of handwriting is to ordinary men. It is a truism to say that individuality is the last quality to be developed in a man.

This account of poetic development, of 'individuality' as 'the last quality to be developed in a man', reproduces as biography the idea of belatedness suggested at the opening of this chapter. The poet repeats in each poem the trajectory of his career, as he struggles with the immanent materials of art and experience which impress themselves upon him. From these, he seeks to wrest those latent qualities and significances which express his own idiosyncratic way of seeing.

[4] Arthur S. Macdowall, 'An Explorer of Reality' in *Thomas Hardy: Poems*, p. 127.

[5] Tim Armstrong, 'Supplementarity: Poetry as the Afterlife of Thomas Hardy', *Victorian Poetry*, 26, 1988, p. 386. However, it must be conceded that Armstrong's Derridean argument identifies Hardy the poet predominantly in terms of his reactions to life's disappointments and losses, in terms of defensive withdrawals and spectral self-fashionings.

[6] Of course, I would not want to deny, for instance, Macdowall's qualification that even Hardy's most lyrical poems cannot be termed ecstatic in so far as 'their sense of the actual is too strong; they seem to imply a fact within their feeling' (p. 128). Contrarily, though, and more fundamentally, I would agree with Jean Brooks's comment that his 'inability to put misery out of view is a direct corollary of the intense wish to justify life and joy, and the interaction of these two emotions [is] a major source of his resonant power.' (Jean Brooks, 'The Homeliest of Heart-Stirrings', in *Thomas Hardy: Poems*, p. 209)

[7] John Lucas, *Modern English Poetry: from Hardy to Hughes* (London: Batsford, 1986), p. 32.

[8] Timothy Clark, *The Theory of Inspiration* (Manchester: Manchester University Press, 1997), p. 3. Clark brilliantly explores the paradoxes of inspiration which also surface in this discussion too: inspiration is the highest expression of selfhood, while its sources are incomprehensible and uncontrollable; the inspired poet can on various interpretations appear as *both* addressor *and* addressee (or *neither* addressor *nor*

addressee) of the poem that comes to him or her. Again, Clark notes how the ancient cliché of the poet as a medium for the unfathomable voices of the muses, conveys this mysterious and enigmatic agency, and describes how such a logic of transmission can be detected by an etymological analysis of the term 'inspiration', whereby it involves:

> the notion of breathing, of an empowering breath or 'spirit', the communication of a sounding energy or power of speech. It thus imposes an oral model on the process of writing, which is troped as an animated voice. (p. 3)

My differences with Clark lie in the deconstructive framework he adopts, whereby his account of such paradoxes become sharpened into Derridean aporias. For similar reasons, my admiration of the Derridean readings of Hardy's poetry offered by Tim Armstrong (in his 'Supplementarity: Poetry as the Afterlife of Thomas Hardy', *Victorian Poetry*, 26, 1988, p. 386) is qualified by his adoption of the Derridean paralogic of 'supplementarity' so that poetry becomes ultimately seen as a ghostly, testamentary activity, one where 'Writing is linked to death' (p. 384).

   9   One could mention here, for instance, the work of Dennis Taylor or Peter Widdowson on the poetry, or the thorough and fascinating notes in Tim Armstrong's *Selected Poems*, each of which indicates these intertextual aspects.

   10   'Apology' to *Late Lyrics, Complete Poems*, p. 561.

   11   In a more general context, John Marks emphasizes what he sees as Hardy's central ethical values of 'kindness', and links this with a cautious 'awareness of the "many-sidedness of things"'. Practically and personally, Marks's ideas have to do with an acknowledgment of the unknown diversity of the other person, whereby one becomes 'circumspect and careful of the feelings of others.' 'Christmastide' can also be said to involve circumspection of another kind, in that its reticence allows many sides to be seen, and acknowledges the reader's function in this respect. John Marks, 'Hardy and Kindness', *The Thomas Hardy Journal*, Vol. XI (February 1995), p. 53.

   12   Most obviously, of course, there are echoes of *Resolution and Independence*, but also perhaps the more intriguing comparison would be with the two versions of the poem about the old man journeying to collect his soldier son's body, *Animal Tranquillity and Decay*.

   13   Similarly, P. E. Mitchell argues that Hardy's poetry retains, beyond religious faith, a sense of enduring aesthetic and communal values. Like Lucas, he sees these as evident in his use of effects of ballad and folk-song:

> While it can be argued, therefore, that Hardy could not justify and systematize his values by reference to traditional notions of transcendental order and harmony, he could and did possess a range of values that are given significance by reference to the impersonal, enduring idea of community extended in history and transcending the individual "human span of durance". P. E. Mitchell, 'Music and Hardy's Poetry', *English Literature in Transition*, Vol. 37, no 3 (1987), p. 319.

   14   Roger Ebbatson has pointed out to me also the links between this vocabulary and Tennyson's language.

   15   Paul Valéry, 'Poetry and abstract thought: dancing and walking', in *20th Century Literary Criticism*, edited by David Lodge (London: Longman, 1979), p. 254.

   16   See the footnotes to the poem in Armstrong's *Thomas Hardy: Selected Poems*, pp. 145-48. Similarly, Dennis Taylor's analysis of the poem indicates how its

versification and diction also echo Swinburne's own, and I return to his discussion in section IV here.

[17] Daniel Karlin, 'The Figure of the Singer in the Poetry of Thomas Hardy', p. 24. (I am indebted to Professor Karlin for allowing me to cite from this lecture for the Thomas Hardy Society, delivered at Dorchester in 1998.)

[18] This is again a poem which seemingly consciously evokes Wordsworth. Like the singing of Wordsworth's solitary reaper, the singing of the other person here is also said to promise the speaker some resources of long term mental or emotional sustenance (though the closing statement of this is also qualified by a defensive and self-satirical overtone).

[19] It is worth remarking that there are several other examples where the pleasures of sound and the responsibility of meaning are thrown into immediate and confusing contact in the poem (*'Aye, I* will wait each note you trill,/Though *duties due* that press to *do... For daytide passes too, too* soon!').

[20] Admittedly, 'Concerning Agnes' ends with the facts of her death, but my point is that the mood that motivates the poem is a longing to relive the past scene more than a desire to emphasize mortality or the transience of love.

[21] Lytton Strachey, *Thomas Hardy: The Critical Heritage* (edited by R. G. Cox, London: Routledge, 1979), p. 437. For full references to original sources for this and the other reviews of Hardy's poetry, please see bibliography.

[22] Lawrence Binyon, *The Critical Heritage*. The first quotation here is from page 440, the other two from page 442.

[23] Unsigned review of *Poems of the Past and Present, Thomas Hardy: The Critical Heritage*, p. 331.

[24] T. H. Warren, *Thomas Hardy: The Critical Heritage*, p. 332-33.

[25] Edmund Gosse, 'Mr Hardy's Lyrical Poems', *The Critical Heritage*, p. 463. There is a passage earlier in Gosse's piece, where he comments on *Time's Laughingstocks*, that is worth citing in so far as it anticipates the following discussion:

> We notice here more than elsewhere in his poems Mr Hardy's sympathy with the local music of Wessex, and especially with its expression by the village choir, which he uses as a spiritual symbol. Quite a large section of *Time's Laughingstocks* takes us to the old-fashioned gallery of some church, where the minstrels are bowing 'New Sabbath' or 'Mount Ephraim', or to a later scene where the ghosts, in whose melancholy apparition Mr Hardy takes such pleasure, chant their goblin melodies and strum 'the viols of the dead' in the moonlit churchyard. The very essence of Mr Hardy's reverie at his moment of his career is to be found, for instance, in 'The Dead Quire', where the ancient phantom-minstrels revenge themselves on their gross grandsons outside the alehouse. ('Mr Hardy's Lyrical Poems', p. 450)

[26] *The Personal Notebooks of Thomas Hardy* (edited by Richard H. Taylor, London: Macmillan, 1978), p. 57.

[27] See, for instance, in Volume 2 of his notebooks, such instances as Hardy's citing of Pater's remark as to 'music being the ideal of all art whatever' (*Literary Notebooks*, Vol. 2, p. 18); a discussion by Ernest Newman of Symbolism, which turns on the musicality of language in poetry as the means by which an 'emotionalized vision' as 'the essence of what we call our knowledge of external things' is conveyed; (*Literary Notebooks*, Vol. 2, p. 119); a quotation of A. C. Bradley's remark that 'in poetry

the meaning and the sounds are one' (*Literary Notebooks*, Vol. 2, p. 162). There are many others.

28 Dennis Taylor, *Hardy's Metres and Victorian Prosody* (Oxford: Clarendon Press, 1988), p. 5.

29 As well as Dennis Taylor's book, and the various biographies and the *Life*, see for instance, the works cited in the bibliography by Gunn, Lucas, Jackson-Houlston, Paulin, Maidment and Maddon.

30 Cited by Taylor, *Hardy's Metres*, p. 119.

31 Cited by Taylor, *Hardy's Metres*, p. 32.

32 Robert Louis Stevenson, 'On Style in Literature: its Technical Elements', *Contemporary Review*, 47 (1885), p. 555.

33 Quoted by Bayley, *An Essay on Hardy*, p. 3.

34 Philip Larkin, 'Philip Larkin Praises the Poetry of Thomas Hardy', *The Listener* (25 July 1968), p. 111.

35 Thom Gunn, 'Hardy and the Ballads', *Agenda*, Vol. 10 (1972), p. 38.

36 Robert Langbaum, *Thomas Hardy in Our Time* (London: Macmillan, 1995), p. 53.

37 Robert Gittings, *Young Thomas Hardy* (London: Penguin, 1980), p. 78.

38 C. Day Lewis, 'The Lyrical Poetry of Thomas Hardy', *Proceedings of the British Academy*, Vol. 37 (1951), p. 161.

39 See Tim Armstrong's discussion of the poem, in his *Selected Poems*, pp. 145-48.

40 See Widdowson's essay, 'Recasting Hardy the Poet' (*Late Essays and Earlier*, pp. 134-167). For Widdowson, the reliance on anthologies has tended to mean that the reception of Hardy's poetry remains too framed by the ideological assumptions, the personal prejudices or conformity, or the thematic arrangements that shape such selections. The poems take on a spurious homogeneity and portentousness through their elevation into being anthology pieces. The inner diversity and dynamism of the poems is reduced by this, as is in J. Hillis Miller's account of the poems (cited by Widdowson). Hillis Miller writes of how 'the uniqueness of each moment of experience' which each poem 'record[s] in words' makes for incommensurability and discontinuity in the collection as a whole (*Late Essays and Earlier*, p. 146). Further, as Widdowson indicates, the undeniable logic of anthologies is that the vast majority of poems are left out, and so will tend to remain unread, even as those that are read lack their appropriate context in the sheer variety and abundance of the *Complete Poems*.

41 Interestingly, after having written this passage, I came across Yeats's different use of the same term, when he wrote that Hardy's poetic work 'lacked technical accomplishment.' (Introduction to the *Oxford Book of Modern Verse* [London: Oxford University Press, 1937], p. xiv.) As an even more negative response to Hardy by a poet, one could also cite R. S. Thomas's reference to Hardy in his poem, 'Taste' from the collection, *Laboratories of the Spirit* (London: Macmillan, 1975):

Then Hardy, for many a major
poet, is for me just an old-stager,

shuffling about a bogus heath
cobwebbed with his Victorian breath. (*Laboratories of the Spirit*, p. 35)

42 Of course, one could also compile such a list for the writings of novelists on Hardy's novels also - J. M. Barrie, D. H. Lawrence, Edmund Gosse, Marcel Proust,

John Cowper Powys, Arnold Bennett, Max Beerbohm, Virginia Woolf, E. M Forster, John Fowles, J. I. M. Stewart, John Bayley and David Lodge in the pro-camp, and G. K. Chesterton, Mrs Oliphant, George Moore, Henry James, Somerset Maugham on the other side.

[43] Gilles Deleuze and Felix Guattari, *A Thousand Plateaus* (translated by Brian Massumi, London: Athlone, 1988), p. 314.

Chapter 4

'Till Time Seemed Fiction'

The previous chapter traced music's association in Hardy's poetry with moments of lyrical inspiration that set up a syncopation between timeless moments of vision, and everyday chronology. The emphasis here is on music's power to effect turns and tricks of memory, and visitations from the ancestral past, that similarly interrupt the present. Certainly, it is hard to think of another poet who possesses Hardy's sentiment for the past in itself, or who so sedulously seeks it out and lives with it in poem after poem. He meditates on this in 'The Ghost of the Past', where he writes of living with its visions, 'gentle echoes' and 'old rapturings':

> Its moving meek companionship
>   I wished might ever be,
> There was in that companionship
>   Something of ecstasy. (*Complete Poems*, p. 308)

The discussion begins by investigating how Hardy's sense of historical and social dislocation led to his placing in the past of the significances of community and love associated with music. There then follows an account of the specifics of how music has the power to reanimate periods and traditions from the distant past, as in the many poems that follow musical trails into the culture and history of Hardy's family and elsewhere. This leads to the more personal case of individual memory, where music is endlessly and variously employed by Hardy as a link between the different temporal dimensions of experience. As F. L. Lucas put it, '[h]e saw things instinctively in three tenses as in three dimensions.'[1] In this connection, the third section explores some of those many poems where the individual's susceptibility to music is at one with its anachronistic power to resist chronology, and to surprise age or loss by affects which summon up a revitalized sense of past times and relationships. Music is a privileged tool of memory, capable of recapturing the ecstasies of the past. However, this is inevitably ambiguous, since current sadness is so obviously and inescapably mixed in with the recovered emotion.

A further aspect of temporal self-division is explored in the fourth section which takes up John Lucas's speculative point that one can detect in Hardy's poetry a covert guilt over the fact that his literary aspirations involved a turning-away from his background, at the same time as he continued to benefit from the demise of the rural culture of the 'village tradition' that became his great resource as an aspiring writer. In this context, music becomes associated with an ethical drama of innocence and guilt that is often played out in connection with music, and configured as a temporal drama. The fifth section explores how a poem's capacity to hold together the painful alternation of different layers of time can be discerned in its expressive effects of sound. In many poems, the constitutive alternations of memory and actuality coexist with incidental evocations of the forms and sounds of the past, as metrical visitations or balladic echoes, for instance, expand the reader's sense of these temporal complexities. This also involves a certain overcoming of time, though, since Hardy's inimitable way of expressively incorporating different strands and dimensions of time is at the heart of his survival as a poet. Leading on from this, the final section explores issues of literary tradition, and poetic influence and viewpoint, which arise out of the commonly individuating, transmissive, qualities of music and poetry.

Finally, although this chapter's survey is not primarily biographical, it is impossible not to refer in passing to the wealth of biographical material available connecting Hardy and music. Because so much of the *Life* concerns itself with music, it is unsurprising that biographical discussions of Hardy emphasize the musical associations of his upbringing. Elna Sherman describes how:

> evenings at home were spent in playing and singing. The boy's mother had a sympathetic voice and was fond of singing songs and ballads of the time [...]; his father played innumerable folk-songs and dance tunes, to which little Thomas reacted with great sensitiveness, dancing ecstatically to the jigs, reels, and hornpipes (of which his father showed him some traditional steps) and being moved to tears by some, whereupon he would dance even more frantically to hide his embarrassment.[2]

There are many such incidents and individuals one could mention here: one could refer to the toy concertina and then the violin given to the young Thomas; the musical tie with his sister Mary; the dances, opera and singing of his London days, associated with home, office and concert hall; the quadrille classes and the music making with Emma;

his later conversations with Grieg and Holst; his avowed desire, expressed as an old man, for the life of a church organist; his passion for collecting music, such as hymn music;[3] and above all, the folk music of his family environment (this latter enthusiasm evident in his authoritative contributions to *English Folk Dance Society Notes* and the *Journal of the English Folk Dance Society*).

I

In his article, 'Hardy's Fiction and English Traditional Music', Brian Maidment points out that Hardy's awareness of music was from the first allied to a sense of history and of loss. In the *Life*, he notes, Hardy dated his coming to consciousness in terms of the passing of the Stinsford parish choir. Maidment sees in Hardy a certain defensiveness about both his susceptibility to 'the *expressive* power of simple traditional music',[4] as well as a complex feeling for traditional music as itself the expression of a vanishing rural culture in a sophisticated world:

> Yet how could his belief in the emotional strength and communal occasions of traditional music - the one embarrassingly personal and the other aggressively unfashionable, even archaic - be made accessible to readers not just excluded from such performances, but entirely ignorant of their continuing existence and historical significance? ('Hardy's Fiction and English Traditional Music', p. 17)

For Maidment, such difficulties or embarrassment led Hardy initially into pre-emptive kinds of satirical treatment of the communal, time-honoured practices of music-making, as in *Under the Greenwood Tree*. Later regretting this, he wrote of his father's parish choir:

> He was accustomed to say that [...] he had rather burlesqued them, the story not so adequately reflecting as he could have wished in later years the poetry and romance that coloured their time-honoured observances. (*Life*, p. 12)

Maidment continues that the protective camouflage afforded by this early tendency to burlesque was replaced in the later fiction by ironic modes which fulfilled a similar function, testifying to the difficulties of conveying directly the historical, local and personal associations of music for him.⁵ Later, Hardy is said to have found in poetry the most satisfactory means 'for describing musical expressivity and intensity' ('Hardy's Fiction and English Traditional Music', p. 17).

Maidment's article usefully suggests Hardy's need, at the time when he turned to poetry, to find appropriate ways to conserve (or at least, commemorate) an oral and rural culture which he felt to be in the process of dissolution. The desire is evident in the General Preface to the Wessex Edition in 1912 which reports this aim to 'preserve for my own satisfaction a fairly true record of a vanishing life'.⁶ The mixed tones of this statement - half of a chronicler, half of someone dispossessed - raises many of the issues and ambivalences implicit in Hardy's position as a writer who was writing for an essentially metropolitan audience. As well as feeling that he inhabited historically a time between times, Hardy felt characteristically that he was himself caught between different classes and locations. Hardy reflects on the passing away of the local culture, and 'the migration to towns', in a letter to H. Rider Haggard of 1902 reprinted in the *Life*:

> For one thing, village tradition - a vast mass of unwritten folklore, local chronicle, local topography, and nomenclature - is absolutely sinking, has nearly sunk, into eternal oblivion. I cannot recall a single instance of a labourer who still lives on the farm where he was born, and I can only recall a few who have been five years on their present farms. Thus you see, there being no continuity of environment in their lives, there is no continuity of information, the names, stories and relics of one place being speedily forgotten under the incoming facts of the next. For example, if you ask one of the workfolk (they always used to be called "workfolk" hereabout - "labourers" is an imported word) the names of surrounding hills, streams; the character and circumstances of people buried in particular graves; at what spots parish personages lie interred; questions on local fairies, ghosts, herbs, etc., they can give no answer: yet I can recollect the time when the places of burial even of the poor and tombless were all remembered, and the history of the parish and the squire's family for 150 years back known. Such and such ballads appertained to such and such a locality, ghost tales were attached to particular sites, and nooks wherein wild herbs grew for the cure of divers maladies were pointed out readily. (*Life*, pp. 312-13)

Like Lyonnesse under the sea, this 'village tradition' is 'nearly sunk' 'into eternal oblivion'. Indeed, as both Maidment's and Hardy's comments indicate, the oral and musical culture that Hardy was concerned to record had in important features already disappeared by the time of his birth. His tone is one of mournful sobriety, that of a surviving witness caught at a cultural cross-roads, and compelled by an historical responsibility to describe and remember.

In another way, though, Hardy was, with respect to his urban readership, inevitably a beneficiary of this painful process of loss, becoming both historian *and* laureate of the passing rural tradition. Ruth Firor has shown the extent to which Hardy continued to collect oral materials throughout his life, and at the same time to draw, in his own work, both on these and on the tales and songs he had heard from childhood.[7] Hardy's work, in this aspect, is readable as a living monument to this culture, a record in the altered medium of print to its verbal history, its lore, its songs and ballads. Norman Arkans emphasizes how Hardy, as he turned to poetry, intensified his search for ancient ballads and stories by talking to old people. He points out also the twofold nature of Hardy's motivation, consisting of an antiquarian or folk historian's desire to collect, and a poet's desire to learn, accommodate, adapt, utilize:

> And perhaps, we may speculate, for the first time in his life, he felt his own past, linked to that of his ancestors, coming together with his present, lending purpose and direction to his movements. ('Hardy's Narrative Muse and the Ballad Connection', p. 135)

To talk of how poetry can bring about this type of convergence of past and present, though, is to imply that one is talking of an essentially aesthetic enterprise, one predicated on an acknowledgment that the ancestral world is now fading from view, and can only be experienced in memory or otherwise imaginatively reconstructed from its traces.[8] Music becomes a crucial and natural device for Hardy in communicating this predicament, and for carrying out this twin project of documenting the past and bringing it to life. Repeatedly, he exploits its power to tantalize the present with flickers of past affections and associations. At its most extreme, it works as a veritable time-machine, signalling to Hardy from times long gone, as in 'Rome: On the Palatine' where a Strauss waltz heard in Rome raises in his mind a sense of:

> old routs Imperial lyres had led,

> And blended pulsing life with lives long done,
> Till Time seemed fiction, Past and Present one. (*Complete Poems*, p. 103)

Hardy's socio-historical dislocation emerges clearly in his use of balladic modes. Arkans draws a useful distinction between the ballad proper, where, within the immemorial and impersonal customs of 'village tradition', one finds oneself 'having a story to tell', and the deracinated experience of 'having to tell a story' ('Hardy's Narrative Muse and the Ballad Connection', p. 152), where one needs to create an audience for one's acutely personal experience of social upheaval. Arkans identifies Hardy's poetry as tending towards this latter type, the implication being that Hardy was writing of a community which no longer existed to one that did not yet exist. Although this last formulation is obviously something of an overstatement, it has the benefit of suggesting the affective charge of the old ballads for Hardy, and of reiterating the way in which Hardy's historical predicament was to be caught in between cultures. Indeed, it is the urgency and complexity of the feeling of historical and social severance which most often compels Hardy to his activity of meticulous commemoration and evocation:

> He could recall to old age the scene of the young women in their light gowns sitting on a bench against the wall in the barn, and leaning against each other as they warbled the Dorset version of the ballad [...] variously called 'The Outlandish Knight', 'May Colvine', 'The Western Tragedy', etc. (*Life*, p. 20)

There are many accounts in the *Life* of Hardy playing and listening to these songs at such a dance (or at a wedding or at the manor house). Typically, the verse which describes such events tends to mingle sharply phrased reminiscence ('the benched barn-nook') with the adoption of the essentially anonymous, balladic modes of 'village tradition':

> Nell and the other maids sat in a row
>   Within the benched barn-nook;
> Nell led the songs of long ago
>   She'd learnt from never a book. ('The Harvest Supper', *Complete Poems*, p. 777)

The dislocating complexities of modernity inflect Hardy's employment of the ballad form with retrospective and historical tones. For instance, in poems which relate tales of the vanished Mellstock Band, like 'The Dead Quire' or 'The Paphian Ball', we can detect how the balladic structure is invested with an air of elegy, as well as of fond family recollection. At the close of these poems, the socially connective power of music is firmly and mournfully placed in the past. The poems' anecdotes are explicitly framed as 'phantasies', as if they are cultural ghosts or echoes - stories and anecdotes of a by-gone time, narrated by those soon to die:

> - The sad man ceased; and ceased to heed
> His listener, and crossed the leaze
> From Moaning Hill towards the mead -
> The Mead of Memories. ('The Dead Quire', *Complete Poems*, p. 259)

> - The man who used to tell this tale
> Was the tenor-viol, Michael Mail;
>
> Yes; Mail the tenor, now but earth! -
> I give it for what it may be worth. ('The Paphian Ball', *Complete Poems*, p. 816)

There is a similar sense of a fast disappearing world at the end of another of these poems, 'The Rash Bride', where the bride's burial is described:

> Our old bass player, as I recall - his white hair blown - but why recall!-
> His viol unstrapped, bent figure - doomed to follow her full soon -
> Stood bowing, pale and tremulous; and next to him the rest of us....
> We sang the Ninetieth Psalm to her - set to Saint Stephen's tune.
> (*Complete Poems*, p. 255)

The verse appears to strive, like the old bass player, to hold itself together amid the gathering sense of disconnection. The word 'bowing' might refer to either his 'bent' posture or his playing, but the ambiguity catches the juxtaposition at the end of the poem between loss and death on the one hand, and, on the other, the man's lifelong affectibility where music is concerned. 'Bent' and 'pale', the bass player seems - as he sings with the others - more or less consciously to anticipate his own approaching death, while the word 'tremulous' has an affecting incongruity since it is often used by Hardy about children. Here too it suggests involuntary emotion, but the discomfiting kind of someone who is broken up by age and loss, and for whom the reawakened feelings of childhood are rending.

This emphasis on tonal instability is a way of locating the tensions, the shifts of tone, which Arkans writes of (as marking Hardy's career) within a single poem, as it alternates between celebrating the echoes of community and conveying private sadness and yearning. In similar terms, P. E. Mitchell has written of the distinctive comings and goings of these balladic effects in Hardy's verse. In terms of sound, he writes of how pervasive is the 'employment of rhythmic irregularity for expressive local effects', a description which implies, once again, the generally disjunctive and interruptive mode of Hardy's poetic viewpoint ('Music and Hardy's Poetry', p. 315).

II

Hardy could not prevent himself pursuing the musical threads which bind the present to earlier periods. One can call to mind his running out into the London street in 1879, unsuccessfully to find out from the organ-grinder the name of a quadrille he had not heard for over two decades. In personal terms, it was a tune which had taken on glamorous, and historical, associations for him by the testimony of his senior at Hicks's office, that 'jaunty young man [...] had spread such a bewitching halo [...] by describing the glories of dancing round to its beats on the Cremorne platform or at the Argyle Rooms' (*Life*, p. 123).

This entangling of his own memory with those of other people is typical of Hardy. In the poem inspired by these dancing venues, 'Reminiscences of a Dancing Man', the dancing man seems a compound of Hardy himself (who danced at Willis's, and who may have danced at the Cremorne and the Argyle Rooms) and the jaunty young man whose exuberance and enthusiasm it also seemingly celebrates. Whatever the mixtures of lived experience in the poem, though, its historical reach goes even further, beyond the lives of both the poet and the young man himself. In the first stanza, describing the Almack balls at Willis's Rooms, the scene takes on resonances of 'former days':

> Where as we trod to trilling sound
> The fancied phantoms stood around,
>   Or joined us in the maze,
> Of the powdered Dears from Georgian years.
> Whose dust lay in sightless sealed-up biers.
>   The fairest of former days. (*Complete Poems*, p. 217)

At its outer limit, the poem expresses a type of expanded historical consciousness, one alert even to ghosts, the 'fancied phantoms[...] of Georgian years'.[9]

There are many poems that, like this one, use music to document and revive different times and lives. In them, Hardy reaches outside the temporal bounds of his own life to become a channel for the memories of others. Most importantly, there are the numerous poems and songs he wrote, throughout his career, set in the time of the Napoleonic wars, poems such as 'The Sergeant's Song', 'Budmouth Dears', 'The Night of Trafalgar', 'My Love's Gone a-Fighting', and 'Valenciennes' (as well, clearly, as *The Dynasts* itself). In the case of the last two shorter poems, their careful dedications indicate that they were inspired by verbal testimonies.

This desire to incorporate the voices and tales of the past is a fundamental one, underlying numerous poems. In 'The Bridge of Lodi', the poem turns on the irony that the speaker finds that the denizens of Lodi have no memory of the events of Napoleonic times associated with the tune, 'The Bridge of Lodi'. For the speaker, since boyhood, the tune has been evoked with the vivid and ideal romance of such events, so that it is the present scene which fades before the past one through the stirring melody:

I
When of tender mind and body,
I was moved by minstrelsy,
And that air, 'The Bridge of Lodi'
Brought a strange delight to me.

II
In the battle-breathing jingle
Of its forward-footing tune
I could see the armies mingle [...]

IV
Hence the tune came capering to me
While I traced the Rhone and Po;
Nor could Milan's marvel woo me
From the spot englamoured so [....]

And so, in the penultimate verse he ponders whether the collective forgetfulness, of tune and historical conflict alike (evident also in the lack of any memorial 'stone to fame the fight'), might not be for the best, before concluding:

XVII

Nay; I'll sing 'The Bridge of Lodi' -
    That long-loved, romantic thing,
Though none show by smile or nod he
    Guesses why and what I sing! (*Complete Poems*, pp. 107-8)

In this poem, music is once again the magic thread which
connects Hardy and the reader to times outside his own life and to his
family past. In other poems actually set in the Napoleonic times, the
connotations of music are more dramatically personal, as in 'San
Sebastian' (another work attributed to an historical individual). Here,
the sight and sounds for the Sergeant, of his daughter dancing round
the may-pole bring back to his mind the painful memories of the
Spanish woman he raped, whose eyes he sees when he looks at his own
daughter's eyes:

    For the mother of my child is not
    The mother of her eyes. (*Complete Poems*, p. 23)

A musical scene once again brings back the past in 'Leipzig', where the
tune of an old street-fiddler moves 'Old Norbert' to tears as he thinks of
its associations with his mother, and *for* his mother, and her eventful
youth in the Napoleonic wars. What is remarkable about the poem is
the sense the reader gets of old Norbert, his experiences and memories,
so that in reading it his life opens up for us and becomes the means of
reaching into other lives, summoning other times, as with all the
soldiers and characters who are mentioned in the poem.

   To describe the resonances of these Napoleonic times for Hardy,
one has to refer to his grandmother, Mary Hardy, who taught him so
many old songs and tales of a Dorset threatened by Napoleonic
invasion. She was the 'member of the writer's family' whose exploits as
a volunteer inspired 'The Alarm', a poem suitably conceived in the form
of a traditional song, its sensational narration delayed by the evocative
opening stanza:

        In a ferny byway
        Near the great South-Wessex Highway,
    A homestead raised its breakfast-smoke aloft;
    The dew-damps still lay steamless, for the sun had made no
    skyway,
            And twilight cloaked the croft. (*Complete Poems*, p.
35)

Ballads often begin with scene-setting, but the self-sufficient expansiveness of this is closer perhaps to simple story-telling. Certainly, in terms of effect, the intent and preparatory air and the rhythmically phased detailing of this opening bring about in the reader something of the child's spellbound involvement in this shared activity. In this respect among others, the poem is a homage to his grandmother, designed to make available to the reader the type of imaginative satisfactions that the young Thomas and his sister Mary, would have experienced with one who, as Gosse wrote in 1918, was the direct source of countless poems ('Mr Hardy's Lyrical Poems', p. 460). More directly, the older Mary Hardy's facility for description is captured in the remarkable 'One We Knew', that relates among other things her telling how in her youth they would dance to 'the light of the guttering wax in the panelled manses' (p. 274). Moreover, like her grandson, she is said to be one who had a peculiar inwardness with the past, an hallucinatory capacity to 'dwell on such dead themes, not as one who remembers/ But rather as one who sees':

> Past things retold were to her as things existent,
>   Things present but as a tale. (*Complete Poems*, p. 275)

In these poems, commemoration of past times is a reanimation of them, and of the people whose voices, and eyes and ears are also brought to life in the telling. Under the sway of music, the individual moves from the actualities of his or her lived experience into an even remoter past. Hardy seeks to convey to the reader his felt imaginings of the world of his ancestors. In the process, though, the writing goes beyond retrospection or documentation, since the lost world is vitally transmuted by art, re-dedicated to the imaginings of future readers.

These twin powers of projection and recollection, associated with poetry, are, of course, associated too with music in many poems, as in 'A Church Romance', a striking example of a poem that uses music to reach forward to the future as well as back to the past. Hardy envisages the experience of music which drew together his parents in Mellstock Church:

> She turned again; and in her pride's despite
> One strenuous viol's inspirer seemed to throw
> A message from his string to her below,
> Which said: 'I claim thee as my own forthright!'

Poetry repeats that orientation to the future which gives this meeting its meaning, as Hardy entrusts to the reader his image of it. In fact, the poem works by such imaginative leaps across time, by anticipations and turning back. In the first place, everything depends on the effectiveness of the leaping messages of the single string's melody, as it announces and brings about the new relationship between the violinist and the otherwise proud woman below. Music literally establishes connections across time and space, uniting the couple for the future. At the end of the poem, differently, this musical scene is placed in the context of the past. Published after his mother's death, the poet, at the end of the poem, affectingly imagines his mother in old age, herself envisaging her husband as a young man again ('as minstrel, ardent, young, and trim') and imagining that she hears him play those tunes again. Now those same tunes go back, as the vehicles of his mother's reminiscences. At the same time, they are essential to the poem's transcendence of time, as they allow Hardy to enter into his mother's mind and connect with readers yet unborn:

> long years thence, when Age had scared Romance,
> At some old attitude of his or glance
> That gallery-scene would break upon her mind,
> With him as minstrel, ardent, young, and trim,
> Bowing 'New Sabbath' or 'Mount Ephraim'. (*Complete Poems*, p. 252)

III

Alongside the many important poems in which Hardy imaginatively and expressively enters into (and makes available to the reader) the remoter past of his family, we can place the even greater number of poems in which memory returns to the lived past of a central figure or speaker. In these cases, also, it is often music which brings about such transpositions. Indeed, in poem after poem, Hardy narrates experience of the kind that made him remark to Ernest Brennecke in 1923 that:

> I can't even always fathom quite the charm of the ancient church musicians about here. They serenaded me with some old tunes the other evening. That sort of thing carries me back to the fifties - even to the forties.[10]

Music reawakens real continuities with the past, even as these are incompatible with the current situation. In many poems, this is a matter of growing old, as in 'The Dance at the Phoenix', where Jenny, aged and married, recovers her youth at the dance, having slipped out to join 'The King's - Own Cavalry' one more time before returning to die next to her sleeping and unsuspecting husband. Similarly, it has been mentioned how in 'Julie-Jane', the old lovers carry Julie-Jane to her grave, musing over the music which they associate with her youth: 'Sing; how a' would sing!'. The use of the motif of music to contrast age with the emotional promptings of youth which it reawakens, is apparent again in 'The Singing Woman'. The old woman finds that no one listens to the singing that pleased so many when she was young, a theme revisited in 'The Maid of Keinton Mandeville'. Though 'a beldame now,/Time-trenched on cheek and brow', it is the young lady in the latter poem who can still be seen and heard by the poet years later.[11] Typically, Hardy's concentration is primarily corporeal, as it conveys the effect of her performance, how she looked and sounded. And as we read, it is these physical effects which take over the language of the poem, as we see her, '[r]ose-necked, in sky-gray gown', and as the wafts, the flights and falls, of her singing rhythmically possess the poem:

> Singing, in flights that played
> As wind-wafts through us all,
> Till they made our mood a thrall
> To their aery rise and fall... (*Complete Poems*, pp. 563-64)

In a lighter vein, Hardy displays similar linguistic or musical virtuosity in another poem which remembers the musical attractions of a young female, 'To Lizbie Browne'. The insistent simplicities of syntax and rhyme in this poem convey Hardy's memories of the girl's vivacious delight in her own powers to charm. In the second stanza, we gain the most intense sense of this as, with an invasion of memory, the language makes Lizbie's influence felt again, dissolving away time. Once again, as she did as a young girl, she forces from the poet an amorous response. The reversed syntax of the fourth and fifth lines, the reversed phrasing of 'glance-giving', the artful use of pauses, and the conversion of 'wile' from noun into dynamic verb, summon for the reader Lizbie's flirtatious power to wrong-foot and delightfully confound young men. Like an illustration in a child's pop-up book, the topsy-turvy lines surprise the reader with the actuality of what is being represented, and draw out an answering spontaneity. The language becomes overrun by the heart-flipping sense of Lizbie's youthful wiles, her innate virtuosity at the arts of love, of twisting boys around her finger, overturning their defences:

> Sweet Lizbie Browne,
> How you could smile,
> How you could sing!
> How archly wile
> In glance-giving,
> Sweet Lizbie Browne! (*Complete Poems*, p. 130)

Working as a pleasurable means of affective transmission between Lizbie, Hardy and the reader, the poem is less typical than many other poems which deal with the lost scenes of youth, where the tone is overtly regretful, sorrowful, even desolate. 'In the Small Hours' is one such poem, where the speaker rues these transitions - the snakes-and-ladders game which memory plays with feeling. It begins:

> I lay in my bed and fiddled
>   With a dreamland viol and bow,
> And the tunes flew back to my fingers
>   I had melodied years ago.
> It was two or three in the morning
>   When I fancy-fiddled so
> Long reels and country-dances,
>   And hornpipes swift and slow.

After a vision of a joyful wedding full of 'Figures of jigging fieldfolk', the poem returns painfully to the present:

> It seemed a thing for weeping
>   To find, at slumber's wane
> And morning's sly increeping,
>   That Now, not Then, held reign. (*Complete Poems*, p. 648)

In many other poems, the disparity between 'Now' and 'Then' is less a matter of youth and age, than of the before and after of 'Lost Love'. In the poem of that title, music provides the speaker with the cruel evidence of her vanished power. The falling flat of her playing is caught in the lowering rhyme of 'balk' and 'walk':

> I play my sweet old airs -
>   The airs he knew
>   When our love was true -

But he does not balk
His determined walk,
And passes up the stairs. (*Complete Poems*, p. 318)

Music criss-crosses actuality with inappropriate associations of happier times, as in 'Singing Lovers' where the speaker rows a boat in whose moonlit stern sit two lovers and regretfully remembers a similar occasion in his past with 'she of a bygone vow/[who] Joined in the song not now!' (*Complete Poems*, p. 719). To take another example, in 'In the Nuptial Chamber', the townspeople's waltz for the newly-weds makes the bride spring up like 'a lace-robed phantome' as she hears again the 'passionate air' associated with her 'old Love'. As she does, she is reawakened to her past pact:

'And I swore as we spun that none should share
My home, my kisses, till death, save he!
And he dominates me and thrills me through,
And it's he I embrace while embracing you!' (*Complete Poems*, p. 421)

These poems of lost youth or lost love commonly turn on human beings who are knocked out of kilter by the unpredictable promptings of the past. And it is repeatedly music that gets round the defences of the conscious self to reveal the soul's repertoire of old passions. Further, though, as these poems tend to show, the past offers real joys, as well as present grief, and the central figures in Hardy's poems often seek and welcome the reveries and ambushes of the past. In even the most obviously grief-stricken of Hardy's own poems, such as those written after Emma's death, for instance, there is a discernible desire to relive the past, to recreate the conditions in which it can return to, and overwhelm the present. This is testimony not to Hardy's masochism, but to what Bergson might call the ontological reality of the past. If Hardy himself revisits the scenes of the past, it is to make the past revisit him. The self cannot control the signals of the past, but like a radio, it must be switched on, tuned-in so as to catch them. In 'Song from Heine', for instance, the speaker must wait, scanning a picture and emptily dreaming, until it decides to live again for him, to arrive within the chronological frame of the present, and suspend succession with the overwhelming actuality of recollection:

I scanned her picture, dreaming,
   Till each dear line and hue
Was imaged, to my seeming,

As if it lived anew. (*Complete Poems*, p. 182)

Again, in another poem designated as a song, 'Come Not; Yet Come!', the focus is this readiness for the bitter-sweet intensities of memory, for that opening up so that '[o]ld fires new burn me':

> So I say, Come: deign again shine
>   Upon this place,
> Even if unslackened smart be mine
>   From that sweet face,
> And I faint to a phantom past all trace. (*Complete Poems*, pp. 709-10)

As with inspiration, memory of this kind is, like Marcel's involuntary memory, a matter of the associations of the past overwhelming the present when accidentally triggered by some seemingly innocuous object or event.[12] Repeatedly, for Hardy, musical scenes carry such a condensed affective signal, bringing about these transmissions of the past. In 'Molly Gone', the speaker's current sense of disconnection, as he misses his absent loved one, eventually comes to be pushed aside in this way by music. We participate in the speaker's implicit surrender to the spell of the remembered musical incident:

> No more singing by Molly to me
>   In the evenings when she
> Was in mood and in voice, and the candles were lit,
>   And past the porch-quoin
> The rays would spring out on the laurels; and dumbledores hit
>   On the pane, as if wishing to join. (*Complete Poems*, p. 497)

In the same way, in the balladic poem, 'Her Immortality', the speaker's reverie of his dead love is linked to his memory of her voice, and 'the moving tone/ It bore ere she was wed'. Lying on the ground, the past returns to him:

> It seemed as if my body pressed
>   The very ground she trod.
>
> I lay, and thought; and in a trance
>   She came and stood thereby -
> The same, even to the marvellous ray
>   That used to light her eye. (*Complete Poems*, p. 55)

Although these joys are real, the value they involve is always clearly ambivalent, as has been said, since the pleasures proceed from, and perpetuate, the affective impoverishment of the present. The soul of the speaker reverberates with the echoes and the images of the past, but he knows that these will fade and vanish. Further the past involves claims of its own since, like the woman in 'Her Immortality', it depends on the survivor for its own survival, its 'sweet continuance' (*Complete Poems*, p. 56). The poem ends:

> But grows my grief. When I surcease,
>   Through whom alone lives she,
> Her spirit ends its living lease,
>   Never again to be!

In 'The Change', similarly, the speaker ends by opining over his reduced emotional predicament as one who hankers after the 'heart whose sweet reverberances are all time leaves to me' (*Complete Poems*, pp, 455-56). Fixatedly, the poem dwells on the vanished 'magic' of that week where he heard her singing: 'Could that song have a mocking note/As it trilled out warm from the singer's throat'?

In many poems, Hardy probes this type of plight of memory, where the rememberer, as the medium of the influences, voices and ghosts of the past, intensifies his division from the present. To live in the past is to let life pass one by. By another analogy, which attracted Hardy, the body of the one who remembers can be said in such cases to be converted thereby into a kind of disused and displaced musical instrument, one which stores within its fabric the fading airs of bygone times. Hardy probes this intimate correspondence between memory and musical instruments in several poems. In 'Haunting Fingers', the regimental drum, the theatre lyre, the dance viol, the church shawm languishing in a museum are imagined pitifully as themselves feeling 'Old players' dead fingers touch them' (*Complete Poems*, p. 590), and thus reliving their various powers of inspiration - before the 'grayer' light of morning crawls in again. In two other, more openly personal, poems, 'A Duettist to Her Pianoforte' and 'To My Father's Violin', it is possible to detect the close, if implicit, identification between the instrument and the speaker in the poem, both of whom exist in a limbo of lost joy. In these poems, interestingly, there are few of the consolatory glimmerings of memory, even of the admittedly forlorn and fanciful type of 'Haunting Fingers'. In both, Hardy is, rather, concerned to portray the unrelieved intractability of loss, through this concentration on the joyless after-life of the dead person's musical instrument. The poems are

unusually unsparing as musical poems, in this refusal of the bitter-
sweet pleasures, afforded by the surgings and hauntings of memory.

   In 'To My Father's Violin' the syntactical contortions work as if
the poem itself were being turned inside out by a returning feeling of
grief. So too, in terms of the sound, the obdurately unpleasing
('dragging... grind') and the banally repetitive ('there [...]   where [...]
Round and round') communicate the combination of emptiness and
grimly dawning repetition which are characteristic of such a state of
mind. This sense surfaces in the strange nominalization of the word
'profound'. No longer a quality of resonant meaning, it now refers to a
state of absence:

> Does he want you down there
> In the Nether Glooms where
> The hours may be a dragging load upon him,
>   As he hears the axle grind
>   Round and round
>   Of the great world, in the blind
>   Still profound
> Of the night time? He might liven at the sound
> Of your string, revealing you had not forgone him. (*Complete
> Poems*, pp. 451-52)

The poem becomes drained of the pleasures of sound and of suggestion,
as it describes a situation of unmeaning material existence:

> [...] your strings a tangled wreck,
>   Once smart drawn,
>   Ten worm-wounds in your neck,
>   Purflings wan
> With dust-hoar, here alone I sadly con
> Your present dumbness, shape your olden story. (*Complete Poems*,
> p. 452)

As well as this evacuation of pleasure in the poem, this rigorous
concentration on privation, a large part of the power of 'To My Father's
Violin' comes from its occupation of the terrain of loss in a way that is
obviously proleptic of the speaker's own death. Like the violin itself, the
poem inhabits a diminished present, an unresounding interval between
life and death. A similar image for is given by the house in 'Silences',
whose entombed emptiness is referred to in terms of the absence of
music:

Past are remembered songs and music-strains
  Once audible there:
  Roofs, rafters, panes
Look absent-thoughted, tranced, or locked in prayer.

It seems no power on earth can waken it
  Or rouse its rooms,
  Or its past permit
The present to stir a torpor like a tomb's. (*Complete Poems*, p. 866)

In its lack of consolatory elements, though, 'To My Father's Violin' merely indicates in a different way how Hardy's poems are open not only to the past, but to the future too. In many of the poems discussed earlier, the opening to the future was identified with the ways the poem uses its expressive resources to reanimate and so perpetuate, through the act of reading, the emotions, the culture and scenes of the past that it describes. In a bleaker and more pointed way, though, these poems of grieving, like 'A Duettist to Her Pianoforte'. 'To My Father's Violin' or 'Silences', are shadowed by the speaker's own mortality. In such poems, the idea of the speaker's death is not obscured or overcome by his turning to the past, but is intensified by it. Even more explicitly, in 'The Chapel-Organist' or 'The Last Performance', such a sad foreknowledge is dramatically located within the consciousness of the central figure in the poem, as the woman in each case (Emma in the latter) consciously foresees her imminent end. Each woman commemorates her life by performing music, an act that combines the turn to the future with the return to the past.

'At the Piano' is a further graphic instance of how the future and death can haunt the present, with a chilling ironic insistence. It is a poem which turns on the contrast between a man observing a woman playing, and the apparition, in the second stanza, of a phantom being to whose monitory and hidden presence the couple remain oblivious throughout. In the first stanza, the mesmeric detail of the scene casts its entrancing spell. The poem seems to occupy a charmed scene of shared intensities, in which pain is banished:

A woman was playing,
  A man looking on;
  And the mould of her face,
  And her neck, and her hair.
  Which the rays fell upon
  Of the two candles there,
Sent him mentally straying

> In some fancy-place
> Where pain had no trace.

But in the second stanza, this enchanted state becomes prey to the incursions and decompositions of time. The past and the future already inhabit the present:

> A cowled Apparition
>   Came pushing between;
>   And her notes seemed to sigh;
>   And the lights to burn pale,
>   As a spell numbed the scene.
>   But the maid saw no bale,
> And the man no monition;
>   And Time laughed awry,
>   And the Phantom hid nigh. (*Complete Poems*, pp. 530-31)

This interruptive work of time and death is, indeed, often figured as an interrupting of the process of music-making, as in 'To an Unborn Pauper-Child' which tells of how 'Time-wraiths turn our songsingings to fear' (*Complete Poems*, p. 127), or as in 'The Head Above the Fog' where the speaker describes how he customarily imagines in a familiar meadow scene the incursions of the spectral figure of a dead beloved as 'nighted birds break off their song' (*Complete Poems*, p. 481).

IV

At first glance, 'During Wind and Rain' is another poem which uses music to capture the complexities of a present moment that in the poet's mind has its final meaning in relation to the future whose past it will be. The final line in each stanza extracts from its scene of collective blitheness a portent of transience:

> They sing their dearest songs-
> He, she, all of them -
> Treble and tenor and bass,
>   And one to play;
> With candles mooning each face....
>   Ah, no; the years O!
> How the sick leaves reel down in throngs! ('During Wind and Rain', *Complete Poems*, p. 495)

Nevertheless, more than this, as Lucas puts it, 'During Wind and Rain' is a 'truly visionary poem', one in which the present opens onto the eternal, as well as onto the past and the future. The poem, he writes, catches in its scenes a genuinely 'timeless vision balanced', though it is, 'against the steady progress of time' (*Modern English Poetry*, p. 47). This section pursues this capacity of music to signal to the 'timeless' in Lucas's phrase, beyond its capacity to introduce into a scene the signs of the past and of the future.

Once again, as the lines quoted make clear, we can link music to what is affirmed as transcendent in the transient present, to those 'timeless' values, in Lucas's phrase, of individual expression and relatedness that Hardy always associates with it. In a general way, the ontological complexities of music itself account in part for its capacity to participate in these temporal shifts and interpolations. As an art of duration, in the first place, it ties together sensation and memory. In the second place, even in the most mundane description, music is also an art of the 'timeless', since it retains an ideality, a power of self-differentiation, outside the logic of the calendar: a musical work necessarily transcends the successive circumstances in which it is variably instantiated and interpreted.

In this latter respect, one can describe how music reawakens in the hearer a sense of spiritual possibility that can, for a short time, alleviate alienation. Beyond its own intrinsic pleasures, as we have seen, the transcendent effects of music make it possible to relive remembered joys. However, in personal terms, what often appears most important and valuable is not simply that musical experiences bring back the past, but that they revive in the older poet enduring values of selfhood more fully expressed in the affective readiness, pliancy and intensity of youth.[13] The imperative in 'The Self-Unseeing', for example, would only superficially be to confront the present self with the past self, since this is at best an ambivalent joy. In fact, the poem courts the harrowing pain of temporal divergence not only to reconnect the present with the past self, but, more importantly, to uncover what is common to both. My concern here is to focus on how Hardy's poems employ musical incidents to reveal the unchanging, virtual, core of individuality.

In its nature, such a focus becomes an ethical enquiry, because it inevitably involves notions of expression and of innocence. So, one needs to read 'Afternoon Service at Mellstock', for instance, as a poem which is spiritually regenerative as well as merely nostalgic or regretful. The quiet simplicity of the language is certainly evocative of lost times, but it also seeks to renew in the poet, and pass on to the reader, that which may have became lost or soured in the meantime: that quality of individuality remembered in 'Wessex Heights' as more clearly evident in 'my simple self that was' (*Complete Poems*, p. 319). In the poem the speaker remembers how:

> On afternoons of drowsy calm
>   We stood in the panelled pew,
> Singing one-voiced a Tate-and-Brady psalm
>   To the tune of 'Cambridge New'.
>
> We watched the elms, we watched the rooks,
>   The clouds upon the breeze,
> Between the whiles of glancing at our books,
>   And swaying like the trees.
>
> So mindless were those outpourings! -
>   Though I am not aware
> That I have gained by subtle thought on things
>   Since we stood psalming there. (*Complete Poems*, p. 429)

The emotion in the poem comes from the dynamic it captures between the older self and its younger version. In the first place, it sharpens our sense of what time has taken away through the language of the first two stanzas. The miraculous rhythmical ease of the verse conveys the singing of the children: the communal 'we' who sing 'one-voiced', and who are implicitly in tune with the natural world, as they absent-mindedly sway 'like the trees' while watching the elms and the rooks. In terms of its content, the many-sided contrast between this and the deflated reflections of the 'I' whose comments conclude the poem could not be clearer. At the same time, though, the poem in itself reveals the poet's capacity mesmerizingly to connect through his language with the concord, promise, and expressive physical spontaneity of the earlier time. In this aspect, the poem is not simply as a vehicle of memory, but an expressive means of reaffirming and rediscovering the 'timeless' values inherent in the past scene. Music and language both testify to a sense of innocence with which the poet reconnects, a sense of innate spiritual potentials that are reawakened both *in* and *by* the poem. This underlying meaning of the poem is only accentuated by the agonizing implication for the speaker that these potentials can no longer be readily actualized in the present. So, the reticent last stanza suggests the way in which he has become oppressed by his capacity for 'subtle thoughts', and how age, wry self-consciousness, and, implicitly, loneliness have further divided him from the boys who 'stood in the panelled pew'.

'The House of Hospitalities' similarly uses music to catch and revive the echoes of past innocence in the self:

> Here we broached the Christmas barrel,
>   Pushed up the charred log-ends;
> Here we sang the Christmas carol,
>   And called in friends.
>
> Time has tired me since we met here
>   When the folks now dead were young,
> Since the viands were outset here
>   And quaint songs sung.
>
> And the worm has bored the viol
>   That used to lead the tune,
> Rusts eaten out the dial
>   That struck night's noon.
>
> Now no Christmas brings in neighbours,
>   And the New Year comes unlit;
> Where we sang the mole now labours,
>   And spiders knit.
>
> Yet at midnight if here walking,
>   When the moon sheets wall and tree,
> I see forms of old time talking,
>   Who smile on me. (*Complete Poems*, p. 206)

What is affirmed in the past is what is lost in the benighted and destructive present - music, hospitality, youthful spontaneity. Community and self-expression survive in memory, but also by poetic language, as it summons the relationships of the past and makes new associations with its readers.[14] For the poet, the necessity again is that he holds on to the past context because it was one in which his individuality had meaning:

> Yet at midnight if here walking,
>   When the moon sheets wall and tree,
> I see forms of old time talking,
>   Who smile on me.

While acknowledging, then, the poignancy of the ways in which music continually floods the conscious self with the affects of the past, the value of such feelings is that they testify to enduring, essential, potentials of selfhood otherwise obscured by habit and circumstance. Which is to reiterate that the significances of such resurgences and revisitings for Hardy are not only biographical, historical, or cultural, but also ethical. When music breaks through the defensive shell of consciousness, it is the soul that it addresses for Hardy.[15]

In terms of the specific relations between Hardy's own life, and these ethical dimensions and issues in the poetry, John Lucas has speculated in subtle ways on what may be involved. He argues that Hardy's 'persistent locating' of 'his vision of community' in the past, and his desire to return to it, can be connected with the poet's guilt about how his literary aspirations would necessarily have involved a secretive betrayal of his humble origins. For Lucas, the poetry is marked by this turning away, by ambition and its attendant self-alienation:

> Nevertheless, Hardy's distancing himself from family and community will help to explain why, in his poems, the gap between past and present is so achingly recorded, but also why the process by which the gap is created is never much more than sketched in [...] In other words, Hardy covers over the causes of those discontinuities out of which much of his poetry is made. As a result, these same discontinuities are presented as a fact. (*Modern English Poetry*, pp. 48-49)

The poetry repeatedly testifies, as an expression of a longing, to wilful betrayals which it glosses over - and so repeats. The sheer dynamism and inescapability of this recursive psychic and moral process is, we might imagine, one reason why, for Lucas, Hardy's vision of community is 'persistent', but never simple or sentimental:

> the very intensity of Hardy's longing for community throngs his poems with voices and visions whose vitality keeps nostalgia at bay. (*Modern English Poetry*, p. 49)

Lucas's analysis of the sense of personal failure is a convincing one, and it raises the question as to how such a notion of guilt coexists with the affirmative emphases that he also describes. His argument emerges in his analysis of 'The Self-Unseeing', an obviously central poem for any discussion of the place of music in Hardy's poetry:

> Here is the ancient floor,
> Footworn and hollowed and thin,
> Here was the former door
> Where the dead feet walked in.

She sat here in her chair,
Smiling into the fire;
He who played stood there,
Bowing it higher and higher.

Childlike, I danced in a dream;
Blessings emblazoned that day;
Everything glowed with a gleam;
Yet we were looking away! (*Complete Poems*, pp. 166-67)

Although Lucas reads the representation of the past scene as subject to a sharply sardonic reading (the characters are, he says, 'looking away': perhaps wrapped in their own dreams, their own amorous betrayals of hearth and home?), he also sees the poem as emphatically committed to an undeniable and compelling vision of harmony:

> Yet against all this we have to set the vision. Betrayed or not, its vitality is beyond doubt: it is 'here' in the emphatic, alliterated lines of the last stanza; and as we have seen, and will do again, *glow* and *gleam* are essential elements in Hardy's visioning. (pp. 32-33)

Lucas's paradox (betrayal or harmony?) is in one clear sense only an apparent one since, according to the argumentative apparatus of this book, unconscious experiences of harmony such as this can coexist with wholly divergent conscious preoccupations. The visionary 'glowings', the ideal 'gleams' of musical togetherness are perfectly compatible with the other ways in which the characters are 'looking away' or falling short. Indeed, the poem could be taken as an exemplary case of an individuating event that operates according to different affective and experiential principles than those which govern the contents and intentions of the self-conscious mind.

However, while this epistemological issue can be resolved like this, it is less easy to resolve the ethical issue. In the cryptic brevity of Lucas's account, we remain uncertain how far we should read the poem as a poem of bad faith: is it one which covertly repeats the acts of betrayal that it equally covertly describes?; or, contrarily, is it a poem that keeps the faith, since it affirms the collective visions of the past? I think the difficulty can be reduced by spelling out the links between guilt and innocence in the poem. Certainly, one can speculate that the idealization of the past which Lucas identifies in the poem is itself connected to the mechanics of guilt, since guilt, one could say, always must involve an ideal version of the self. Guilt is a debt paid by the actual self to an abiding ideal counterpart, whose sense of potential tends to be more clearly detectable in, or associable with, the 'childlike' world than in that of the adult. The poet's *desire* to surrender to the spell of the past (since no music is actually heard in its present scene) would then be connected to a fear lest the traces of the past be obliterated, since guilt fears, above all, the loss of the locus of innocence to which it clings. Innocence is another word for individuality, for a vitality and readiness which expresses itself through what the poem calls the 'blessings' of events of unconscious relatedness.

In this way, the equivocation which Lucas identifies corresponds to the ethical self-division within the speaker, as he strives to connect with his youthful self. As a further complication, though, the innocence of this former self, identified with the musical expressiveness of the family scene, could itself be taken as both affirmed and queried in the poem. As we have seen it is affirmed as a necessary fiction of the soul, but also, on a further reading, innocence is queried as a historical reality, as when Lucas suggests that the poem even allows us to think of how the young Hardy himself was perhaps already 'looking away', like Pip in *Great Expectations,* to the 'city, and a new, more ambitious life' (*Modern English Poetry*, p. 32). In such ways, the poem locates itself complicatedly on the threshold of past and present, guilt and innocence, selfhood and community, 'village tradition' and ambition, harmony and irony, simplicity and complexity, fiction and fact.

Further, such a reading of the poem, in terms of its open-ended, inclusive complexity, suggests, in psychological terms, how it could function simultaneously as an oblique expression of guilt and also as a release from it. Perhaps more fundamentally still, though, the poem's own expressive complexity and openness proves again, as in 'Afternoon Service at Mellstock' its best means of keeping faith with the spiritual potentials, the projection into the future, of the childhood soul, however fallible the child was or proved to be. Formally, the poem would essentially revitalize the sense of the innocent 'blessings' of the past through its dedication to the possible: the fluency and interchange of music are the values which inform its own constitutive repetition of play and possibility, its unfinalized circulation of contrary senses and nuances, its suspension of final judgments. The innocence of art as play and pleasure offers a form of redemption, since artistic values align themselves against the static qualities of subjectivity, not least its needs to know and to blame.

The innate refusal of poetic language to be identified with mere representation thus has an intrinsic link with the unresolved potentiality of the soul, as expressed through music in 'The Self-

Unseeing'. A comparable scene occurs in 'At the Railway Station - Upway', as the pitying boy fiddles, and the cuffed prisoner sings "This life so free". Predominantly, the scene appears as one of obvious and marked irony, full of an abyssal sense of bitter absurdity. This is the second stanza:

> The man in the handcuffs smiled;
> The constable looked, and he smiled too,
>   As the fiddle began to twang;
> And the man in the handcuffs suddenly sang
>   With grimful glee:
>   'This life so free
>   Is the thing for me!'
> And the constable smiled, and said no word,
> As if unconscious of what he heard;
> And so they went on till the train came in -
> The convict, and the boy with the violin. (*Complete Poems*, p. 607)

The twanging fiddle obviously cannot set up any genuine intermission in the sequence of guilt and punishment. Nonetheless, the figures in the scene continue 'till the train came in', and the poet is similarly transfixed. It is as if everyone clings once again to the values and potentials of expression and communality associated with music - all the more so where the scene is, like this, unredeemably sad and contaminated by isolation and judgment. The prisoner tries to relate to the boy in recognition of the child's sympathetic impulse, but he does so in a fitful and self-mocking way. The poet appears paralyzed by the awful sadness of the scene, though in another sense his air of quiet amazement corresponds to a contrary set of significances. These succeed and coexist each other in the reader's mind, creating an expressive continuity between the language of the poem and the way in which its scene holds open, through the influences of music, the poet's sense of the underlying possibilities of the self.

These gaps between youth and age, and between the custom and sympathy, are again revealed through music in 'The Bird-Catcher's Boy', a poem that similarly uses music as a metaphor for its own underlying imperative of an expressive, sympathetic, connection identified with youth. The boy desires to escape his father's attempts to trap him within his own profession:

> 'Father, I fear your trade:
>   Surely it's wrong!
> Little birds limed and made

Captive life-long.

'Larks bruise and bleed in jail,
 Trying to rise;
Every caged nightingale
 Soon pines and dies.'

'Don't be a dolt, my boy!
 Birds must be caught;
My lot is such employ,
 Yours to be taught. (*Complete Poems*, p. 825)

The next day he runs away to sea, where he is drowned. Music comes into the poem in association with the boy's habitual and intimate gesture, by which his fingers, 'harp-like', would 'sweep on the wires of their cage'. The sound is first described in the poem as the boy goes to bed after fatefully quarrelling with his father. At this point it shows the conflict between the boy's spontaneity and his desire for autonomy, and the father's resentful and divisive desire for control:

Lightless, without a word
 Bedwise he fares;
Groping his way is heard
 Seek the dark stairs.

Through the long passage, where
 Hang the caged choirs;
Harp-like his fingers there
 Sweep on the wires. (*Complete Poems*, p. 825)

By the end of the poem, though, when the sound is heard or imagined by his parents on the night of his death, the boy's absent-minded reflex has taken on a powerful eloquence of a different kind. Movingly, it illuminates the father's self-ignorance, touching his consciousness with the revelation of the true depth of his feelings for his son, feelings that anger and familiarity had recently obscured:

Then some one seemed to flit
 Soft in below;
'Freddy's come!' Up they sit,
 Faces aglow.

Thereat a groping touch

Dragged on the wires
Lightly and softly - much
    As they were lyres;

'Just as it used to be
    When he came in,
Feeling in darkness the
    Stairway to win!' (*Complete Poems*, p. 826)

The tragic displacement of the unregarded world of the familiar in the poem is conveyed even by the line break which moves the definite article to the end of the line, 'the / Stairway to win', and so makes the reader for an instant grope for an instant in what seems an impossible absence.

Once again, this poem skilfully counterpoises its various differentiated elements of meaning and feeling while preserving through its seeming artlessness, the most direct emotional concentration. Language makes available, and produces, the essential affects of innocence that the poem is organized around. Words share the qualities of inconclusiveness and promise that the poem's content stages in association with music's power to connect up people, and to traverse the different, incommensurable worlds of age and youth. This can be further seen in the autobiographical poem, 'Middle-Age Enthusiasms', that Hardy dedicated to his sister Mary, the church-organist. The speaker tells how the two of them, grown middle-aged, would fasten onto small pleasures all the more because of their shared sense of transience and mortality:

We passed where flag and flower
Signalled a jocund throng;
We said: 'Go to, the hour
Is apt!' - and joined the song;
And, kindling, laughed at life and care,
Although we knew no laugh lay there. (*Complete Poems*, p. 63)

The word 'kindling' suggests that the two were able to forget themselves and to revive their childhood bond, '[a]lthough we knew no laugh lay there'. As in 'The Bird-Catcher's Boy', or 'The Self-Unseeing', or 'Afternoon Service at Mellstock', the underlying ironic mismatch between social, adult, identity and emotion is played out in a narrative of innocence and experience, while the language captures the values associated with music.

These dualities, and this ethical aspect of the texts, are also evident in the last poem here, 'At Madam Tussaud's in Victorian Years'. This poem is somewhat different, on the face of it, in that its focus is on an individual who is remarkable simply because he has retained the secret in age of youthful, unself-conscious, joy. The speaker observes that the first fiddler in the band is the same as he who '[h]ere fiddled four decades' ago, and that he still 'wears the same babe-like smile of self-centred delight'. It appears he has led 'a blissful existence [...] with his lyre,/In a trance of his own, where no wearing or tearing had sway'. Music has insulated him from time and care, although the poem also details how his face, 'if regarded, is woefully wanner, and drier,/And his once dark beard has grown straggling and gray'. Nonetheless, the poem ends with an apostrophe to the man's enduring innocence:

> Ah, but he played staunchly - that fiddler - whoever he was,
>   With the innocent heart and the soul-touching string:
> May he find the Fair Haven! For did he not smile with good cause?
> Yes; gamuts that graced forty years' - flight were not a small thing!
> (*Complete Poems*, p. 492)

V

This section ponders these ideas of aesthetic survival and renewal in relation to the common rhythmical element of poetry and music. In the context of the larger discussion of time here, the concentration is on two important ways in which rhythm in itself resists chronology, and exemplifies the temporal complexities that run through the argument of the chapter. In the first place, rhythm, in commonplace ways, always involves an overcoming of the separation of time into moments, since its logic is of the unity of larger, undivided movements. In the second, in its ideal aspect as a pattern, a particular rhythm obviously can be repeated, anew and differently, on various occasions. A rhythm retains an ideality beyond its concrete forms, a power of differentiation and becoming by which it both manifests and transcends its materiality. This immediate discussion examines several poems to bring out how the treatment of rhythm and sound, in intimate association with the topic of music, contributes to the temporal dramas of Hardy's poems.

To begin with, I want to take up some of the points raised by Denis Taylor's discussion, in his work on Hardy's prosody, on the relations of metre and sound with the temporal and historical issues that the poems deal with. Taylor's work provides an invaluable resource in that it shows in various ways how metrical analysis can open up these complex issues of time. There then follows a close reading of a poem not discussed by Tayor, 'I Found Her Out There'.

The first poem, 'Concerning Agnes', is another one that has been oddly underestimated or ignored as Peter Widdowson has shown.[16] Its pretext is typically a sad one, proceeding as it does from the longing of the speaker who cannot escape his wish to 'dance with that fair woman yet once more' - although she is dead, and 'lies white, straight, features marble-keen/ Unapproachable, mute, in a nook I have never seen'. In the earlier discussion in Chapter Three, the emphasis fell on how Agnes was reanimated in the poem by the transformative spell of memory, as the surviving poet remembers 'when the wide-faced moon looked through/ The boughs at the faery lamps of the Larmer Avenue'. The extraordinary physical precision of the poet's language conveys the relation between regret and imaginative recapture that underlies the poem:

> The while I held her hand, and, to the booms
> Of contrabassos, feet still pulsed from the distant rooms. (*Complete Poems*, p. 878)

In relation to the poem's metrical argument, Taylor has shown how the dance music of the past scene is intermittently evoked, as in these lines, by effects of rhythm and rhyme. These faint pulses provide a ghostly backing track to the different quality of the speech rhythms which overlay it, and which firmly reiterate the present sense of loss:

> I am stopped from hoping what I have hoped before -
> Yes, many a time!

In such ways, the phantoms of memory which overcome the speaker are duplicated by the echoic effects of sound which come to inhabit the poem and the speaker's mind. The association between such movements of feeling and the ideality of art that overcomes death is caught at the end of the poem in the poet's imaginings of Agnes's burial place, through a series of comparisons with the goddesses of ancient mythology and literature:

> There she may rest like some vague goddess, shaped
>   As out of snow:
> Say Aphrodite sleeping; or bedraped
>   Like Kalupso;

> Or Amphitrite stretched on the Mid-sea swell,
> Or one of the Nine grown stiff from thought. I cannot tell!

In these ways, the poem's language matches the complexity of Hardy's meditation on the different survivals effected by memory and art. Further, it is an ironic implication of the subtlety of Hardy's poetic dramatization and registration of mortality and transience that it secures his own poetic survival.

In relation to another poem mentioned earlier, 'Reminiscences of a Dancing Man', Taylor develops a similar account of how sound mimics or expresses the important layerings of time itself. We noted earlier how the concentric, inclusive, kinds of temporal referencing in the poem (the poem going beyond the experiences of Hardy himself, and the young man at Hicks's, to take in even those of 'the powdered Dears from Georgian years') is also a matter of the language's own metrical and other effects of sound. Taylor points out, further, that the poem is one of those in which 'Hardy imitates the pulse of remembered song', as well as adopting for its ten line stanzas a 'common eighteenth-century ode rhyme scheme' (*Hardy's Metres*, p. 136). Similarly, in discussing 'To My Father's Violin', Taylor asserts that 'the father's rhythms live on in the son's metrical impressions' (*Hardy's Metres*, p. 145). In both these cases, again, sound becomes associated with the poem's meditation on the endurance of artistic works.

This artistic persistence emerges in a related way in another of Taylor's striking metrical readings, of 'Apostrophe to an Old Psalm Tune':

> So, your quired oracles beat till they make me tremble
> As I discern your mien in the old attire,
> Here in these turmoiled years of belligerent fire
>   Living on still - and onward, maybe,
>   Till Doom's great day be! (*Complete Poems*, p. 432)

For Taylor, the 'dimeter boom' of the last line ('Till *Doom's* great *day* be') is a moment where the metrical overlays the spoken content, 'somewhat like the power of music casting its spell on the consciousness of the speaker' (*Hardy's Metres*, p. 144). At this moment, the metrical pattern which has haunted the poem is most insistent, implying how the psalm tune has lived on, and will continue to do so:

> That more hypnotic rhythm was, we discover, implicit all along; and its echo now seems, eerily, to outlive life itself. (*Hardy's Metres*, p. 144)

Taylor's knowledge of the history of prosody and of the Victorian context, in such examples, provides further dimensions to this study of history and temporality in Hardy's poetry. The battle of dislocation and continuance that marks the poetry in so many ways - culturally, personally, poetically, ethically - has, as a further aspect, this wish to incorporate old metrical foundations as an echoic reference within the poem's own original stanza form. Rhythmical enfoldings embody the poem's emotionally charged sense of change and permanence, and implicitly identify the poem itself with that power to live on attributed to music.

Although not explicitly a poem about Emma's musical talents, 'I Found Her Out There' is a useful poem to consider here, since it is one which employs what can be called innately musical features and themes in its exploration of death, love, art and survival:

I found her out there
On a slope few see,
That falls westwardly
To the salt-edged air,
Where the ocean breaks
On the purple strand,
And the hurricane shakes
The solid land.

I brought her here,
And have laid her to rest
In a noiseless nest
No sea beats near.
She will never be stirred
In her loamy cell
By the waves long heard
And loved so well.

So she does not sleep
By those haunted heights
The Atlantic smites
And the blind gales sweep,
Whence she often would gaze
At Dundagel's famed head,
While the dipping blaze
Dyed her face fire-red;

And would sigh at the tale
Of sunk Lyonnesse,

As a wind-tugged tress
Flapped her cheek like a flail;
Or listen at whiles
With a thought-bound brow
To the murmuring miles
She is far from now.

Yet her shade, maybe,
Will creep underground
Till it catch the sound
Of that western sea
As it swells and sobs
Where she domiciled,
And joy in its throbs
With the heart of a child. (*Complete Poems*, pp. 342-43)

The poem ends by imagining Emma's ghost returning from the inland spot of her burial to the place it has left behind - the Cornish coast of her childhood and youth where Hardy met her, as in the title and the first stanza. The dominant idea is that Emma's spirit and individuality were so strongly attached to the environment of the coast that the sea might even wake her now, were its sounds to be brought into proximity with her body. As well as this idea of the possible reunion of her ghost with the sea, brought about by sound, the poem meditates on the old Arthurian tale, equally fanciful, of the mythical beauty of the sunken city of Lyonnesse. These places are described as enclosed within the girl's memory and imagination, her 'thought-bound brow'. Further, as Lyonnesse transcends the accidents of time through the story and Emma's imagination, so ironically she lives on in the poem. The reader's imagination brings her back to life, as we enter into Hardy's sense of her as indissociable from the coast itself. The poem's central trope of reanimation is accordingly performed as we are introduced into the series of embedded, or nested, individual viewpoints which the poem articulates.

However, at the same time as it sets up a literary chain of reanimation, the poem also sets up a chain of meditations on death - Emma thinks of 'sunk Lyonnesse'; the poet thinks of her in 'her loamy cell'; the reader thinks of her, and of Hardy, for whom the poem is a monument of sorts, and so on. A further implication, of course, is that the reader is the next in this chain of association. Our reading, which meditates on death, becomes implicitly an anticipation of it: we are absorbed by this literary patterning into confronting our own mortality, at the same time as the poem, and the poet, take on their continuing life within us. The poem seems itself, in an important aspect, an expressive meditation both on death, and on the immortality, the transcendent modes, of literary art. In terms of the larger argument of this chapter, the implication is that the two are connected, since art, like memory and history, bases its powers of virtual continuity on actual separation. In probing these points further, I want to concentrate more closely on the physical material of the poem, its effective features of sound and rhythm.

In the first stanza, we know that the poet remembers their first accidental meeting in an obscure coastal spot, a place of natural encounters, with the slope meeting the air, the air edged with the salt of the sea, the ocean breaking on the beach, the strand taking on the purple of the sky, the land shaken by the winds, and so on. The emphasis on such conjunctions and reverberations is caught at the level of sound by the mobility of the rhythm as it rises into successive percussive peaks in its two-line waves. The stresses congregate and fall before the transitional pause introduced by the comma in each case:

> I found her out there
> On a *slope few see*,
> That falls westwardly
> To the *salt-edged air*,
> Where the ocean breaks
> On the *purple strand*,
> And the hurricane shakes
> The *solid land*.

This play of the rhythmical effect of turbulent concordance and the separations of the line-breaks can be seen as expressive of the poem's overall contrast between the percussive intensities of the earlier meeting and the eventual passing of Emma into the 'noiseless' world of death itself. In the second stanza it is this latter fact which dominates, and the rhythmical motif of the opening stanza has faded to a remote echo:

> I brought her here,
> And have laid her to rest
> In a noiseless nest
> No sea beats near.
> She will never be stirred
> In her loamy cell
> By the waves long heard
> And loved so well.

The initial links between the encounters of love, and the compoundings of nature return in the following stanzas, where the emphasis on 'those haunted heights [...where] the blind gales sweep' sets up the intimate picture of Emma given in the fourth. The poet describes, in this verse, how Emma would become distracted from her circumstances, moved by the story of Lyonnesse or the sounds of the sea. It is this distraction by art and sound which moves the poet, as he observes her. His falling in love with her, the beginning of a lifelong association, is remembered as provoked by her touching capacity for following her own trail of rapt imaginings or rememberings. The reader becomes entranced or affected in a similar way - as we look within to imagine her visualizing Lyonnesse - in that embedding effect that I have mentioned earlier:

> And would sigh at the tale
> Of sunk Lyonnesse,
> As a wind-tugged tress
> Flapped her cheek like a flail;
> Or listen at whiles
> With a thought-bound brow
> To the murmuring miles
> She is far from now.

The reader's visualization throughout is a crucial part of that process which introduces us into the imaginative and felt 'inside' of the poem. Here, it is clearly secured by the evocative imagery, such as that image of the wind which tugs her tresses, as her tresses flap against 'her cheek like a flail'. The image of the flapping hair is precise, and the woman herself is unconscious of it. What is also moving about this detail is the further sense that it took memory to raise such an accidental sensation to consciousness, and to articulate its many-faceted evocative power. The joy which the poet might have taken in it at the time would obviously have been far more an unconscious one, caught up in all the unfolding complexities, anxieties and strategies of the moment. It is only in the concentrated medium of poetic language that the stray and accidental detail is appropriately isolated, recovered and relived, becoming a means not only of delivering the affects and associations of the past for the poet, but of transferring them to the reader. As this implies, the meaning of the picture of Emma which we are offered is not reducible to what was perceived or remembered, since the poem seeks, above all, to convey to the reader those defining features of her soul which attracted him to her. The poem, that is, offers a vision of

Emma which trails a sense of her essence as a person, at the same time as it offers an account of the poet's relationship with her.

One final important feature of what I am inclined to call the general musicality of the poem is Hardy's use of verbal echoes. Consider, for instance the 'fl' sound in the last line referred to, 'Flapped her cheek like a flail'. The line suggests, through the precise placement of the sounds, the unpredictable but violent flapping motion of hair against cheek. In this way, it again exemplifies the percussive logic of physical conjunction at the heart of the poem, and links it to the joyous encounter which is celebrated within it, and given in the title. However, there is more to such uses of sound here than mere evocation of a past scene. An echo, after all, is a paradoxical entity, since it is like the ghost or after-image of a sound, half-way between the physical and the ideal. For instance, when we hear the first sound 'fl', we are unconscious of it. We then become conscious of it with the second sound, in so far as the second sound echoes it, defining an alliterative pattern. This pattern thus utilizes sensation and memory (since it is revealed by these divergent yet conjoined means), while also transcending both as artistic form. At the level of sound as well as theme, language becomes open to sympathetic resonances which pertain not primarily to the memory (which moves from past to present and back again), but to the ideal potentials for association embedded within the purely physical, and which, according to the effective logic of this poem, are articulated expressively both in love and in art.

In many ways, then, the poem sets up a string of physical encounters out of whose contiguous yet uncommunicating elements emerge new arrangements which are spontaneous and accidental, as well as unwilled, yet whose singular beauty and associations the poet strives above all else to convey. The sea and the land, Emma and Hardy, the sounds of the words themselves: everything in the poem comes into an expressive conjunction whose principles are not rational or conscious, but aesthetic, affective, unconscious:

> Whence she often would gaze
> At Dundagel's famed head,
> While the dipping blaze
> Dyed her face fire-red;

The writing revives and transmits the sense of Emma's youthful susceptibility to which Hardy was himself susceptible, and so affirms these associative and individuating values which this book has identified in Hardy's writing about music, and in the ethical world-view at work in the texts. Once more individuality is here a function of the associations which are established in the poem, not a resource of consciousness, and the poem's premiss is that art can perpetuate these associations across the gaps of time. Finally, like many of the other poems discussed in the chapter, the treatment of time in 'I Found Her Out There' goes beyond the merely elegiac in so far as, like many of the other poems discussed in this chapter, it seeks not simply to remember the past, but to reanimate it and capture its spiritual qualities. In so doing, it sets up a chain of resonances which transcends age and death, as Emma herself, 'with the heart of a child', is fancifully imagined doing at the poem's close, as she hears what can be called the music of the sea:

> Yet her shade, maybe,
> Will creep underground
> Till it catch the sound
> Of that western sea
> As it swells and sobs
> Where she domiciled,
> And joy in its throbs
> With the heart of a child.

VI

Time as personal history, as family history, as national history and local history: in each of these contexts, then, music has the power to transport listeners from their circumstances into other kinds of certainty and experience. The associations of sound open up files of past lives and time, and disjoin the present from itself. Music places the hearer on-line to other people's souls, and stimulates the exercise of his or her own in an experience which is affective: at once physical and spiritual, but also inter-personal or communal. John Lucas, taking up a similar point about the effects of kinds of ventriloquism in Hardy's verse, refers to:

> those poems where Hardy's own voice is invaded by another, or where the isolated 'I' gives way to the communal 'we' or 'they' [...] In other words, community is not so much affirmed as rediscovered, repossessed in the act of speech, in the voiced imagining. ('Hardy Among the Poets', p. 200)

The important point is simply that music is often the force that provokes such intimations of community. Lucas takes up from Seamus

Heaney the connected idea that Hardy carried within him a 'ghost life', that his poems were transmissions. Lucas comments on:

> those [poems] which seem to have been set down in an unforced, uninvented manner, as though, unbidden, voices and visions have come thronging to him. ('Hardy Among the Poets', p. 201)

Lucas sees Hardy's accessibility to such inspirations or invasions as a paradoxical responsiveness in which his voice is conjoined with those of other people. In a compatible way, Nicholas Royle and Andrew Bennett identify weird telepathic effects in 'The Voice', seeing Hardy's poem in one aspect as an uncanny switchboard in which the voices of Emma and Keats inhabit Hardy's voice, mingling with it as independent elements inseparable from an ensemblic dimension of effects in the poem.[17] To take another example, if Keats or Arnold could be said to be ghostly presences in 'The Darkling Thrush', so too, for John Bayley, is Shelley (*An Essay on Hardy*, p. 37), whereas for Robert Langbaum '[b]ehind the whole poem stands Wordsworth' (*Thomas Hardy in Our Time*, p. 68). Indeed, one could add other voices, as does Tim Armstrong who says that 'The Darkling Thrush' is '[p]erhaps Hardy's most allusive poem', as he relates it by way of its diction to further works by Milton, Keble, Cowper, Meredith, and, by way of its hymn-like stanza form, to William Barnes, among others (*Selected Poems*, pp. 88-91). In such ways, this poem of the turn of the century, becomes implicitly both a meditation on literary history and also a celebration of the power of poets to endure, if the reader can respond in a suitable way to its mode of communication.

By extension, as has been suggested, it is in the reader that Hardy's voice and vision have forms of after-life. To a degree this corresponds to Hardy's lifelong wish to celebrate the music he had known in childhood and youth, as in, for instance, 'Song to an Old Burden', and in his desire to preserve the memory and songs of his family's music-making. The profoundly personal 'To My Father's Violin', we have seen, movingly describes the associations of music for Hardy himself, and conveys the desire to pass them on to the reader. Nonetheless, there is much more to this than merely a personal impulse to be remembered and to survive. Hardy described art as the means by which a distinctive viewpoint on the world can be preserved, a viewpoint which is at once wholly individual and yet which transcends the personality of the writer, both in so far as it incorporates other lives and because it is amenable to being renewed in the lives of the readers with whom the author's perceptions are compounded. An idea like this can be seen in the following famous remark:

> Art consists in so depicting the common events of life as to bring out the features which illustrate the author's idiosyncratic mode of regard; making old incidents and things seem new. (*Life*, p. 225)

Again, it can be seen in the musical analogy that 'the new poet [...] comes with a new note' (*Life*, p. 300), or in his early puzzled perception of the shared qualities of 'two marches of totally opposite sentiment', before he discovered that they were both by Handel (*Life*, p. 16). Once again, these elements of the discussion are reminiscent of Proust, not simply of the idea of art as the means of regaining lost time ('making old incidents and things seem new'), but also because the original viewpoint of an artist is his or her means of transcending chronology. This is connected to Proust's conception of each artist as an exile from a native land that differs from that of any other's, and to which his or her different works pay an unvarying testimony, revealing 'this unknown quality of an unique world.' (*Remembrance of Things Past*, Vol. 2, p. 382). The narrator reflects, as Marcel desultorily plays Vinteuil's sonata:

> Was there in art a more profound reality, in which our true personality finds an expression that is not afforded by it in the activities of life? For every great artist seems so different from all the rest, and gives us so strongly that sensation of individuality for which we seek in vain in our everyday existence. (*Remembrance of Things Past*, Vol. 2, p. 156)

Most importantly, then, Hardy, like Proust, overcomes time by extracting from it the timeless qualities that correspond to his own individuality.

Hardy's poetry, then, is adjusted to a dual and conscious sense both of the necessity as well as the impermanence of values and experiences of relatedness. The representation of music in the *Complete Poems* unlocks, I have argued, a range of ways to explore the topics of memory, feeling and society involved. Hardy's intensely conscious attitude towards the precarious and fleeting nature of personal happiness (when Hardy had dedicated himself to poetry, after the mid-1890s), perhaps has to do with the onset of age as well as with temperamental traits, or his marital loneliness. Nonetheless, Hardy the poet's enhanced sense of physical impermanence coexists with an equally enhanced sense of spiritual and affective continuities that do not change, a coexistence that can obviously be experienced as a kind of irony, a widening gap. As has been shown, in the aesthetic meditations of the late 1880s onwards, this sense recurs many times, as in this recorded comment from November 1891 in the *Life*, quoted in Chapter One:

> The highest flights of the pen are mostly the excursions and revelations of souls unreconciled to life [...] (*Life*, p. 240)

Such an emphasis on a life configured as disappointment is inseparable, though, from the ineradicable revisitings of hope. There always seem in Hardy's poems - even the most bleak - grains or seeds of joy disobedient to the consciousness of time and place. In 'The Colonel's Soliloquy', for example, the speaker embarks on another campaign:

> 'My years mount somewhat, but here's to't again!
>   And if I fall, I must.

And the poem ends:

> 'Now sounds "The Girl I've left behind me", - Ah,
> The years, the ardours, wakened by that tune!
> Time was when, with the crowd's farewell "Hurrah!"
>   'Twould lift me to the moon.
>
> 'But now it's late to leave behind me one
> Who if, poor soul, her man goes underground,
> Will not recover as she might have done
>   In days when hopes abound.
>
> 'She's waving from the wharfside, palely grieving,
> As down we draw.... Her tears make little show,
> Yet now she suffers more than at my leaving
>   Some twenty years ago!
>
> 'I pray those left at home will care for her;
> I shall come back; I have before; though when
> The Girl you leave behind you is a grandmother,
>   Things may not be as then.' (*Complete Poems*, pp. 87-88)

VII

This chapter, then, has explored how music serves in Hardy's poems to reawaken the values and pleasures associated with the past, conceived of as a time when self-expression was more natural and communal. Hardy's imagination is gripped by several main forms of temporal dislocation: the alienation brought about by historical change and social mobility; the self-exile associated with ambition; the sense of loss associated with love, death and age. In each case, within a poem music simplifies what is complex and oppressive in the present state of affairs, producing affects which link one back to what are conceived of as more innocent times. In numerous poems, we have seen, music has this power to off-set the present, reanimating the lost world of the past and the immemorial ideality of the soul itself. While no-one would deny that Hardy's poems are, in the last analysis, ironic meditations on transience, it also remains true that they are also celebrations of these revisitings and invocations, these instances of counter-times that complicate chronology and reveal the true intricacies of temporality and experience.

If individuality can overcome time in these respects, so too, in a further sense art is, for Hardy a way in which individuality can be passed on, and can function outside of the life of the artist himself. For all his preoccupation with loss, it has been argued that his poetry is motivated by this belief in the connective, individuating, function of art. In poem after poem, musical experience focuses Hardy's fascination with the counter-reality of art as a transmission of relatedness by other means. For all that Hardy is the great poet of transience and death, he subscribes through the very practice of his art to the poet's own impulse *as* poet to overcome time, and to use poetry as a means of survival, of living on, in and through the reader who responds to his work.

Notes

[1]   *Casebook*, p. 132.

[2]   Elna Sherman, 'Music in Thomas Hardy's Life and Work', *The Musical Quarterly*, Vol. XXVI, no. 4 (1940), p. 421.

[3]   See, for instance, F. B. Pinion, *A Hardy Companion* (London: Macmillan, 1968), pp. 187-88.

[4]   B. E. Maidment, 'Hardy's Fiction and English Traditional Music', *Thomas Hardy Annual*, No. 4 (1986), p. 7.

[5]   This heartfelt regret is articulated in the following extract, from the second of the two paragraphs which Hardy added in 1912 to the Preface of 1896:

> In rereading the narrative after a long interval there occurs the inevitable reflection that the realities out of which it was spun were material for another kind of study of this little group of church musicians than is found in the chapters here penned so lightly, even so farcically and flippantly at times. But circumstances would have rendered any aim at a deeper, more essential, more transcendent handling unadvisable at the date of writing; and the exhibition of the Mellstock Quire in the following pages must remain the only extant one, except for the few glimpses of that perished band which I have given in verse elsewhere. (*Under the Greenwood Tree*, pp. 28-29).

It is interesting here to note a similar qualification in the preface to *The Hand of Ethelberta*, where Hardy appears to regret elements of the satirical treatment of the Chickerel family:

> The artificial treatment perceptible in many of the pages was adopted for reasons that seemed good at the date of writing for a story of that class, and has not been changed. (*The Hand of Ethelberta*, p. 32)

[6]   Thomas Hardy, *General Preface to the Novels and Poems*, Wessex Edition, I, 1912, in *Thomas Hardy's Personal Writings* (edited by Harold Orel, Lawrence: University of Kansas Press, 1966), p. 46.

[7]   Ruth Firor, *Folkways in Thomas Hardy* (Philadelphia: University of Pennsylvania Press, 1931).

[8]   Arkans has also suggested the loss of the connections of family and local history is a factor accounting for the fact that the undertones of the ballad tradition in Hardy's poetry have become muted for us:

> contemporary readers seemed to hear in Hardy's verse something we have not heard to the same extent: the presence of ancestral voices descended from more primitive, bardic voices spinning yarns, singing tales, weaving stories about plaintive lovers, mismatched couples, unfortunate wrongdoers, or supernatural visitants. ('Hardy's Narrative Muse and the Ballad Connection', *Thomas Hardy Annual*, No. 2 [1984], p. 134)

Similarly, Michael Pollard, among others, has commented that:

> Hardy knew country music when it was a reality in people's lives [...] But it is a matter of regret that we have only the teasing echoes of the musical culture that filled such an important place in the store of Hardy's literary and personal resources. ('Thomas Hardy & Folk Music', *The Thomas Hardy Journal*, Vol. VIII, no. 1 [1992], p. 44)

⁹ Once again this strand in Hardy's writing is compellingly close to a strand in Proust's thought. Often for Hardy the substance of the soul, like that of the body, appears composed out of ancestral material, so that the souls of our ancestors populate our own, and can be revived within us, by a form of extra-personal family-memory. This kind of virtual connection and spiritual continuity, as bearing on unlived experience, would still be real at the level of affect. If our epistemology might struggle with such a sense of spiritual connection and transfer, the idea is in another way simply connected with common kinds of childhood experience (and with superstition, which was for Freud, of course, a residual trace of cultural infancy). It is common, for instance, for music to lead the young in particular to have what we might call affects, or visions, or projections, of a past that is felt in this way as compellingly, hauntingly, uncannily, real, yet which pre-dates them. Fanciful as this common feeling might be when one tries to articulate it, it remains obviously true that Hardy is recurrently fascinated by such a paradoxical access to family history, social history, and national history, and all its manifestations. In the following chapter, in relation to a discussion of Bergson's concept of duration, I have cited a passage from a letter that is also of relevance in this different context:

> 'You must not think me a hard-hearted rationalist for all this. Half my time - particularly when writing verse - I "believe" (in the modern sense of the word) not only in the things Bergson believes in, but in spectres, mysterious voices, intuitions, omens, dreams, haunted places, etc., etc.' (*Life*, pp. 369-70)

¹⁰ Ernest Brennecke, Jr., *The Life of Thomas Hardy* (New York: Haskell House, 1973), p. 5.

¹¹ The poem bears on the incident discussed in the *Life* and the introduction above, where the woman sang 'Should he Upbraid!', one of Hardy's favourite songs.

¹² We can imagine Hardy towards the end of his life reading Proust's marvellous description of this:

> I feel that there is much to be said for the Celtic belief that the souls of those whom we have lost are held captive in some inferior being, in an animal, in a plant, in some inanimate object, and thus effectively lost to us until the day (which to many never comes) when we happen to pass by the tree or to obtain possession of the object which forms their prison. Then they start and tremble, they call us by our name, and as soon as we have recognised their voice the spell is broken. Delivered by us, they have overcome death and return to share our life.
>
> And so it is with our own past. It is a labour in vain to attempt to recapture it: all the efforts of our intellect must prove futile. The past is hidden somewhere outside the realm, beyond the reach of intellect, in some material object (in the sensation which the material object will give us) of which we have no inkling. And it depends on chance whether or not we come upon this object before we ourselves must die. (Marcel

Proust, *Rememberance of Things Past*, trans. C. K. Scott Moncrieff and T. Kilmartin; and A. Mayor, London: Penguin, 1989, I, pp. 47-48)

[13] A comparison with Wordsworth or Blake suggests itself, whereby music can work as a means for reconnecting the individual, if only fleetingly, with an abiding innocence, which transcends the phases and habits of chronological ageing. 'The Self-Unseeing' in this connection could be called Hardy's 'My Heart Leaps Up'.

[14] P. E. Mitchell argues that Hardy's use of musical topics and his employment of the effects of ballad and folk-song help him affirm a secular evaluation of life, based on the continuities of these communal art forms:

> While it can be argued, therefore, that Hardy could not justify and systematize his values by reference to traditional notions of transcendental order and harmony, he could and did possess a range of values that are given significance by reference to the impersonal, enduring idea of community extended in history and transcending the individual "human span of durance". ('Music and Hardy's Poetry', p. 319)

[15] As always in this book, the soul is understood as a power of self-differentiation which manifests itself expressively through its relations.

[16] See Peter Widdowson, *Thomas Hardy: Selected Poetry and Non-Fictional Prose*.

[17] Andrew Bennett and Nicholas Royle, *An Introduction to Literature, Theory, Practice* (Hemel Hempstead: Harvester, 1995), p. 68.

Chapter 5

'Let Every Man Make a Philosophy for Himself out of His Own Experience'

Robert Gittings observed how Hardy's 'lifelong self-discipline in reading and note-taking' became more and more orientated towards 'poetry and to theories of how to write poems', and towards philosophy, so that 'extracts from Schopenhauer, Haeckel, and von Hartmann are prominent'. From the 1880s onwards these preoccupations are reflected intensively in the notebooks. Gittings even concludes that Hardy's 'intellectual life seemed to burn brighter as his body grew feebler'.[1] This chapter sets out to consolidate the book's central emphases, but by revisiting them in a different context - through a concentration on what emerges from studying Hardy's reading of writers such as Schopenhauer, von Hartmann, Bergson, and William James. Above all, the aim is to note the points of contact between his work and the work of these philosophical writers who increasingly fascinated him. However, the question is not in what ways did the work of each influence him, but in what ways did it attract him? What were the continuities between his work and theirs, and what light can these correlations throw on our conception of his work?

That is to say, the chapter is a study of intellectual affinities and curiosities, not of intellectual debts. In terms of the ideas, we have seen in previous chapters how music allows Hardy the artist to engage with a host of interrelated issues of interest to the philosopher - issues of temporality, individuality, aesthetic experience, community, affectivity, corporeality, memory, the spirit. What will be of interest in reading the philosophy that Hardy read will be to see some of the ways in which the explicit metaphysical investigations undertaken by the philosophers (often interestingly entwined with musical terminology and concepts) corresponded to Hardy's own literary ways of staging ethical and epistemological questions. The aim is to come full circle, using this foray into Hardy's reading to establish a further context for considering his writing, and its uses of music. Further, it is also incidentally interesting to note how music provides a strategic access to the work of these writers. Music as idea, experience, and metaphor, is important for Bergson, James and von Hartmann, as well as for Schopenhauer and Nietzsche.

I

To begin with, though, there would clearly be many reasons why we might suspect attempts to establish Hardy's intellectual dependence on these major thinkers, or to draw other kinds of straight-line connection between his work and theirs.[2] As Millgate points out:

> Edmund Gosse told an inquiring scholar in 1909 that Hardy did 'not admit any influence from Schopenhauer on his work'. He went on: 'The ideas which have animated Mr Hardy's books were already present in his mind and conversation, and were the result of temperament and observation, rather than of "influence"'.
> (*Thomas Hardy: A Biography*, p. 199)

William R. Rutland made similar points in 1938, demonstrating that Hardy 'did not read Schopenhauer until he was over forty'.[3] Nor does it seem that he could have read von Hartmann until he was over fifty, or James, Nietzsche or Bergson until he was older still. Indubitably, Rutland is correct also to criticize the critical genre (burgeoning up until 1938) which sought to expound Hardy's work in terms of the various kinds of master-discourse offered by the work of philosophers like these. Moreover, Rutland argues persuasively that Hardy's most abiding intellectual debts were not to continental or American figures but to earlier, English writers, to Charles Darwin, John Stuart Mill, Herbert Spencer, Leslie Stephen, and Thomas Huxley.

Nevertheless, it is also arguable that the distinctions between these British figures and their later translated or transatlantic counterparts are less important than the similarities. Rutland cites C. C. J. Webb's comments about the philosophical climate in which Hardy grew up in the 1850s and 1860s, identifying its crucial ingredient as the concept of evolution:

> Regarded as the enunciation of a principle valid throughout the Universe, it [evolution] seemed, at any rate to some minds, to explain by processes going on *within* the universe what it had previously been commonly maintained that an intelligent Power *beyond* and *above* the Universe was required to account for. If this use of the idea of evolution was to be reconciled with religion at

all, it must plainly be by some doctrine of divine *immanence*, which should replace an instantaneous operation of *transcendent* divine power [...] Moreover, if the world process were thus to be conceived after the analysis of the known facts of organic life, it would almost inevitably follow that individual members of any species, and therefore individual human beings among the rest, would come to be envisaged rather as transitory embodiments of relatively abiding types than as themselves supremely important realities for the sake of which the whole process exists.[4]

The main emphases of this passage - on contingency, change, materiality, and on those evolutionary principles by which emerges what Rutland calls 'the production of conscious mind by unconscious processes' (*Critical Assessments*, Vol. 4, p. 277): these are not only common to Darwin, Mill and Spencer, but are also central to the work of Bergson, Schopenhauer, James and von Hartmann. Similarly and crucially, each of these writers is concerned with the crucial task, identified in the passage, of thinking about the limits and possibilities of individuality and community in a world deprived of a corresponding transcendent realm and purpose.

The particular question persists though: what did Hardy read these writers for, and with such industry? Gosse's comments quoted earlier have the virtue of stressing that Hardy was intellectually a self-starter in the sense that he was possessed of an original intelligence, as well as of a genuine and compelling interest in issues of philosophy and science. This is important given the familiar red-herring that sees Hardy's reading simply as 'autodidacticism', or as an aspirational activity fuelled mostly by social self-doubt and insecurity about his general education. While it is true that Hardy did seem to envy (as well as wryly evaluate) the synoptic outpourings of the trained philosophers and men of letters, Gosse highlights what is characteristically different about Hardy's way of thinking: that he was temperamentally given to 'observation' rather than to 'influence', and to incidental acts of articulation rather than to *a priori* prescriptions and system-building. Presumably, this very mental difference was an important factor in Hardy's continuing to read writers who possessed the elevation of tone, the argumentative consistency and scope, that he admired but did not share. To simplify, one could say that Hardy's mind was untheoretical, so long as one adds, as I did earlier, that it was also highly philosophical and individual. He generated ideas and insights not out of logic and precept, but out of the materials of 'temperament and observation'.

Gosse's remarks, then, suggestively allow for a description of Hardy's thought as both exact in its details, but also piecemeal and provisional, and tending to reject general syntheses. Certainly, Hardy's distrust of closed systems is evident in his repeated disavowal that he possessed a system of his own, as in the often exasperated prefaces. Moreover, as Rutland put it, he was one of those philosophical artists, for whom 'arguments continued by the mind' were nonetheless 'apt to be initiated by the heart' (*Critical Assessments*, Vol. 4, p. 263). However, he did possess the keenest sense of philosophical imperatives. In 1901 he jotted:

> After reading various philosophic systems, and being struck with their contradictions and futilities, I have come to this: *Let every man make a philosophy for himself out of his own experience.* (*Life* p. 310)

Read literal-mindedly, this remark suggests a predisposition to empiricism. Hardy's poems and fiction were seen recurrently to work through sensory scenes where the mind finds itself in the middle of things. Empiricism's emphases on the priority of sensory experience and the secondariness of reflexive subjectivity are obviously consonant with the materiality of such a practice and drama. According to this general model, too, Hardy's relation to these other writers can be construed not, as Gosse says, as one of 'influence', but more as one of response and interlocution, more as a matter of finding confirmation and stimulation for one's own thinking in another person's.

For these reasons, it is obviously important to insist on the differences of tone and method between Hardy's intellectual outlook and those of the thinkers that he read as he grew older. As well, though, it is interesting to trace the incidental continuities with types of aesthetic, metaphysical and social speculation which were in concert with his own, and which appealed to him. It has been suggested that one such thinker who becomes interesting to us in these respects, is Henri Bergson, to whose work Hardy was to be drawn in his seventies. Now, once again, it is possible to downplay this connection, and there are reasons to be cautious.[5] Yet a brief discussion of Bergson does indicate real associations between his metaphysics and the affirmative metaphysics which I have been attempting to tease out through this book, as a necessary and underlying component in Hardy's fiction and poetry. For instance, in *The Two Sources of Morality and Religion*, Bergson wrote some suggestive passages about the unpredictable and collective aspects of musical emotion. Music has a transcendent power, as the listeners are worked over by what it expresses to them:

We feel, while we listen, as though we could not desire anything else but what the music is suggesting to us, and that this is just as we should naturally and necessarily act did we refrain from action to listen. Let the music express joy or grief, pity or love, every moment we are what it expresses. Not only ourselves, but many others, too. When music weeps, all humanity, all nature weeps with it. In point of fact it does not introduce these feelings into us; it introduces us into them, as passers-by are forced into a street dance.[6]

Music goes between and beyond different people, who are 'forced' by it into an essentially involuntary response, and introduced into 'what it expresses'. Reflecting on the actual motions of dance, as Bergson describes it, one can see in the creative values and collocations of such undivided movements, some of the main preoccupations of Bergson's metaphysics, as it sought to develop its critique of rationalism as a philosophy dedicated, conversely, to the ordering of experience and knowledge according to the divisible, momentary, logic of space and the self-reflexive subject. Likewise, for the Bergson of *Creative Evolution* (a text which Hardy was to enjoy, though not wholly uncritically), life itself, as evolution, is seen to follow such quasi-musical principles. Life is a mobile cosmic inspiration, a process of becoming, out of whose endless passages and modulations definite and closed forms are produced, before these too evolve and mutate again in their turn. Stability of identity, at the level of species, for instance, is only relative to such movements and transformations. This is analogous to the way, in the quotation, that the closed solitudes of the various listeners were broken for a time by their introduction, by music, into an altered and collective state.

These comments reiterate why duration is a key concept for Bergson. It is a mode of time which affects everything, opening up closed orders of being to changes in which inherent, perhaps undisclosed, characteristics, qualities and traits become actualized and intuited as new relationships are established. Out of the patterns of resonance, vibration and rhythm which play between them the elements of the physical world are unformed and reformed, introduced into destructive and creative intervals of indetermination or becoming. In *The Two Sources of Morality and Religion*, Bergson identifies this metaphysics of emergence and conductivity at the level of artistic inspiration with an emotion 'capable of crystallising into representations' (*Two Sources*, p. 47). At the same time, the generative processes and affective properties of this creative activity cannot be identified with the objective features of the art-work. Interpretation, insofar as it deals in the representative content of a work, short-changes this important expressive and individual dimension. What is important is that out of such vital affective sources the artistic sensibility, for Bergson, becomes the origin for new, infectious types of thought and feeling available to others:

> [T]he emotion excited within us by a great dramatic work is of quite a distinct character. Unique of its kind, it has sprung up in the soul of the poet and there alone, before stirring our own. (*Two Sources*, p. 47)

Describing how 'each new musical work brings with it new feelings', Bergson writes of how a new piece's distinctive grammar of sound, and the feelings which it creates, are not 'extracted from life by art' according to some principle of resemblance or artistic precedent (*Two Sources*, p. 41). Instead, the artist essentially creates a new and individuating affect, as in Bergson's description of another, non-musical, case. Pursuing a musical metaphor nonetheless, Bergson relates how Rousseau invented a new style of responding to nature, a new emotion for mountains:[7]

> But Rousseau created in connection with them a new and original emotion [...] True, there are reasons why this emotion, sprung from the heart of Jean-Jacques, should fasten on to mountains rather than any other object; the elementary feelings, akin to sensations, which were directly aroused by mountains must have been able to harmonize with the new emotion. But Rousseau gathered them together, gave them their places, henceforth as new harmonics in a sound for which he provided, by a true creation, the principal tone. (*Two Sources*, p. 41)

In a broad way, then, there are illuminating correspondences between these features of Bergson's work and those general issues of thought and emotion, community and memory, that have been identified in Hardy's writing. Specifically, the operative Bergsonian notions discussed here (of movement, of collective emotion, of expression, originality, creativity, duration, life, and the specific emphasis on literary art as an affective relation of 'souls') are consonant with the themes and methods of Hardy's work described so far. To this degree, the explicit philosophical articulations of Bergson function as a sort of developing reagent, so that one can clearly see innate philosophical characteristics of Hardy's own work. Where Hardy's writing draws in literature on affects, sensations, and kinds of indetermination which overturn the normative logic of the subject, so

Bergson operated with conceptual equivalents to diagnose the rationalist architectonic which he saw as dominant in European thought.

Such a line of approach, of course, is selective in that it corresponds, as has been said, to the affirmative strains in Hardy's work. Nevertheless, it does indicate the nature of Hardy's originality, and make more comprehensible the reasoning behind Deleuze's identification of him as a writer whose work is distinguished by an essentially experimental thought. In a more general way, Deleuze identified this experimentalism with English novelists who, like Hardy, are seen as capable of 'philosophizing as a novelist, of being a novelist in philosophy' (*Dialogues*, p. 55). This involves the novelist in producing distinctive affects, corresponding to the distinctive potentials of thought which it is his task also to phrase and contemplate:

> The writer twists language, making it vibrate, seizes hold of it, and rends it in order to wrest the percept from perceptions, the affect from affections, the sensation from opinion. (*What is Philosophy?*, p. 176)

These emphases allow for an articulation of the ways in which literary writing can be comprehended as, like philosophy, a creative thinking. Where the philosopher invents new concepts, the writer's thought produces new truths, new possibilities, of perception and emotion. Proust makes a point about these individuating possibilities of art in a passage which is close to Bergson's earlier comments about Rousseau:

> [...] the world around us (which was not created once and for all, but is created afresh as often as an original artist is born) appears to us entirely different from the old world, but perfectly clear. Women pass in the street, different from those we formerly saw, because they are Renoirs [...] The carriages, too, are Renoirs, and the water, and the sky [...] Such is the new and perishable universe which has just been created. It will last until the next geological catastrophe is precipitated by a new painter or writer of original talent. (*Remembrance of Things Past*, Vol. 2, pp. 338-39)

In this context of parallel enterprises, Hardy's own thoughts about Bergson are important, though not overriding. Interestingly, his comments are both enthusiastic and cautionary, as in the letter to Dr Saleeby of 16 March 1915:

> I am returning, or shall be in a day or two, your volume of Bergson. It is most interesting reading, and one likes to give way to

> its views and assurances without criticizing them [...] But the most
> fatal objection to his view of creation plus propulsion seems to me
> to lie in the creation of pain. If nature were creative she would
> have created painlessness. (*Life*, p. 451)

Noting this familiar division in attitude allows me to draw together
threads which run through this entire book. Even in this brief
discussion, one can see the sense in which it is true for Bergson and
Deleuze, as for Hardy, that the value of individuality is articulated by
means of a division between the conscious self and the soul.
Individuality, we have argued, is for Hardy a function of the soul,
involuntarily revealed and provoked through events that go beyond the
self's powers of choice and understanding, if not its powers of
unconscious thought and response. To use the word 'provoke' here is to
suggest, once again, that individuation is an effect of the writing for the
reader who is (like Bergson's passer-by at the dance) 'introduced' by the
work into a distinctive and collective region of feeling. For Deleuze, too,
individuality would be expressed for writer, reader and character, from
such dynamic and unformed moments, and would not necessarily
accord with hitherto recognized or predictable traits:

> Individuality is not a characteristic of the Self but, on the contrary,
> forms and sustains the system of the dissolved Self.[8]

Similarly, in the notebooks, there are many points where Hardy
ponders on the involuntary movements and expressive moments in
writing, on what he calls the 'artist's duty to perpetuate... fugitive
perfections' (*Literary Notebooks*, Vol. 2, p. 36). Ceaselessly, he meditates
on his own or other writers' formulations of how literature can seek to
capture and engage such powers of unconscious thought and feeling. In
the following example, he cites Lafenestre's notion that art conveys
highly individualized affects and viewpoints:

> One cannot repeat too often that what makes the work of art is the
> force of the sentiment that an individual fixes in it, & eternizes in
> it; nature is only the arsenal, always open, where he goes to look
> for his means of expression. (*Literary Notebooks*, Vol. 2, p. 11)

Or, in Volume 1, he quotes from de Quincey's comments on style an
insight that is highly applicable to his own practice of writing liminal
and truant impressions:

The skill with which detention or conscious arrest is given to the evanescent, external projection to what is internal, <u>outline to what is fluxionary</u> & body to what is vague ... depends on the command over language. (*Literary Notebooks,* Vol. 1, p. 88)

Bergson's philosophically explicit analysis of what Deleuze calls the 'system of the dissolved self', then, allows us to emphasize the ways in which Hardy also interrogates something similar. Undoubtedly, Hardy's own resistance to dialectical and intellectualist modes of thought would have chimed with such themes in Bergson. More broadly, in his use of the topic of music, Bergson can be linked with some of the other influential thinkers who Hardy was reading, or reading about, at the turn of the century, writers like Schopenhauer, von Hartmann, Pater and Nietzsche. For all their obvious differences of temper and perspective, each placed music at the heart of their metaphysical and aesthetic speculations, of their interrogation of social morality and convention, and of their connecting up of feeling and subjectivity. Music was integral to their questioning of how secular life could find value and meaning, and what contribution artistic experience and pleasure might make to this. The rest of this chapter surveys some of the connections and differences between Hardy and some of these writers.

II

In his careful reading of von Hartmann's *Philosophy of the Unconscious,* Hardy would have found a systematic conception of the unconscious mind that again can be put alongside his own literary practice. For von Hartmann, the unconscious intelligence had instinctual purposes and social functions that far outstrip the conscious mind's capacity to comprehend or control them. The book begins with a quotation from Kant, *'To have ideas, and yet not be conscious of them'*, to whose paradoxical import the whole work can be seen as a response.[9] Von Hartmann's elucidation of such unconscious ideas is interestingly dependent on musical analogies, the mind seen as dependent on the sensitivities of the body. The nerves vibrate like strings in a harmonic responsiveness with the stimulus they receive, producing ideation as a function (in the last analysis) of 'cerebral vibrations', physical resonances (*Philosophy of the Unconscious*, Vol. I, p. 346):

> it is not difficult to see that the so-called slumbering ideas of memory are not ideas *in actu*, in activity, but merely *dispositions* of the brain facilitating the revival of ideas. As a string, when caused to sound by aerial vibrations, always yields the same note A or C, for instance, if it be attuned to A or C; so does one or another idea arise more easily in the brain, according as the distribution and tension of the cerebral molecules induces a more ready response with one or another kind of vibrations on an appropriate stimulus [...] still such an arrangement of passive material molecules, favouring the genesis of certain ideas, cannot be termed *Ideation*, albeit it may, according to circumstances, co-operate as condition in the production of an idea, and, indeed, of a conscious idea. (*Philosophy of the Unconscious*, Vol. I, p. 33-34)

Ideation emerges from sensation by virtue of quasi-musical laws, by which the unconscious extracts from the infinitesimal elements of response a transcendent quality and continuity of perception. The building up of mind as a resonating system in this way provides von Hartmann with an image of co-operation and participation, of synthesis and combination, which has correlative manifestations in the political, and even mystical, moments of his philosophy (a philosophy encyclopaedic in intent as it is, bearing also on evolution and anthropology). Music, or vibration, can be seen as a kind of master-figure at important moments in his work, for the thinking out of how the material and spiritual are to be brought together:

> as in a string caused to move sympathetically by a resonant note, every single vibration taken alone accomplishes too little, and [... we see] that only the effects of many similar vibrations gradually added can gain a perceptible influence which arises above the threshold of stimulation. (*Philosophy of the Unconscious*, Vol. I, p. 347)

A kind of musical principle, that is, appears as the means of unity in difference of sensations, as the physical basis of thought and consciousness itself. The nervous system is like a stringed instrument, producing effective sensory aggregates out of the minute but euphonious resoundings of its parts. A citation from Schelling earlier in von Hartmann's book is a useful way of pulling together some of these ideas:

> 'We see indeed daily [...] the *unconscious*, how the soul without consciousness guides the fingers according to the laws of harmony, whilst it incites consciousness to new relations and actions. When

we behold the complicated relations of muscle and nerve, we are astonished at contractions and pressures of the most delicate kind without conscious volition'. (*Philosophy of the Unconscious*, Vol. 1, p. 27)

Music offers a model or metaphor for the operations and creativity of the unconscious intelligence. The body is like an aeolian harp: the 'soul without consciousness' expresses itself in more or less fortuitous ways, depending on the interactions of the individual sensibility and environment.[10] Thought is firmly conceived of as engendered out of accident and sensibility, and self-consciousness is conceived of as a laggardly function of representation.

In short, von Hartmann explores systematically, and over three volumes and its various addenda, a line of thought which would have been familiar to Hardy from his reading of Mill's *Essays on Religion*, dating from the late 1860s, in which Mill briskly sketches the conceptual distinctions necessary to such a materialist notion of the evolution of consciousness:

> The assertion is that physical nature must have been produced by a will because nothing but will is known to us as having the power of originating the production of phenomena.... That nothing can *consciously* produce Mind but Mind is self-evident, being involved in the meaning of the words; but that there cannot be *unconscious* production cannot be assumed.[11]

Further, von Hartmann's work, in developing so rigorously a materialist notion of nature as a domain of unconscious physical desire, came to be identified with what was often described as nineteenth-century philosophical pessimism, and thereby with Schopenhauer's work, in particular. In this latter case, it is famously the case that music retains a peculiar privilege in his metaphysics. Schopenhauer's world is driven by pitiless unconscious forces (as in Hardy's similar, derived concept of 'immanent Will', [*The Dynasts*, p. 2]), and he generalizes this automatic, self-preserving, activity of animal desire into a cosmic principle which he calls 'Will'. Opposed to this is the world of conscious experience, of phenomenal appearance. This is the domain of experience amenable to conceptual or pictorial representation and to rational discourse. However, the instances of subjectivity which emerge here can never be distinguished from the seething contaminants of unconscious desire which compass and condition them. (Unsurprisingly, Freud and Nietzsche recognized in Schopenhauer a great precursor.)

Specifically, music is famously of fundamental importance for Schopenhauer insofar as it offers human beings an emancipation from the bonds of desire, of Will. It is able to do this because it alone can express Will adequately, and so offer a measure of aesthetic distance and ascetic detachment from it. Music, as a non-representational art, provides a sonic image for the strivings and violence of the Will itself, and the inherent affects of joy and sorrow. He writes of a Beethoven symphony that:

> It is *rerum concordia discors*, a true and complete picture of the nature of the world, which rolls on in the boundless confusion of innumerable forms, and maintains itself by constant destruction. But at the same time, all the human passions and emotions speak from this symphony: joy, grief, love, hatred, terror, hope, and so on in innumerable shades, yet all, as it were, only in the abstract and without any particularization; it is their mere form without the material, like a mere spirit world without matter.[12]

As we listen to music, we both confront and renounce the 'real and true nature', the 'innermost soul', of the world. Music 'is able to express every movement of the will, every feeling', and in so doing redeems us from it, purgatively confronting us with what Schopenhauer tends to see as the true pathos and absurdity of our enthralment by the illusions of subjectivity (*The World as Will and Representation*, Vol. 2, p. 449).

A more extended discussion could follow up the connections of Schopenhauer's ideas with those of other post-Kantian thinkers who employ music as a means and figure for the bridging of the domains of representation and ideality.[13] But what of Hardy's connection to Schopenhauer's work? To begin with, there are explicit connections between his ideas and the pessimistic 'philosophy' which many critics have identified in Hardy? In particular, there is Hardy's notion of the 'immanent will', that 'viewless, voiceless Turner of the Wheel' which works the universe, to no discernible purpose, like a giant kaleidoscope.[14] In the words of the 'Spirit of the Years', it:

> works unconsciously, as heretofore,
> Eternal artistries in Circumstance.
> Whose patterns, wrought by rapt aesthetic rote,
> Seem in themselves Its single listless aim. (*The Dynasts*, p. 1)

Without forethought or afterthought, the immanent will produces endless effects of patterning:

In the Foretime, even to the germ of Being,
Nothing appears of shape to indicate
That cognizance has marshalled things terrene,
Or will (such is my thinking) in my span.
Rather they show that, like a knitter drowsed.
Whose fingers play in skilled unmindfulness,
The Will has woven with an absent heed
Since life first was; and ever will so weave. (*The Dynasts*, p. 2)

The thought behind the universe is likened to that of an absent-minded or dozy knitter rather than a creative genius: or, to vary the metaphor, to that of a mindless cosmic doodler rather than a divine architect. Forms succeed each other and are productive of suffering and pleasure, but they do not reveal divine intention.[15] This Schopenhauerian conception of the play of forces underlying the universe obviously has more affinity with Nietzsche's dice-thrower than with Kant's watchmaker.

Further, it is true that there are often Schopenhauerian strands in many of Hardy's own aesthetic pronouncements:

The "simply natural" is interesting no longer. The much decried, mad, late-Turner rendering is now necessary to create my interest. The exact truth as to material fact ceases to be of importance in art - it is a student's style - the style of a period when the mind is serene and unawakened to the tragical mysteries of life; when it does not bring anything to the object that coalesces with and translates the qualities that are already there, - half-hidden, it may be - and the two united are depicted as the All. (*Life*, p. 185)

The function of art or literature can be seen as approximating to that which Schopenhauer identified with music, bridging expressively the phenomenal and the noumenal, and embodying the 'tragic mysteries' of life and a sense of 'the All'.

However, it is vitally important not to misconstrue the incidental alignments that can be made between certain strains in Hardy's work, or certain aspects of his temperament, with the work of writers and philosophers like Schopenhauer or von Hartmann. In the first place, the values of a self-elevating philosophical renunciation which Schopenhauer identifies with musical experience are alien to Hardy's ecstatic and socially situated sense of music. The pleasures of music offer not so much a reprieve from the bonds of unconscious desire for Hardy, as an involuntary and transporting experience of it. Music is about feeling, and the possibilities of desire. It is an expression of an enthusiasm for life, not of a world-weary desire for emancipation from it. The testimony of J. Vera Mardon's conveys this sense that music for Hardy was linked not to an escape from individuality but to a lifelong modification and expression of it. She describes many instances of his characteristic powers of recall:

> In the production of *The Mellstock Quire* old country dances were performed and Hardy helped the cast by lending copies of his old manuscript scores and he wrote down particulars of the figures to be danced. In 1918 at a rehearsal at which I was present with my father, Hardy was most dissatisfied with the evolutions of the dancers in the dance "The Triumph". He took a lady as his partner and then, despite his age (77), he nimbly demonstrated to the assembled company the correct steps and positions. Nor was the musical accompaniment, provided by one violin, to his liking. He was displeased with the tempo, and borrowing the violin he played in a lively manner all the required tunes from memory. He was what we should now call a perfectionist. Everything had to be as he wanted it to be - correct to the smallest detail.[16]

It might be said that Hardy consciously was something of a cosmic pessimist, but was, when he forgot himself, an inveterate vitalist. Margaret Elvy would go further, saying that 'Hardy can [even] be seen as ultimately an optimist', though one who:

> tries to look honestly and clearly at life - to go after the 'offensive truth'. His pessimism is really 'evolutionary meliorism' [...] He is an optimist blasted by life's shocks into a bitter realism.[17]

In 1922, in the 'Apology' to *Late Lyrics*, Hardy described himself as one who, albeit 'forlornly', continued to 'hope' for human advancement, 'notwithstanding the supercilious disregard of hope by Schopenhauer, von Hartmann, and other philosophers down to Einstein who have my respect' (*Complete Poems*, p. 562). He certainly appeared bemused to have been categorized in this latter way himself. In the 'Introductory Note' to *Winter Words* we read:

> My last volume of poems was pronounced wholly gloomy and pessimistic by reviewers - even by some of the more able class. My sense of the oddity of this verdict may be imagined when, in selecting them, I had been, as I thought, rather too liberal in admitting flippant, not to say farcical, pieces into the collection. (*Complete Poems*, p. 834)

Once again, it is important to mention Hardy's repeated claims that his work did not attempt a systematic or 'harmonious philosophy'. In this connection, we may remember C. Day Lewis's apposite words:

> What critics called his philosophical tenets were, he said, only 'impressions' or rationalizations of moods. He vigorously disclaimed the title of pessimist, preferring to be thought of as a meliorist, and showing in his idea of an emergent consciousness in the universe a certain affinity with the doctrine of Emergent Evolution. ('The Lyrical Poetry of Thomas Hardy', p. 163)

Relatively early poems like 'Nature's Questioning' in fact, though, show a versatility and compression of reflection that many a philosopher might envy. The poetic voice ponders variously whether nature is a product of 'some Vast Imbecility', or of 'an Automaton', or of a 'Godhead' fallen on bad times, or of an incomprehensible 'high plan' of Good. Ultimately, the poem is proof against such inevitable speculations, and the final stanza concludes in unknowing:

> Thus things around. No answerer I...
>   Meanwhile the winds, and rains,
>   And Earth's old glooms and pains
> Are still the same, and Life and Death are neighbours nigh.
> (*Complete Poems*, p. 67)

Such a watchful and questioning reticence, shaping and multiplying speculations while withdrawing from any endorsement of them, brings to mind John Bayley's remark that Hardy's mind was 'stubbornly unsynthesising', as in his imaginings of God:

> As an external personality - that was indeed for Hardy the only true meaning of the word, God must exist, if he exists at all, in the same absolute and indifferent sense as the thrush and the winter's day, the years, the separate fields [...]
> In the history of lost faith Hardy has a unique place. Right up to our time he has been patronised, it seems to me, for his inability to do what most other artists and thinkers, who lost theirs, did: intellectualise, moralise, build new theologies [...] He could not substitute 'grounds of being', or George Eliot's humanistic idealism, Bergson's vitalism, the pragmatism of William James, the rational hedonism and 'states of mind' of G. E. Moore and Bloomsbury. (*An Essay on Hardy*, p. 45)

Similarly, Rutland emphasizes how this speculative modesty or limitation on Hardy's part would have found its correlative in his reading as a young man of Herbert Spencer's *First Principles*, in which he would have come across the argumentative demonstration that any power informing the universe was necessarily 'inscrutable' and incomprehensible (*Critical Assessments*, Vol. 4, p. 269).

III

While accepting Bayley's point about Hardy's refusal of philosophy's answers to life's questions, it is still illuminating to reflect on the appeal that the work of Bergson and William James might have had for Hardy at points, based, as their work is, on the refusal of rationalism and on the affirmation of the sensible. For instance, in *A Pluralistic Universe*, a collection of Manchester College lectures (which Hardy read not long after they were published in 1909 as a *A Pluralistic Universe*), James scorned the notion that thought could begin outside the material and temporal stuff of bodily experience and emotion. In this connection James offered, as well as a form of empiricism, a bravura puncturing of alternative views, as with his assault on T. H. Green's neo-Kantian account of the transcendental subject. Green's conception is seen as misreading the unified and concerted acts of the mind in conscious experience for the acts of an essentially unified and concerted mind. This illusory mind precedes experience, confident of its own self-knowability:

> If we open Green, we get nothing but the transcendental ego of apperception (Kant's name for the fact that to be counted in experience a thing has to be witnessed), blown up into a sort of soap bubble large enough to mirror the whole universe. Nature, Green keeps insisting, consists only in relations, and these imply the action of a mind that is eternal; a self-distinguishing consciousness which itself escapes from the relations by which it determines other things. Present to whatever is in succession, it is not in succession itself.[18]

Against this for James (as we can say for Hardy too), the mind is not a distinct and coherent entity outside of time and place, but is tied to the body and its local environment. In this vein, throughout *A Pluralistic Universe* James is wonderfully scathing about Kant's notion of the subject, and its philosophical legacy in 'thin' conceptions, obscure formulations, and dialectical dodges. James opposes to these things the work of Fechner and Bergson, above all, work which calls 'upon you to look towards the sensational life for the fuller knowledge of reality', and which offers the means for a critique of the presumptions of abstract intellectual thought. For James, Bergson allows philosophy to approach the 'essence of life', which is 'its continually changing character', a power of movement and qualitative alteration opposed to the artificial distinctions of the concept. Such thinkers as Bergson and Fechner become for James, accordingly, an inspiration for his own form of renovated empiricism or 'pluralism':

> Pragmatically interpreted, pluralism or the doctrine that it is many means only that the sundry parts of reality may be externally related. Everything you can think of, however vast or inclusive, has on the pluralistic view a genuinely 'external' environment. (*A Pluralistic Universe*, p. 321)

James's book is a highly engaging anti-rationalist *tour de force* which opposes, in terms explicitly indebted to Bergson, the fluctuating nature of life to the demarcated representations of it available to the identity logic of 'the reflective intellect' (*A Pluralistic Universe*, p. 347). Against such purely logically derived distortions of thought, the principles of the universe, in James's view, are those activities of interaction and becoming by which bodies are affected, and by which reflection is conditioned as a secondary activity of intelligence. Each body necessarily participates in an external environment, and in so doing alters and changes, becoming drawn up into small and multiple processes of change. The analogy between living beings and pieces of music was explicitly drawn by Bergson, as Deleuze and Guattari have indicated:

> According to Bergson, musical beings are like living beings that compensate for their individuating closure by an openness created by modulation, repetition, transposition, juxtaposition [...][19]

More accurately, perhaps, one should say that for Bergson (or Deleuze) this is an artifice intrinsic to the creative evolution of life itself, in its self-differentiating and multiple kinds of adaptation and formal variation. In such compoundings, the body contributes, destructively and productively, to that open-ended process which is the whole. In his more poetic moments, James identifies such cosmic processes as the moments and movements of an endless symphony. As with Bergsonian intuition, the immediate continuities and diversities of this temporal process demand a kind of thought opposed to the *a priori* dictates of pure logic, which shatter and reduce it.[20] Rationalism cannot account for the range of active and sensory ways in which human beings interact with each other and the world, the multiple and modulating aspects of their momentary experience, their antipathies and sympathies:

> Hasn't every bit of experience its quality, its duration, its extension, its urgency, its clearness, and many aspects besides, no one of which can exist in the isolation in which our verbalized logic keeps it? They exist only *durcheinander*. Reality always is, in M. Bergson's phrase, an enosis or conflux of the same with the different: they copenetrate and telescope [...] real life laughs at logic's veto. (*A Pluralistic Universe*, p. 257)

> Distinctions may be insulators in logic as much as they like, but in life distinct things can and do commune together every moment. (*A Pluralistic Universe*, p. 259)

James becomes lyrical when he likens Bergson's work to being 'like [...] the song of the birds' (*A Pluralistic Universe*, p. 265), or when he writes of the response which is characteristic of Bergsonians when they enter into their master's work. James's passage is wholly gripped by musical metaphors:

> They have understood in the fashion in which one loves, they have caught the whole melody and can therefore admire at their leisure the originality, the fecundity, and the imaginative genius with which its author develops, transposes, and varies in a thousand ways by the orchestration of his style and dialectic, the original theme. (*A Pluralistic Universe*, p. 266)

James's comments reiterate how Bergson's vitalism offered ways of unchaining our description of individuality from the limiting, formal, concepts of person and time available to merely analytical thought:

> Get at the expanding centre of a human character, the *élan vital* of a man, as Bergson calls it, by living sympathy, and at a stroke you see how it makes those who see it from without interpret it in such diverse ways. (*A Pluralistic Universe*, p. 262)

> Reality *falls* in passing into conceptual analysis; it *mounts* in living its own undivided life - it buds and burgeons, changes and creates [...] (*A Pluralistic Universe*, p. 264)

Of course, what could be said to be Bergson's great contribution to philosophy - his thinking of the undivided movement of duration - would have been evident to Hardy in his reading of *Creative Evolution*. Having said this, Hardy's interest in evolution would have been evident in his reading of those other and earlier writers, otherwise diverse, who all placed it at the heart of their work - Pater, von Hartmann, James himself, Darwin, Huxley, Haeckel, Spencer, Spengler, Symonds and others. Each can broadly be seen as concerned with studying how, in James's memorable phrase 'real life laughs at logic's veto'. In their different ways, as what could generally be called 'evolutionists', they were anti-rationalists, students not of 'logic's veto', but of physical, aesthetic, zoological, economic or cultural processes of transition and transformation. Certainly, each was concerned with the ways in which wholly new kinds of organization could emerge from the encounter of different forces and elements, within a common external milieu. Thinking in terms of evolution, then, necessarily makes one place observation over reflection. It commits thought to the study of relativity and transience, and the extra-rational conditions of reason itself. For these reasons, it involves also an implicit scepticism towards the totalizing claims of theory, its own speculations included.

Indeed, music often appears to be less an image of evolution or duration than an indispensable exemplar of their logic. Where evolutionary thinking defines the world as a physical domain of change and combination, so music gives an image of this, while also conveying through its effects and communality a sense of how such a world might continue to find value in the immediate. Of Freud and Darwin, in a similar connection, Adam Phillips writes that they 'wanted to convert us to the beauty of ephemera':

> their work was scandalous because it disfigured people's cherished ideals, and so compelled people to revise their hopes for themselves. Havoc was played with people's priorities, but always with the implicit assumption that such redescriptions could change people for the better; that if we ditched redemption, say, or dreams of perfect happiness or complete knowledge, or took our histories more to heart, we might be more happily in this world rather than any other one. But this involved, on the one hand, simply taking for granted that certain kinds of suffering were just part of life, built in to what it is to be a human being; and, on the other hand, wondering in new ways why transience had always been so daunting.[21]

For all that Bergson was, like Hardy himself, also a great thinker of the ephemeral, Hardy's sympathy for Bergson (presumably based on his reading of *Creative Evolution*) was tempered by a self-consciously divided reserve, at least in the letter to Dr C. W. Saleeby cited earlier in the chapter:

> His theories are much pleasanter ones than those they contest, and I for one would gladly believe them; but I cannot help feeling all the time that his is rather an imaginative and poetical mind than a reasoner's [...]
>
> You will see how much I want to have the pleasure of being a Bergsonian. But I fear his theory is, in the bulk, only our old friend Dualism in a new suit of clothes [...]

Despite this conscious display of scepticism, though, Hardy interestingly closes this particular discussion by writing:

> You must not think me a hard-hearted rationalist for all this. Half my time - particularly when writing verse - I "believe" (in the modern sense of the word) not only in the things Bergson believes in, but in spectres, mysterious voices, intuitions, omens, dreams, haunted places, etc., etc. (*Life*, pp. 369-70)

Hardy's attitude to Bergson's work might seem inadequate, but it is interesting to note his responsiveness to the mysterious communications of the real that Bergson explores. Hardy's self-critical account of his own superstitious credulity can perhaps even be seen as one way of smuggling to the fore-front of the reader's attention those extra-subjective forces, those extra-rational influences, which shape experience, but which in William James's words above bear out how 'real life laughs at logic's veto'.

More specifically, it is worth briefly here reiterating some of the main reasons why Bergson remains a central figure in this study. In relation to Bergson's broader thinking of duration, music was termed, in an earlier chapter of this book, an 'art of duration', and described as an art-form which allows for, and (literally in the case of dance) provokes, movement. In Bergson's scheme of things, it was said, such a change in the position of bodies expresses not merely their transposition in space, but also a qualitative change in their relations, since they now make up a new ensemble. This new transpersonal whole or ensemble allows for an indirect image of the open whole which is the universe itself, within which such changing sets are articulated, and which they express. The logic of temporal multiplicity at play essentially differs from the type of organization which characterizes space, in terms of quantities, of divisible patches and points.[22] So, when Bergson distinguishes the intensive multiplicities of time from the extensive multiplicities of space, it seems natural to construe the former as musical, as an unfolding mobile composition whose identity is inseparable from the qualitative alterations which express it. And this indivisible unity of different moments as duration is also memory.

In these respects and others, then, the area of interest which connects Hardy and Bergson is in aspects of experience which elude, as in James's formulations, the discursive language of the rational subject. Each invokes music to explore this, as in Bergson's provision, at the heart of his work, of a melodic notion of time which describes the real connections of past, present, and future and which sidesteps the paradoxes thrown up by logic. So Susanne K. Langer remarked that 'only art can fulfil [...] the demand Bergson makes upon experience - to set forth the dynamic forms of subjective experience'. For her, Bergson was for this reason the artist's (and especially the musician's) philosopher *par excellence*.[23] By the same token, Hardy's literary meditations on music can be said to be implicitly philosophical to the extent that they also open up these real complications of temporality and identity. Further study could develop an account of the overlappings and parallels between the two in terms of a range of ideas, ideas which Bergson reflects on, though for Hardy they are most evident as drama and effect - ideas of sensation, comedy, sympathy, community, location and so on. In this context, then, we can further imagine the attraction which Bergson's work, or William James's, held for Hardy: James for whom 'theoretic knowledge, which is knowledge *about* things as distinguished from living or sympathetic acquaintance with them, touches only the outer surface of reality' (*A Pluralistic Universe*, pp. 249-50). Above all, then, the fixities and demarcations of conceptual thought are powerless to grasp the profundity of change and movement that James spells out, in a passage inspired by Bergson:

> The essence of life is its continuously changing character; but our concepts are all discontinuous and fixed, and the only mode of making them coincide with life is by arbitrarily supposing positions of arrest therein [...] and you can no more dip up the substance of reality with them than you can dip up water with a net, however finely meshed [...] (*A Pluralistic Universe*, p. 253)

Music, because it fluently resists cognition, obviously retains an inwardness with these empiricist emphases on the immanent conditions of experience. Wittgenstein, who loved James's work, in a similar fashion distinguished the expressive from the cognitive workings of a work of art, in terms drawn from music:

> And you could say too that in so far as people understand it, they 'resonate' in harmony with it, respond to it. You might say: the work of art does not aim to convey *something else*, just itself.[24]

IV

The unconscious is a predominant and recurrent theme of Hardy's notebooks, particularly in relation to aesthetic experience. By way of introduction, we can recognise these ideas in Hardy's note from von Hartmann, in which Carrière is described as placing the drama of the mind's two modes at the heart of all art: '[i]n <u>Aesthetics</u>, Carrière, after Schelling, shows the interposition of conscs and unconscs mental activity to be indispensable for every artistic achievement' (*Literary Notebooks*, Vol. 2, p. 110). More specifically, and slightly differently, there are many other notes which approve an identification of the originality and individuality of literary art with its unconscious sources. The first is once again from von Hartmann's *Philosophy of the Unconscious* (from the addenda to the third volume):

> All that is *original*, and therefore *all that is genuine* in man, acts as such *unconsciously*, like the forces of Nature. What has passed through consciousness has thereby become a representation. Accordingly, *all genuine and sterling* qualities of the *character* and of the *mind* are originally *unconscious*, and only as such do they make a deep impression.[25]

Similarly, in some notes made in 1891, (the first a quotation, the second a summary) from Schopenhauer's *Studies in Pessimism*, Hardy writes:

> Everything that is really fundamental in man, & therefore genuine, works, as such, unconsciously; in this respect like the power of Nature. (*Literary Notebooks*, Vol. 2, p. 29)

> Unconscious origin ... those fundamental ideas which form the pith & marrow of all genuine work. (*Literary Notebooks*, Vol. 2, p. 29)

My earlier linking of Hardy's notion of the soul with manifestations of individuality is suggested by such judgments. It is even more explicitly evident, in relation to the author, in the following general extract from an article by Mabie in *The Bookman* in 1899. The context is Mabie's discussion of Goethe and Herder's notions of a vital original impulse as the genuine informing source of art:

> In other words, a work of art is an expression of a man's whole nature and life; something that grows out of him and not something which he puts together with mechanical dexterity. (*Literary Notebooks*, Vol. 2, p. 82)

More specifically, the following notes make similar points about Brahms, and English landscape painters. The first is from Groves, the second from Palgrave's *Decline of Art*:

> Brahms - The individual character of his ideas ... With him beauty seems to hold a place subordinate to expression. (*Literary Notebooks*, Vol. 2, p. 5)

> Landscape ... can only move us much when the spectator's soul feels that the artist's soul is speaking through the forms & colours of his canvas. This was the secret of our gt landsts from Gainsb. to Turner... & Mason'. (*Literary Notebooks*, Vol. 1, p. 195)

In so far as a work of art, or a piece of music, or a work of fiction, takes on these expressive powers in relation to its audience, it thereby reveals, according to the general logic of individuation, the qualities not only of its artist or performers, but also those of its recipient, its viewers, or listeners or readers: response is always self-revelation. In relation to this latter point, we can cite a note of Hardy's own, from 1886, in which he identified in the impressionist school of painters a principle 'even more suggestive in the direction of literature than in that of art'. Although it refers primarily to a painter, it could equally apply to the spectator, or to the reader of a book. It is the principle that:

> what you carry away with you from a scene is the true feature to grasp; or in other words, *what appeals to your own individual eye and heart in particular* amid much that does not so appeal, and which you therefore omit to record. (*Life*, p. 184)

In accordance with many such comments of the time, the point of this last note appears to be that the essential condition of art is an affective echo between writer and subject-matter. Once again, this is an aesthetic which has little to do with subjective interiority or objective realism as such, but rather with capturing a rapport, a 'coalescence', between writer and world in which ideal features are expressed:

> I want to see the deeper reality underlying the scenic, the expression of what are sometimes called abstract imaginings [...] The exact truth as to material fact ceases to be of importance in art - it is a student's style - the style of a period when the mind is serene and unawakened to the tragical mysteries of life; when it does not bring anything to the object that coalesces with and translates the qualities that are already there, - half-hidden, it may be - and the two united are depicted as the All. (*Life*, p. 185)

> Art is a changing of the actual proportions and order of things, so as to bring out more forcibly [...] that feature in them which appeals most strongly to the idiosyncrasy of the artist [...] Art is a disproportioning - (i.e. distorting, throwing out of proportion) - of realities, to show more clearly the features that matter in those realities, which, if merely copied or reported inventorially, might possibly be observed, but would more probably be overlooked. Hence "realism" is not Art. (*Life*, p. 229)

After a visit to the Royal Academy on January 9, 1889, Hardy affirmed those aesthetic effects of Turner's painting which he said were essentially concerned with producing in the reader not representations of the real, but affective modifications of the 'soul'. The painting is less an approximation to the objective than a means, like light, of visibility itself. To reiterate a point made earlier, there is a way of seeing which belongs to Turner himself, but which becomes available through his work, a way of seeing which depends on the revelation of light itself as its real topic:

> each is a landscape *plus* a man's soul... What he paints chiefly is *light as modified by objects*[...] He said, in his maddest and greatest days: "What pictorial drug can I dose man with, which shall affect his eyes somewhat in the manner of this reality which I cannot carry to him?" (*Life*, p. 216)

This emphasis on the individuality of art (and poetry particularly) is endlessly reiterated through the notebooks, as in the citation from Courthorpe that 'the real superiority of the painter or the poet' lies in his 'ability to find expression for imaginative ideas of nature floating unexpressed' (*Literary Notebooks*, Vol. 2, p. 399). From this same source (Courthorpe's *A History of English Poetics*) Hardy also took down the remark, which could be a motto for this book, that the 'secret of enduring poetical life lies in individualizing the universal, not in universalizing the individual'.

According to such ideas, art for a painter like Turner conveys to others less the objective depiction of an event than the power of a creative response. The artist sets out to catch and stimulate the dynamic commerce of the world and 'man's soul', in a way analogous to Hardy's notion of the writer as one who seeks to catch and expressively arrange the individuating significances which haunt him in accidental encounters:

> July 13. After being in the street: What was it on the faces of those horses? Resignation. Their eyes looked at me, haunted me. The absoluteness of their resignation was terrible. When afterwards I heard their tramp as I lay in bed, the ghosts of their eyes came in to me, saying, "Where is your justice, O man and ruler?" (*Life*, p. 211)

The notebooks are peppered with remarks and extracts which reiterate this preoccupation with the unconscious in matters relating to aesthetics and literature. There is one extract from the *Nation* in 1910 which turns on the sense of literary art as to do less with the communication of explicit meanings, or 'expressions', than with the conveying of 'impressions': that is to say, with sensible signs which imply nuances, and which activate the mind to read and interpret:

> Benedetto Croce, in his book on "Aesthetics" says 'Art is the expression of <u>im</u>pressions, & not the expression of <u>ex</u>pressions'. (*Literary Notebooks*, Vol. 2, p. 207)

Again, in an extract from *Mozley's Sermons*, Hardy takes down a remark which bears on such a conception: 'Language is everywhere half sign; its hieroglyphics, the dumb modes of expression, surpass the speech. All action, indeed, is besides being action, language' (*Literary Notebooks*, Vol. 2, p. 69). The important point to précis is the notion of interpretation or reading involved in these last two comments. In both cases, a notion of language is implied which refuses to conform to the purely communicative function of representation. Instead, the intelligence is compelled to unpack those aspects and potentials of meaning which are cryptically signalled by a physical gesture, or by intonation, or by an impression.[26]

This idea of reading obviously relates, at the level of expression, to the writer's exploitation of the material aspects and intensities of language. In relation to poetry, a citation from a discussion by Ernest

Newman of Symbolism emphasizes the musicality of language in poetry as the means by which an 'emotionalized vision' as 'the essence of what we call our knowledge of external things' is conveyed (*Literary Notebooks*, Vol. 2, p. 119). Unsurprisingly, there are many quotations from Pater in the notebooks that similarly insist on the resistance of art to simple representation, and on the elevating and transfiguring powers of expression identified with music as 'the ideal of all art whatever' (*Literary Notebooks*, Vol. 2, p. 18). Also, in relation to poetry, there are many more interesting observations about the importance of sound. The following remark by A. C. Bradley suggests the twin aspects of linguistic materiality that I identified in Hardy's poetry in Chapter Three (a productive indetermination of meaning, a significant determining of sound): 'in poetry the meaning and the sounds are one; there is, if I may put it so, a resonant meaning, or, a meaning resonance'. (*Literary Notebooks*, Vol. 2, p. 162). This could be linked as well to Symonds's dictum that 'Art is bound to introduce an equivalent for what it cannot represent'. (*Literary Notebooks*, Vol. 2, p. 36). Finally, it is worth briefly quoting two remarks, presumably by Hardy himself, which reiterate this book's emphasis on the way that Hardy's poetry often works to create an affectively productive suspense between the inevitability of disappointment and the possibility of hope. The first offers a definition of literature, the second considers what gives worth to a poet's work:

> Literature. The best poetry is that which reproduces the most of life, or its intensest moments. (*Literary Notebooks*, Vol. 2, p. 34)

> Has he anything to say... looking back on to the irrevocable & forward to the unknown. (*Literary Notebooks*, Vol. 2, p. 19)

Indeed, insofar as Hardy appears to have a philosophy as such, it is, as Paul Turner has maintained, a consciously adopted agnosticism.[27] Turner identifies this with the thematic and technical attributes of Hardy's writing, but it is an attitude which surfaces also in references such as the following. The first, from Fiske, follows a discussion of Kant's unknowable noumenon, the thing-in-itself: 'Beyond our consciousness of things lies their unknown Reality' (*Literary Notebooks*, Vol. 2, p. 108). The second is from Spencer: 'All things known to us are manifestations of the Unknowable' (*Literary Notebooks*, Vol. 2, p. 108).

There are many other extracts which bear on various facets of the idea of the unconscious, though it is only possible to cite a few more. In an early entry, Hardy quotes (and paraphrases in the parenthesis) from Comte's *Social Dynamics*:

> "Thought depends on Sensation" (- sensation on Environment -) "Aristotle's aphorism, 'There is nothing in the Understanding that did not originally spring from Sensation'". (*Literary Notebooks*, Vol. 1, p. 74)

Again, in 1885 he transcribed extracts from an article by F. W. H. Myers, entitled 'Human Personality', in the *Fortnightly Review*:

> The unity of an individual organism - "a unity aggregated from multiplicity"[...] Does my consciousness testify that I am a single entity? This only means that a stable cænesthesia exists in me just now; a sufficient number of my nervous centres are acting in unison. (*Literary Notebooks*, Vol. 1, p. 167)

Approximately three years later, he made a note from Maudsley's *Natural Causes*:

> The mind is not a single function or faculty, but a confederation... (*Literary Notebooks*, Vol. 1, p. 198.)

Similarly, the ideas of transpersonal becoming, associated with rhythm and nature in Chapter 3, could be linked with the following two quotations. The first is from von Hartmann:

> Leibnitz assumed an unconscious thinking ... which is incessant. He declares unconscious ideas to be the bond wh. unites every being with all the rest of the universe. (*Literary Notebooks*, Vol. 2, p. 109)

The second is from a *Times* review of a book called *Symbiogenesis* by Hermann Reinheimer:

> Symbiogeneis, in Nature ... Cooperation thus begins to approximate to a moral law in Nature... (*Literary Notebooks*, Vol. 2, p. 241)

Finally, many of these threads can be briefly drawn together with two quotations from John Addington Symonds's *Essays Speculative and Suggestive*. The book opposes immanence and evolution to Christian and philosophical notions of transcendence, and identifies music as an implicitly social and civic tool, a cultural means of recreation and transformation:

> By penetrating our minds with the conviction that all things are in process, that the whole universe is literally in perpetual *Becoming*, it has rendered it impossible for us to believe that any one creed or set of opinions possesses finality.[28]

> The ancients [...] without pretending to assign an intellectual significance to music [...] held it for an axiom that one type of music bred one type of character, another type another [...] music creates a spiritual world, in which the spirit cannot live and move without contracting habits of emotion. In this vagueness of significance but intensity of feeling lies the magic of music. (*Essays*, Vol. 1, p. 141)

V

This chapter has sought to elaborate the ideas of unconscious thought and becoming which have been identified in Hardy's work. In its critical aspect, this has involved, following Deleuze's conception of empiricism, two denials: first, that the human mind can be construed on the model of a prior and transcendent subjectivity, and second, that human autonomy can be construed on the model of conscious volition.[29] The thinkers cited in this chapter have offered a foil for Hardy's literary investigation of the unconscious, pithily described in a note for *The Dynasts* of 1892, where Hardy writes of how he '[c]onsidered methods for the Napoleon drama. Forces, emotions, tendencies. The characters do not act under the influence of reason'.[30] Thought is here to do with the manifold fluctuations, the accidents of passion and sensation, as in Margaret Elvy's striking discussion of how:

> Sue and Jude drift apart and come back together in waves. They fuse then fragment, like particles in some subatomic experiment [...] Hardy depicts love-in-flux, always being modulated, changed, destroyed, rebuilt, transfigured. Sue and Jude fly together involuntarily - such as in their kiss on the silent road, when they 'kissed close and long'. But they soon fall apart again. (*Sexing Hardy*, p. 42)

Essentially, music has offers both a model and an occasion for Hardy's writing in these respects. I quoted earlier Brennecke's remark, after meeting Hardy in 1923, that the writer possessed 'a sentiment that trembles at the touch of things' (*The Life of Thomas Hardy*, p. 11). Artistry emerges from such involuntary responses, and the unconscious participation they involve:

> Style - Consider the Wordsworthian dictum (the more perfectly the natural object is reproduced, the more truly poetic the picture). This reproduction is achieved by seeing into the *heart of a thing* (as rain, wind, for instance), and is realism, in fact, though through being pursued by means of the imagination it is confounded by invention, which is pursued by the same means. It is, in short, what M. Arnold calls "the imaginative reason". (*Life*, p. 147)

Seeing into the heart of things, for the writer, is accordingly also to see into oneself, to discover that distinctive medium or style which is brought out by chance encounters. For the reader, too, this logic of response is revealing. Hardy's work finds a language for the subliminal life of sensation and passion, and makes expressive, conflictual drama out of the disjunctions of our conscious and unconscious selves.

Finally, Hardy's texts use music to affirm and exemplify the pleasures of immediacy, since music embodies in insistent form the indisputable values of physical expression and relatedness. Hardy's texts are complex, but it has been one of the main arguments of this book that their better-known sardonic and elegiac aspects have, as a less overt counterpart, this more positive investigation of the conditions of a secular ethics, this politics of the here and now. Thought, feeling, relatedness and individuality are best conceived in terms of conduction, resonance, vibration, transmission - as in Schelling's formulation, which condenses many of the themes of this book's discussion of Hardy's work:

> All resonance, however, is conduction, and no body resounds except insomuch as it simultaneously conducts sound.[31]

Notes

¹   Robert Gittings, *The Older Hardy* (London: Penguin, 1980), p. 257.

² There is no intention in this chapter to attempt to map the work and thought of any of these other writers onto Hardy's own work.

³ William R. Rutland, from *Thomas Hardy: A Study of his Writings and their Background*, reprinted in Vol. 4, *Thomas Hardy: Critical Assessments* (edited by Graham Clarke, Mountfield: Helm, 1993), p. 262.

⁴ C. C. J. Webb, cited by Rutland, p. 268.

⁵ Philosophically Hardy, as we shall see, felt that Bergson's vitalism paid insufficient notice to those themes of cosmic tragedy that Hardy was to respond to in Schopenhauer. In 'Our Old Friend Dualism', Hardy pokes fun at Bergson's monist tendencies. Similarly, one could emphasize the apparent differences of background, discipline and temperament between the two men, and indicate the tenuous connection between them (since Hardy's reading of Bergson was both limited and took place late in his life).

⁶ Henri Bergson, *The Two Sources of Morality and Religion* (translated by R. Ashley Audra and Cloudesley Brereton, with W. Horsfall Carter, University of Notre Dame Press: Notre Dame, 1977), p. 40.

⁷ There is an interesting parallel here, with Ruskin's conception of Turner. In Francis O' Gorman's words :

> Turner was a landscape artist of exceptional power, Ruskin said, whose paintings showed a grasp of natural fact fused with emotion, and revealed an imagination capable of entering the essence of natural form. He was, Ruskin wrote, 'the only painter who ever drew a mountain, or a stone.' (*Ruskin*, Stroud: Sutton, 1999, p. 15)

⁸ Gilles Deleuze, *Difference and Repetition* (translated by Paul Patton, London: Athlone, 1994), p. 254.

⁹ Eduard von Hartmann, *Philosophy of the Unconscious*, Vol. I (translated by W. C. Coupland, London: Kegan Paul, 1893), p. 1. In one of the fascinating addenda to the third volume of the book (in Coupland's translation published also in 1893), von Hartmann also draws out the ways in which he sees his own work prefigured in the work of Kant, Schopenhauer and, even, Hegel. His analyses of passages in their writings are designed to indicate a more thorough acknowledgment of, and dependence on, the notion of a transcendental unconscious than they might wish explicitly to make.

¹⁰ There are many other connections one could make between von Hartmann's work and the rest of this discussion - for instance, his celebration of the metaphysics of Spinoza, his identification of individuality with the unconscious, his sense of the unconscious as a power of becoming that works through kinds of relatedness, his sense of the co-operative and collective nature of much unconscious activity as social and affective phenomena, and so on.

¹¹ Cited by Rutland, p. 277.

¹² Arthur Schopenhauer, *The World as Will and Representation* Vol. 2 (translated by E. F. J. Payne, New York: Dover, 1958), p. 450.

¹³ See for instance, Andrew Bowie's fascinating *Aesthetics and Subjectivity* (Manchester: Manchester University Press, 1993), which considers the centrality of musical experience in the meditations of continental philosophers from the late

eighteenth century onwards.

¹⁴ The phrase is given to the 'Spirit of the Pities' (*The Dynasts*, p. 2).

¹⁵ The notion of such an interwoven design is prefigured in the well-known note cited in the *Life*, from the time when Hardy was writing *The Woodlanders*:

> The human race to be shown as one great network or tissue which quivers in every part when one point is shaken, like a spider's web if touched. (*Life*, p. 177)

¹⁶ J. Vera Mardon, *Thomas Hardy as a Musician*, (edited by J. Stevens Cox, Beaminster: Toucan Press, 1964), p. 9.

¹⁷ Margaret Elvy, *Sexing Hardy: Thomas Hardy and Feminism* (London: Crescent Moon, 1998). The first quotation is from p. 48, the main one from p. 47.

¹⁸ William James, *A Pluralistic Universe* (London: Longman, 1909), p. 137.

¹⁹ Gilles Deleuze and Felix Guattari, *What is Philosophy?* (translated by Hugh Tomlinson and Graham Burchell, New York: Columbia University Press, 1994), p. 190.

²⁰ James cites Fechner at length, with his notion of the Earth-Soul, in this connection. However, one can also make the connection with what would later be familiar as a Bergsonian notion of creative evolution.

²¹ Adam Phillips, *Darwin's Worms* (London: Faber, 1999), p. 7.

²² Deleuze glosses the difference between these two types of multiplicity succinctly in *Bergsonism*:

> One is represented by space [...] It is a multiplicity of exteriority, of simultaneity, of juxtaposition, of order, of quantitative differentiation, of *difference in degree*; it is a numerical multiplicity, *discontinuous and actual*. The other type of multiplicity appears in pure duration: It is an internal multiplicity of succession, of fusion, of organization, of heterogeneity, of qualitative discrimination, or of *difference in kind*; it is a *virtual and continuous* multiplicity that cannot be reduced to numbers. (p. 38)

²³ Susanne K. Langer, *Feeling and Form* (London: RKP, 1953), p. 114. Within a discussion linking Bergson's notions of temporality and the philosophy of music, Susanne K. Langer makes some interesting references to two French writers on music, Gabriel Marcel and Charles Koechlin, who had indicated, in Proust's Marcel's words, that 'a certain philosophy of music is wrapped up in the theory of concrete time' (cited by Langer, *Feeling and Form*, p. 115). Music, that is to say, is the best symbol of time, the best way of comprehending how, as Langer writes, 'the direct intuition of time must be our measure for its philosophical conception' (*Feeling and Form*, p. 115). She formulates the connection again by saying of Bergson's '"concrete duration," "lived time,"' that it is the prototype of "musical time," namely passage in its characteristic forms' (*Feeling and Form*, p. 115).

²⁴ Ludwig Wittgenstein, *Culture and Value* (edited by G. H. Von Wright in collaboration with Heikki Nyman, and translated by Peter Winch, Oxford: Blackwell, 1980), p. 58e.

²⁵ Eduard von Hartmann, *Philosophy of the Unconscious*, Vol.III (translated by W. C. Coupland, London: Kegan Paul, 1893), p. 293.

²⁶ This is a notion of reading as a physically produced and orientated adventure of thought, such as was identified by Deleuze in his *Proust and Signs* (translated by Richard Howard, New York: George Braziller, 1983).

[27] See Paul Turner, *The Life of Thomas Hardy*, pp. 2-3, pp. 225.

[28] John Addington Symonds, *Essays Speculative and Suggestive*, Vol. 1 (London: Chapman and Hall, 1890), p. 7.

[29] The terms of this twin critique correspond to Deleuze's account of Spinoza's ethics in his *Spinoza: Practical Philosophy*. For a contemporaneous account of a similar project, consider William James's taking apart of the Kantian notion of the unity of apperception (of the privileged transcendent instance of a concerted and unifying power of subjectivity), as discussed in the introduction above.

[30] Millgate, *Thomas Hardy*, p. 261.

[31] Friedrich Schelling, *The Philosophy of Art* (edited and translated by Douglas W. Stott, Minneapolis: University of Minnesota Press, 1989), p. 108.

Bibliography

Primary Sources

Works and other writings by Thomas Hardy

Desperate Remedies (London: Penguin, 1995).
Under the Greenwood Tree (London: Macmillan, 1974).
A Pair of Blue Eyes (London: Penguin, 1986).
Far from the Madding Crowd (London: Macmillan, 1974).
The Hand of Ethelberta (London: Macmillan, 1975).
The Return of the Native (London: Macmillan, 1974).
The Trumpet-Major (London: Macmillan, 1974).
A Laodicean (London: Macmillan, 1975).
Two on a Tower (London: Macmillan, 1975).
The Mayor of Casterbridge (London: Macmillan, 1974).
The Woodlanders (London: Macmillan, 1974).
Tess of the d'Urbervilles (London: Dent, 1984).
Jude the Obscure (London: Macmillan, 1974).
The Well-Beloved (Oxford World's Classics, 1986).
The Stories of Thomas Hardy, 3 Volumes (edited by F. B. Pinion, London: Macmillan, 1977).
The Complete Poems (edited by James Gibson, London: Macmillan, 1976).
The Collected Letters of Thomas Hardy, 7 Volumes (edited by Richard Little Purdy and Michael Millgate, Oxford: Clarendon, 1978-88).
The Literary Notebooks of Thomas Hardy, 2 Volumes (edited by Lennart A. Björk, New York: New York University Press, 1985).
The Personal Notebooks of Thomas Hardy (edited by Richard H. Taylor, London: Macmillan, 1978).

Secondary Sources

Abercrombie, Lascelles, *Thomas Hardy: A Critical Study* (London: Secker, 1912).
Abraham, Nicholas, and Maria Torok, 'Psychoanalytical Esthetics: Time, Rhythm, and the Unconscious,' *Diacritics* (Fall 1986), pp. 3-14.
Anderson, Wayne, 'The Rhetoric of Silence in Hardy's Fiction', *Studies in the Novel*, Vol. 17, i (1985), pp. 53-68.
Arkans, Norman, 'Hardy's Narrative Muse and the Ballad Connection', *Thomas Hardy Annual*, No. 2 (1984), pp. 131-156.
Armstrong, Isobel, *Victorian Poetry* (London: Routledge, 1993).
Armstrong, Tim, 'Supplementarity: Poetry as the Afterlife of Thomas Hardy', *Victorian Poetry*, Vol. 26 (1988), pp. 381-393.
Armstrong, Tim, *Thomas Hardy: Selected Poems* (London: Longman, 1993).

Aronson, Alex, *Music and the Novel: A Study in Twentieth Century Fiction* (Totowa, N. J.: Rowman and Littlefield, 1980).

Attali, Jacques, *Noise: The Political Economy of Music* (translated by Brian Massumi, Minneapolis: University of Minnesota Press, 1985).

Bachelard, Gaston, *On Poetic Imagination and Reverie* (selected, translated and introduced by Collette Guadin, revised edition, Dallas: Spring, 1994).

Bakhtin, M. M., *Towards a Philosophy of the Act* (translated and notes by Vadim Liapunov, edited by Vadim Liapunov and Michael Holquist, Austin: University of Texas Press, 1993).

Barthes, Roland, 'Musica Practica', in *Image-Music-Text* (edited and translated by Stephen Heath, London: Fonatana, 1979), pp. 149-64.

Barthes, Roland, 'The Grain of the Voice', in *Image-Music-Text*, pp. 179-89.

Bayley, John, *The Uses of Division* (London: Chatto & Windus, 1976).

Bayley, John, *An Essay on Hardy* (Cambridge: Cambridge University Press, 1978).

Bayley, John, 'A Social Comedy? On Re-reading *The Woodlanders*', in *Thomas Hardy Annual*, No. 5 (edited by Norman Page, London: Macmillan, 1987), pp. 3-21.

Bayley, John and Jedrzejewski, J., editors, *Outside the Gates of the World: Selected Short Stories of Thomas Hardy* (London: Everyman, 1996).

Bebbington, Brian, 'Folksong and Dance in *The Mayor of Casterbridge*', *English Dance and Song*, Vol. 40 (1978), pp. 111-115.

Bennett, Andrew and Royle, Nicholas, *An Introduction to Literature, Theory, Practice*, (Hemel Hempstead: Harvester, 1995).

Berger, Susan, *Thomas Hardy and Visual Structures: Framing, Disruption, Process* (New York: New York University Press, 1990).

Bergson, Henri, *Creative Evolution* (translated by A. Mitchell, London: Macmillan, 1964).

Bergson, Henri, *The Two Sources of Morality and Religion* (translated by R. Ashley Audra and Cloudesley Brereton, with the assistance of W. Horsfall Carter, Notre Dame: University of Notre Dame Press, 1977).

Bergson, Henri, *Matter and Memory* (translated by N. M. Paul and W. S. Palmer, New York: Zone, 1991).

Binyon, Lawrence, Review of *Satires of Circumstance*, *Bookman*, xlvii, (February 1915), pp. 143-44. Reprinted in *Thomas Hardy: The Critical Heritage* (edited by Cox), pp. 440-43.

Bloch, Ernst, *Essays on the Philosophy of Music* (translated by Peter Palmer, introduction by David Drew, Cambridge: Cambridge University Press, 1985).

Bloom, Harold, editor, *Thomas Hardy's The Mayor of Casterbridge* (New York: Chelsea House, 1987).

Bogue, Ronald, 'Gilles Deleuze: The Aesthetics of Force', in *Deleuze: A Critical Reader* (edited by Paul Patton, Oxford: Basil Blackwell, 1996), pp. 257-69.

Borges, Jorge Luis, *Other Inquisitions, 1937-1952* (introduction by James E. Ireby, and translation by Ruth L. C. Simms, London: Souvenir, 1973).

Boumelha, Penny, *Thomas Hardy and Women* (Brighton: Harvester, 1982).

Bowie, Andrew, *Aesthetics and Subjectivity* (Manchester: Manchester University Press, 1993).

Brady, Kirstan, *The Short Stories of Thomas Hardy* (London: Macmillan, 1982).

Brennecke, Ernest, *The Life of Thomas Hardy* (New York: Haskell House, 1973).

Bridges, Robert, 'A Letter to a Musician on English Prosody', *Collected Essays*, No. 15, (London: Oxford University Press, 1933), pp. 54-85.

Brogan, Howard O., " 'Visible Essences' in *The Mayor of Casterbridge*", *English Literary History*, Vol. 17 (1950), pp. 302-23.

Brown, Calvin S., *Music and Literature: A Comparison of the Arts* (Athens: University of Georgia Press, 1948).

Bullen, J. B., *The Expressive Eye: Fiction and Perception in the Work of Thomas Hardy* (Oxford: Clarendon, 1986).

Burgan, Mary, 'Heroines at the Piano', *Victorian Studies*, Vol. 30 (1986), pp. 51-76.

Butler, Lance St. John, editor, *Alternative Hardy* (London: Macmillan, 1989).

Cavell, Stanley, 'Music Discomposed', in *Must We Mean What We Say?* (Cambridge: Cambridge University Press, 1976).

Cecil, David, *Hardy the Novelist* (London: Constable, 1943).

Chesterton, G. K., 'Thomas Hardy', *Illustrated London News*, Vol. clxxii (21 January 1928), p. 94.

Chesterton, G. K., *The Victorian Age in Literature* (Oxford: Oxford University Press, 1961).

Clark, Graham, editor, *Thomas Hardy: Critical Assessments*, 4 Volumes (Mountfield: Helm, 1993).

Clark, Timothy, *The Theory of Inspiration* (Manchester: Manchester University Press, 1997).

Collins, Vere H., *Talks with Thomas Hardy at Max Gate* (London: Duckworth, 1978).

Conrad, Peter, *The Everyman History of English Literature* (London: Dent, 1985).

Cox, R. G., editor, *Thomas Hardy: The Critical Heritage* (London: Routledge, 1979).

D'Agnillo, Renzo, 'Music and Metaphor in *Under the Greenwood Tree*', *The Thomas Hardy Journal*, Vol. IX, no. 2, (1993), pp. 39-50.

Daleski, H. M., *Thomas Hardy and the Paradoxes of Love* (Columbia: University of Missouri Press, 1997).

Davie, Donald, 'Hardy's Virgilian Purples', *Agenda*, Vol. 10 (1972), pp. 138-56.

Davie, Donald, *Thomas Hardy and British Poetry* (London: Routledge and Kegan Paul, 1973).

Davies, Sarah, '*The Hand of Ethelberta*: de-mythologising "woman"', *Critical Survey*, Vol. 5, no. 2 (1993), pp. 123-30.

Day Lewis, Cecil, 'The Lyrical Poetry of Thomas Hardy', *Proceedings of the British Academy*, Vol. 37 (London: Oxford University Press, 1951), pp. 155-74.

Day Lewis, Cecil, *The Lyric Impulse* (London: Chatto and Windus, 1966).

De Man, Paul, *Allegories of Reading* (New Haven: Yale University Press, 1979).

De Man, Paul, *The Resistance to Theory* (Minneapolis: University of Minnesota Press, 1986).

Deleuze, Gilles, *Proust and Signs* (translated by Richard Howard, New York: George Braziller, 1972).

Deleuze, Gilles, *Cinema I: The Movement-Image* (translated by Hugh Tomlinson and Barbara Habberjam, London: Athlone, 1986).

Deleuze, Gilles and Parnet, Claire, *Dialogues* (translated by Hugh Tomlinson and Barbara Habberjam, London: Athlone, 1987).

Deleuze, Gilles, *Bergsonism* (translated by Hugh Tomlinson and Barbara Habberjam, New York: Zone, 1988).

Deleuze, Gilles, *Spinoza: Practical Philosophy,* (translated by Robert Hurley, San Francisco: City Lights, 1988).

Deleuze, Gilles, and Guattari, Felix, *A Thousand Plateaus* (translated by Brian Massumi, London: Athlone, 1988).

Deleuze, Gilles, *Cinema II: The Time-Image* (translated by Hugh Tomlinson and Robert Galeta, London: Athlone, 1989).

Deleuze, Gilles, and Guattari, Felix, *What is Philosophy?* (translated by Hugh Tomlinson and Graham Burchell, New York: Columbia, 1994).

Deleuze, Gilles, *Essays Critical and Clinical* (translated by Daniel W. Smith and Michael A. Greco, London: Verso, 1998).

Deleuze, Gilles, *Negotiations* (translated by Martin Joughin, New York: Columbia University Press, 1995).

Dodge, Alan D., 'Hardy and Wessex Church Music in Transition', *The Thomas Hardy Journal*, Vol. XIV, no. 3 (1998), pp. 56-67.

Draper, R. P., editor *Thomas Hardy: Three Pastoral Novels* (London: Macmillan, 1987).

Draper, R. P., and Ray, Martin, *An Annotated Critical Bibliography of Thomas Hardy* (Hemel Hempstead: Harvester, 1989).

Eagleton, Terry, *Criticism and Ideology* (London: Verso, 1978).

Ebbatson, Roger, editor, *Critical Survey: Thomas Hardy*, Vol. 5, no. 2 (1993).

Ebbatson, Roger, *Hardy: The Margin of the Unexpressed* (Sheffield: Sheffield Academic Press, 1993).

Eliot, George, *The Mill on the Floss* (London: Penguin, 1979).

Eliot, T. S., *After Strange Gods* (London: Faber and Faber, 1934).

Elkin, Stanley, 'Words and Music', *Review of Contemporary Fiction*, Vol. 15 (1995), pp. 27-37.

Elvy, Margaret, *Sexing Hardy: Thomas Hardy and Feminism* (London: Crescent Moon, 1998).

Eva, Phil, 'Home Sweet Home? The "culture of exile" in mid-Victorian popular song', *Popular Music*, Vol. 16, no. 2, pp. 131-150.

Fink, Hilary, 'Andrei Bely and the Music of Bergsonian Duration', *Slavic and East European Journal*, Vol. 41 (1997), pp. 287-302.

Firor, Ruth, *Folkways in Thomas Hardy* (Philadelphia: University of Pennsylvania Press, 1931).

Fisher, Joe, *The Hidden Hardy* (London: Macmillan, 1992).

Fraleigh, Sondra, *Dance and the Lived Body: A Descriptive Aesthetics* (Pittsburgh: University of Pittsburgh Press, 1987).

Frogley, Alain, 'Hardy in the Music of Vaughan Williams', *Thomas Hardy Journal*, Vol. 2, no. 3 (1986), pp. 50-55.

Garson, Marjorie, *Hardy's Fables of Integrity* (Oxford: Clarendon, 1991).

Gatrell, Simon, *Hardy the Creator: A Textual Biography* (Oxford: Clarendon, 1988).

Gatrell, Simon, *Thomas Hardy and the Proper Study of Mankind* (London: Macmillan, 1993).

Gittings, Robert, *Young Thomas Hardy* (London: Penguin, 1980).

Gittings, Robert, *The Older Hardy* (London: Penguin, 1980).

Goddard, Dick, 'As a Boy He Had an Unusual Ear for Music', *English Dance and Song*, Vol. 33 (1971), pp. 14-15.

Goode, John, *Thomas Hardy: The Offensive Truth* (Oxford: Blackwell, 1988).

Gosse, Edmund, 'Mr Hardy's Lyrical Poems', *Edinburgh Review* (April 1918). Reprinted in *Thomas Hardy: The Critical Heritage* (edited by Cox), pp. 444-63.

Gray, Beryl, *George Eliot and Music* (London: Macmillan, 1989).

Grundy, Joan, *Hardy and the Sister Arts* (London: Macmillan, 1979).

Gunn, Thom, 'Hardy and the Ballads', *Agenda*, Vol. 10 (1972), pp. 19-46.

Hanna, Judith Lynne, *To Dance is Human: A Theory of Nonverbal Communication* (Austin and London: University of Texas Press, 1979).

Hardy, Evelyn, *Thomas Hardy: A Critical Biography* (London: Hogarth Press, 1954).

Hardy, Florence Emily, *The Life of Thomas Hardy, 1840-1928* (London: Macmillan, 1975).

Harrison, Charles, and Paul Wood, with Jason Gaiger, editors, *Art in Theory, 1815-1900: An Anthology of Changing Ideas* (Oxford: Blackwell, 1998).

Hartman, Geoffrey, *Criticism in the Wilderness: The Study of Literature Today* (New Haven: Yale University Press, 1971).

Hartmann, Eduard von, *Philosophy of the Unconscious*, 3 Volumes (translated by W. C. Coupland, London: Kegan Paul, 1893). Heaney, Seamus, *Station Island*, London: Faber and Faber, 1984.

Heaney, Seamus, *Station Island* (London; Faber and Faber, 1984).

Heath, Apryl Lea Denny, 'Phelps, Browning, Schopenhauer and Music', *Comparative Literature Studies* (Illinois: University of Illinois Press, 1985), pp. 211-217.

Hollander, John, *The Untuning of the Sky: Ideas of Music in English Poetry, 1500-1700*, (New York: Norton, 1970).

Hollander, John, 'Wordsworth and the Music of Sound' in *New Perspectives on Coleridge and Wordsworth* (edited by Geoffrey Hartman, New York: Columbia University Press, 1972) pp. 41-84.

Hollander, John, *Vision and Resonance: Two Senses of Poetic Form* (New York: Oxford University Press, 1975).

Hollander, John, *The Figure of Echo: A Mode of Illusion in Milton and After* (Berkeley: University of California Press, 1981).

Howe, Irving, *Thomas Hardy* (London: Weidenfeld and Nicolson, 1968).

Hughes, John, 'Hardy and Music', *English*, Vol. 46 (Summer 1997), pp. 113-29.

Hughes, John, *Lines of Flight* (Sheffield: Sheffield Academic Press, 1997).

Hughes, John, 'Hardy and the Life of Birds', *The Thomas Hardy Journal*, Vol. XIV, no. 3 (1998) pp. 68-77.

Ingham, Patricia, 'The Evolution of *Jude the Obscure*', *The Review of English Studies*, Vol. 27 (1966), pp. 27-37 and pp. 159-169.

Ingham, Patricia, *Thomas Hardy* (Hemel Hempstead: Harvester, 1989).

Ingham, Patricia, 'Provisional Narratives: Hardy's Final Trilogy', in *Alternative Hardy* (edited by Lance St John Butler, London: Macmillan, 1989), pp. 49-73.

Jackson-Houlston, Caroline, 'Thomas Hardy's Use of Traditional Song', *Nineteenth-Century Literature* (December 1989), pp. 301-34.

Jackson-Houlston, Caroline, *Ballads, Songs and Snatches: The Appropriation of Folk Song and Popular Culture in British Nineteenth-Century Realist Prose* (Aldershot: Ashgate, 1999).

Jacobs, Robert L., 'The Role of Music in George Eliot's Novels', *Music Review*, Vol. 45, (1984), pp. 277-282.

Jacobson, Howard, *Peeping Tom* (Chatto & Windus: London, 1984).

Jacobus, Mary, 'Sue the Obscure', *Essays in Criticism*, Vol. 25 (1975), pp. 304-28.

Jacobus, Mary, 'Tess's Purity', *Essays in Criticism*, Vol. 26 (1976) pp. 318-38.

James, William, *A Pluralistic Universe* (London: Longman, 1909).

James, William, *Selected Writings* (edited by G. Bird, London: Everyman, 1995).

Johnson, Bruce, *True Correspondence: A Phenomenology of Thomas Hardy's Novels* (Tallahassee: University Presses of Florida, 1983).

Johnson, Trevor, *A Critical Introduction to the Poems of Thomas Hardy* (London: Macmillan, 1991).

Jones, Lawrence, 'The Music Scenes in *The Poor Man and the Lady, Desperate Remedies* and "An Indiscretion in the Life of an Heiress"', *Notes and Queries*, Vol. 24 (1977), pp. 32-34.

Karlin, Daniel, 'The Figure of the Singer in the Poetry of Thomas Hardy', unpublished lecture for the Thomas Hardy Society, delivered at Dorchester in 1998.

Kramer, Dale, editor, *Critical Approaches to the Fiction of Thomas Hardy* (London: Macmillan, 1979).

Kurth, Richard, 'Music and Poetry, a Wilderness of Doubles: Heine - Nietzsche - Schubert - Derrida', *Nineteenth Century Music*, Vol. XXI, no. 1 (Summer 1997), pp. 3- 37.

Langbaum, Robert, *Thomas Hardy in Our Time* (London: Macmillan, 1995).

Langer, Susanne, K., *Feeling and Form* (London: Routledge and Kegan Paul, 1953).

Larkin, Philip, 'Philip Larkin Praises the Poetry of Thomas Hardy', *The Listener* (25 July 1968), p. 111.

Larkin, Philip, 'Wanted: Good Hardy Critic', *Required Writing* (London: Faber, 1971), pp. 13-40.

Lawrence, D. H., 'A Study of Thomas Hardy', *Phoenix* I (1936).

Lawrence, D. H., *Selected Literary Criticism* (London: Heinemann, 1973).

Leavis, F. R., 'Hardy the Poet', *Southern Review*, Vol. 6 (Summer 1940), pp. 87-98.

Leavis, F. R., 'Reality and Sincerity', *Scrutiny*, Vol. 19 (Winter 1952), pp. 90-98.

Lenzer, Getrud, *Auguste Comte and Positivism: The Essential Writings* (New York: Harper and Row, 1975).

Levinas, Emmanuel, 'Art and its Shadow', in *The Levinas Reader* (edited by Seán Hand, Oxford: Blackwell, 1989), pp. 129-43.

Lucas, John, *The Literature of Change: Studies in the Nineteenth-Century Provincial Novel* (Brighton: Harvester, 1977).

Lucas, John, *Modern English Poetry from Hardy to Hughes* (London: Batsford, 1986).

Lucas, John, 'Hardy among the poets', *Critical Survey*, Vol. 5, no. 2 (edited by Ebbatson, 1993), pp. 192-201.

Mahar, Margaret, 'Hardy's Poetry of Renunciation', *English Literary History*, Vol. 45 (1978), pp. 303-24.

Maidment, B. E., 'Hardy's Fiction and English Traditional Music', *Thomas Hardy Annual*, No. 4 (1986), pp. 3-18.

Mallett, Phillip, '*Jude the Obscure*: A Farewell to Wessex', *The Thomas Hardy Journal*, Vol. XI, no. 2 (October 1995), pp. 48-59.

Mansell, Darrell, 'William Holman Hunt's *The Awakening Conscience* and James Joyce's "The Dead"', *James Joyce Quarterly*, Vol. 23 (1986), pp. 487-91.

Marcus, Greil, 'Speaker to Speaker', *Art Forum*, Vol. 24 (1985), p. 13.

Mardon, J. Vera, *Thomas Hardy as Musician* (edited by J. Stevens Cox, Number 15 in *Monographs on the Life of Thomas Hardy* [Toucan Press: Beaminster, 1964]).

Marks, John, 'Hardy and Kindness', *The Thomas Hardy Journal*, Vol. XI, no. 1 (February 1995), pp. 52-59.

Mein, Margaret, 'Proust and Wagner', *Journal of European Studies*, Vol. 19 (1989), pp. 205-22.

Mellown, Elgin W., 'Music and Dance in D. H. Lawrence', *Journal of Modern Literature*, Vol. 21 (1997), pp. 49-60.

Melnick, Daniel C., *Fullness of Dissonance: Modern Fiction and the Aesthetics of Music* (Madison, N. J. : Fairleigh Dickinson University Press, 1994).

Miller, J. Hillis, *Thomas Hardy: Distance and Desire* (Oxford: Oxford University Press, 1970).

Miller, J. Hillis, 'Thomas Hardy, Jacques Derrida, and the "Dislocation of Souls"', in *Taking Chances: Derrida, Psychoanalysis, and Literature* (edited by William Kerrigan and Joseph H. Smith, John Hopkins: Baltimore, 1984), pp. 135-145.

Millgate, Michael, *Thomas Hardy* (Oxford: Oxford University Press, 1982).

Mitchell, P. E., 'Music and Hardy's Poetry', *English Literature in Transition*, Vol. 30, no. 3 (1987), pp. 308-21.

Morgan, Rosemarie, *Women and Sexuality in the Novels of Thomas Hardy* (London: Routledge, 1978).

Morrell, Roy, *Thomas Hardy: The Will and the Way* (Kuala Lumpur: University of Malaya Press, 1965).

Musselwhite, David, '*Tess of the d'Urbervilles*: 'A becoming woman' or Deleuze and Guattari go to Wessex', *Textual Practice*, Vol. 14, no. 3 (2000), pp. 501-18.

Newey, Vincent, *Centring the Self: Subjectivity, Society and Reading from Thomas Gray to Thomas Hardy* (Aldershot: Scolar Press, 1995).

Nicholls, G., 'Reading Hardy for Pleasure', *Thomas Hardy Yearbook*, Vol. 13 (1986), pp. 58-62.

Nietzsche, Friedrich, *The Birth of Tragedy* and *The Genealogy of Morals* (translated by Francis Goffing, New York, Doubleday, 1956).

Nietzsche, Friedrich, *The Will to Power* (translated by Walter Kaufmann and R. J. Hollingdale, New York: Doubleday, 1968).

O' Gorman, Francis, *Ruskin* (Stroud: Sutton, 1999).

Orel, Harold, *Thomas Hardy's Personal Writings* (Lawrence: University of Kansas Press, 1966).

Pater, Walter, *Appreciations* (London: Macmillan, 1924).

Pater, Walter, *Studies in the Renaissance* (Cleveland: World, 1961).

Patmore, Coventry, *The Poems of Coventry Patmore* (edited by Frederick Page, Oxford: Oxford University Press, 1949).

Paulin, Thomas, *Thomas Hardy: The Poetry of Perception* (London: Macmillan, 1986).

Pettit, Charles P. C., 'Hardy's Vision of the Individual in *Tess of the d'Urbervilles*', in *New Perspectives on Thomas Hardy* (edited by Charles P. C. Pettit, New York: St Martin's Press, 1994), pp. 172-90.

Phillips, Adam, *Darwin's Worms*, (London: Faber, 1999).

Pinion, F. B., *A Hardy Companion* (London: Macmillan, 1968).

Pollard, Michael, 'Thomas Hardy and Folk Music,' *The Thomas Hardy Journal*, Vol. VIII, no. 1 (1992), pp. 40-44.

Porter, Katherine Anne, 'Notes on a Criticism of Thomas Hardy', *Southern Review*, Vol. 6 (Autumn 1940), pp. 150-161.

Proust, Marcel, *Remembrance of Things Past*, 3 Volumes (translated by C. K. Scott Moncrieff and T. Kilmartin; and by A. Mayor, London: Penguin, 1989).

Royle, Nicholas, *Telepathy and Literature* (Oxford: Blackwell, 1990).

Ruskin, John, *Modern Painters*, 5 Volumes (London: George Allen, 1905).

Schopenhauer, Arthur, *Studies in Pessimism* (selected and translated by T. Bailey Saunders, London: George Allen and Unwin, 1937).

Schopenhauer, Arthur, *The World as Will and Representation*, 2 Volumes (translated by E. F. J. Payne, Oxford: Oxford University Press, 1958).

Seymour-Smith, Martin, *Hardy* (London: Bloomsbury, 1994).

Shad, John, 'Waiting in "Unhope": Negation in Hardy's Early Poetry', *Critical Survey*, Vol. 5, no. 2 (1993), pp. 174-79.

Sherman, Elna, 'Music in Thomas Hardy's Life and Work', *Musical Quarterly*, Vol. 26 (1940), pp. 143-71.

Showalter, Elaine, 'The Unmanning of *The Mayor of Casterbridge*', in *Critical Approaches to the Fiction of Thomas Hardy* (edited by Kramer), pp. 99-115.

Simpson, P., 'Hardy's "The Self-Unseeing" and the Romantic Problem of Consciousness', *Victorian Poetry*, Vol. 17, 1979, pp. 45-50.

Smith, Daniel W., 'Deleuze's Theory of Sensation: Overcoming the Kantian Duality', in *Deleuze: A Critical Reader* (edited by Paul Patton, Oxford: Basil Blackwell, 1996), pp. 29-56.

Spencer, Herbert, *An Autobiography*, 2 Volumes (London: Williams and Norgate, 1926).

Sprechman, Ellen Lew, *Seeing Women as Men: Role Reversal in the Novels of Thomas Hardy* (New York: University Press of America, 1995).

Stecker, Robert, 'Expression of Emotion In (Some of) The Arts', *Journal of Aesthetics and Art Criticism*, Vol. 42 (1984), pp. 409-18.

Stevenson, Robert Louis, 'On Style in Literature: its Technical Elements', *Contemporary Review*, Vol. 47 (1885), pp. 548-61.

Strachey, Lytton, Review of *Satires of Circumstance*, *New Statesman* (19 December 1914). Reprinted in *Thomas Hardy: The Critical Heritage* (edited by R. G. Cox), pp. 435-39.

Sumner, Rosemary, 'Discoveries of Dissonance; Hardy's Late Fiction', *The Thomas Hardy Journal*, Vol. XI, no. 3 (October 1995), pp. 79-88.

Sutherland, John, 'A Note on the Teasing Narrator in *Jude the Obscure*', *English Literature in Transition*, Vol. 17 (1974), pp. 159-62.

Swinburne, Algernon, *Poems and Ballads, Atalanta in Calydon* (edited by Morse Peckham, New York: Bobbs-Merrill, 1970).

Symonds, John Addington, *Essays Speculative and Suggestive*, 2 Volumes (London: Chapman and Hall, 1890).

Tanner, Tony, 'Colour and Movement in Hardy's *Tess of the d'Urbervilles*', *Critical Quarterly*, Vol. 10 (1968), pp. 219-39.

Taylor, Dennis, *Hardy's Metres and Victorian Prosody* (Oxford: Clarendon, 1988).

Taylor, Richard, H., *The Neglected Hardy* (London: Macmillan, 1982).

Thomas, Edward, *A Language Not To Be Betrayed: Selected Prose of Edward Thomas*, (edited by Edna Longley, Manchester: Carcanet, 1981).

Thomas, Jane, *Thomas Hardy, Femininity and Dissent* (London: Macmillan, 1999).

Turner, Paul, *The Life of Thomas Hardy* (Oxford: Blackwell, 1998).

Unsigned review of *Poems of the Past and Present*, *Saturday Review*, 11 January November 1902. Reprinted in *Thomas Hardy: The Critical Heritage* (edited by Cox), p. 331.

Valéry, Paul, 'Poetry and abstract thought: dancing and walking', in *20th Century Literary Criticism* (edited by David Lodge, London: Longman, 1978), pp. 254-61.

Vendler, Helen, *The Music of What Happens* (Cambridge: Harvard University Press, 1988).

Vendler, Helen, *The Breaking of Style* (Cambridge: Harvard University Press, 1995).

Warren, T. H., Review of *Poems of Past and the Present*, *Spectator* (5 April, 1902). Reprinted in *Thomas Hardy: The Critical Heritage* (edited by Cox), p. 332-35.

Wasserman, 'The Music of Time: Henri Bergson and Willa Cather', *American Literature*, Vol. 57, no. 2 (1985), pp. 226-39.

Weinstein, Philip M., *The Semantics of Desire: Changing Models of Identity from Dickens to Joyce* (Princeton: Princeton University Press, 1984).

Widdowson, Peter, *Hardy in History* (London: Routledge, 1989).

Widdowson, Peter, *Thomas Hardy: Selected Poetry and Non-Fictional Prose* (London: Macmillan, 1997).

Widdowson, Peter, *On Thomas Hardy: Late Essays and Earlier* (London: Macmillan, 1998).

Williams, Raymond, *The English Novel from Dickens to Lawrence* (London: Chatto and Windus, 1970).

Williams, Raymond, *The Country and the City* (London: Chatto and Windus, 1973).

Wiltshire, David, *The Social and Political Thought of Herbert Spencer* (Oxford: Oxford University Press, 1978).

Woolf, Virginia, 'Thomas Hardy's Novels', *Times Literary Supplement* (19 January 1928), p. 33.

Woolf, Virginia, 'The Novels of Thomas Hardy', *Collected Essays*, Vol. 1 (edited by Leonard Woolf, London: Hogarth, 1966), pp. 256-66.

Wotton, George, *Thomas Hardy: Towards a Materialist Criticism* (Dublin: Gill & Macmillan, 1985).

Wright, T. R., 'Rhetorical and Lyrical Imagery in *Tess of the d'Urbervilles*', *Durham University Journal*, Vol. 34 (1973) pp. 79-85.

Wright, T. R., *Hardy and the Erotic* (London: Macmillan, 1989).

Index

Adorno, Theodor, *Introduction to the Sociology of Music* 14
aeolian harp
  and the body 211
  in Hardy 67-68
aestheticism, Bakhtin on 21n. 10
Arkans, Norman 159, 160, 162
Armstrong, Tim 108
art, Hardy on 193-94, 223-25
artist, Proust on role of 194, 207

Bakhtin, Mikhail
  on aestheticism 21n. 10
  Towards a Philosophy of the Act 7
Barnes, William 105
Bayley, John
  An Essay on Hardy 1, 215
  on Hardy's fiction 33, 83
  on Hardy's poetry 139
Bergson, Henri
  Creative Evolution 205
  Hardy's reading of 204-209, 220, 230n. 5
  on movement 81-82
  on music 205-206, 217-18, 220-21
  The Two Sources of Morality and Religion 204-205
Binyon, Lawrence, on Hardy 138
body, the
  and the aeolian harp 211
  and the soul 30
Borges, Jorge Luis 14
Bradley, A.C., on sound 226
Brennecke, Ernest 166, 228-29

character, and music 45, 84-86, 228
Clark, Timothy 110-11
community, and Hardy 151n. 13
Conrad, Peter 50
counterpoint, Robert Louis Stevenson on 141

Davie, Donald 64
Deleuze, Gilles 6, 7, 11, 15, 16, 29-30, 66, 69, 81, 207, 208, 217
  A Thousand Plateaus 146-47
  Cinema 1: The Movement-Image 82

dissonance 14-15

Eliot, George, *The Mill on the Floss* 76
Elvy, Margaret 49
  Sexing Hardy: Thomas Hardy and Feminism 228
evolution, Hardy's interest in 202-203, 219
experience, and music 16-17

Firor, Ruth 159
Fraleigh, Sondra, *Dance and the Lived Body* 80

Gatrell, Simon 80
Gittings, Robert 144, 201
Gosse, Edmund, on Hardy 138, 202-204
Green, T.H. 216
Grundy, Joan, *Hardy and the Sister Arts* 28-29, 80
Guattari, Felix 146-47, 217
Gunn, Thom, on Hardy 143-44

Hardy, Florence Emily, *The Life of Thomas Hardy* 5, 11, 18-19, 23, 24, 25-26, 69, 71-73, 79-80, 137, 141-42, 144, 158, 160, 162, 194, 213, 223, 224
Hardy, Mary 164, 183
Hardy, Thomas
  on art 193-94, 223-25
  Bergson, Hardy's reading of 204-209, 220, 230n. 5
  C. Day Lewis on 215
  character 20n. 5
  and community 151n. 13
  D.H. Lawrence on 39-40, 44
  Edmund Gosse on 138, 202-204
  evolution, Hardy's interest in 202-203, 219
  hope in 34-35
  kindness of 151n. 11
  Lawrence Binyon on 138
  and localism 158-59
  Lytton Strachey on 137-38
  musical influences 140, 156-57
  narrative technique 70, 77-78, 84, 89
  novelists appreciation of 153n. 42

Hardy, Thomas - *continued*
  pessimism of 3, 10-11, 19
  Philip Larkin on 142-43, 146
  philosophers, Hardy's reading of 11-12,
      58n. 10, 201-202, 214-15
  philosophy of 226-28
  plot construction 102n. 27
  poems, anthologies 153n. 40
  poetics 139-146
  poets appreciation of 145-46
  Schopenhauer, Hardy's reading of 212-
      13
  short stories 90-97
  Siegfried Sassoon on 141
  on the soul 19, 23-26, 109, 115, 198n. 9,
      208, 224
  Thom Gunn on 143-44
  on Turner 224-25
  and the unconscious 222-23
  Virginia Woolf on 35-36, 38, 44, 77
  and Wordsworth 152n. 18
  works
    'A Bygone Occasion' 136
    'A Church Romance' 165-66
    A Laodicean 42, 43
    A Pair of Blue Eyes 8, 30-31, 40-41, 44,
        68, 79, 86-87
    'A Singer Asleep' 124-27, 145
    'Absentmindedness in a Parish
        Choir' 94
    'After the Burial' 106
    'Afternoon Service at Mellstock' 175-
        76
    'An East-End Curate' 119-20
    'An Imaginative Woman' 93-94
    'An Indiscretion in the Life of an
        Heiress' 94
    'An Upbraiding' 135-36
    'Apostrophe to an Old Psalm Tune' 186
    'Architectural Masks' 115-16
    'At Madam Tussaud's in Victorian
        Years' 184
    'At the Piano' 173-74
    'At the Railway Station - Upway' 181
    'Barbara of the House of Grebe' 90-91
    'Barthélèmon at Vauxhall' 128-29
    'Christmastide' 111-15, 122
    'Come Not; Yet Come' 170
    'Concerning Agnes' 133, 185-86
    Desperate Remedies 35-8, 43, 65, 78-79,
        83

'During Wind and Rain' 174-75
Far from the Madding Crowd 41, 65, 68,
    70, 77, 80, 82, 88
'Fellow-Townsmen' 35
'For Conscience Sake' 94
'Haunting Fingers' 171
'Her Immortality' 170-71
'I Found Her Out There' 187-192
'In Her Precincts' 137
'In the Nuptial Chamber' 169
'In the Small Hours' 168
'In a Waiting Room' 119
Jude the Obscure 52-53
'Julie-Jane' 117
'Lost Love' 168-69
'Middle-Age Enthusiasms' 183
'Molly Gone' 170
'Music in a Snowy Street' 72
'Nature's Questioning' 215
'Often When Warring' 116
'On a Fine Morning' 118
'On a Midsummer Eve' 127-28
'On Stinsford Hill at Midnight' 109-
    10
'On The Belgium Expatriation' 116
'On the Western Circuit' 33-34, 92-93
'One We Knew' 165
'Our Exploits in West Poley' 94
'Penance' 135
'Reminiscences of a Dancing Man'
    162-63, 186
'Rome: On the Palatine' 159
'San Sebastian' 164
'Silences' 172-73
'Singing Lovers' 169
'Sitting on the Bridge' 136
'Song from Heine' 169-170
Tess of the d'Urbervilles 17-18, 27-28,
    32, 51-52
'The Alarm' 164-65
'The Bird-Catcher's Boy' 13, 181-83
'The Blinded Bird' 117
'The Boy's Dream' 118
'The Bridge of Lodi' 163-64
'The Caged Goldfinch' 12-13, 21n. 16
'The Change' 171
'The Colonel's Soliloquy' 195
'The Darkling Thrush' 1-2, 4-5, 9, 15,
    16, 193
'The Dead Quire' 161
'The Difference' 133-34

Hardy, Thomas (works) - *continued*
  'The Distracted Preacher' 34
  The Dynasts 107-108, 212-13, 228
  'The Fiddler' 107
  'The Fiddler of the Reels' 25, 34, 35
  'The Ghost of the Past' 155
  The Hand of Ethelberta 31, 38-39, 85
  'The Harvest Supper' 136, 160
  'The History of the Hardcomes' 91
  'The House of Hospitalities' 177
  'The Last Signal' 105
  The Literary Notebooks of Thomas Hardy 74, 148, 208-209, 223, 226, 227
  'The Maid of Keinton Mandeville' 167
  The Mayor of Casterbridge 41-42, 45-46, 46-48, 84
  'The Melancholy Hussar of the German Legion' 95
  'The Musical Box' 135
  'The Paphian Ball' 161
  'The Pedestrian' 123
  'The Profitable Reading of Fiction' 63, 70-71
  'The Puzzled Game-Birds' 13
  'The Rash Bride' 161
  The Return of the Native 70, 74-76, 80, 97
  'The Rift' 134-35
  'The Romantic Adventures of a Milkmaid' 94-95
  'The Schreckhorn' 129
  'The Seasons of Her Year' 137
  'The Self-Unseeing' 175, 178-79
  'The Son's Veto' 92
  'The Temporary the All' 134
  'The Three Strangers' 95
  The Trumpet-Major 42-43, 67
  'The Waiting Supper' 91-92
  The Well-Beloved 26-27, 55-56
  The Woodlanders 49, 50, 59n. 28-29, 70
  'The Youth Who Carried a Light' 122
  'To a Lady Playing and Singing in the Morning' 129-132
  'To Lizbie Browne' 167-68
  'To My Father's Violin' 172, 173
  'Two Serenades' 136
  Two on a Tower 64-65
  Under the Greenwood Tree 40, 42, 43, 70, 80, 82, 157, 197
  'Without, Not Within Her' 123
  'You on the Tower' 134
  on writing 23, 108
Hartmann, Eduard von, *Philosophy of the Unconscious* 209-211, 222
Holquist, Michael 7
hope, in Hardy 34-35

ideas, and music 210-11
immanence, philosophy of 98n. 10
inspiration 150n. 8
integration, and music 65-66

Jackson-Houlston, Caroline 27, 44-45, 50
Jacobson, Howard 84
James, William
  A Pluralistic Universe 216-19, 221
  on the mind 216-17

Karlin, Daniel 125-26
kindness, Hardy's 151n. 11

Langbaum, Robert 143
Langer, Susanne K. 221
Larkin, Philip, on Hardy 142-43, 146
Lawrence, D.H., on Hardy 39-40, 44
Levinas, Emmanuel 72, 73
Lewis, C. Day, on Hardy 215
localism, and Hardy 158-59
love, and music 40-44, 88-89, 92-93, 94-95, 96-97, 129-137
Lucas, F.L. 155
Lucas, John 10, 108-109, 120-21, 127-28, 143, 156, 178-180, 192-93

Macdowall, Arthur S. 108
Maidment, Brian 157-58
Mallett, Phillip 49, 50
Malvy, Margaret 214
Man, Paul de 15
Mardon, J. Vera 214
Melnick, Daniel C., *Fullness of Dissonance: Modern Fiction and the Aesthetics of Music* 14-15
memory, and music 159-184, 196
Mill, J.S., *Essays on Religion* 211
Miller, J. Hillis 84
Millgate, Michael 10-11, 83, 202
mind, the, William James on 216-17
Mitchell, P.E. 162

movement
  Bergson on 81-82
  and music 79-84
music
  absence of 50
  Bergson on 205-206, 217-18, 220-21
  and character 45, 84-86, 228
  and experience 16-17
  and ideas 210-11
  and integration 65-66
  and love 40-44, 159-184, 196
  and movement 79-84
  Pater on 226
  philosophy of 231n. 23
  and Proust 58n. 4
  and reader response 117-18
  and rhythm 146-49
  and Schopenhauer 211-12
  and social criticism 50-55
  and the soul 8, 16, 23-24, 26, 29, 80-81,
    97, 192
  and time 17-18
  and tragedy 46-49
  and transcendence 109, 115
  and transformation 72-74, 78-79
  and the unconscious 69

Newman, Ernest, on Symbolism 225-26

past, the, Proust on 198n. 12
Pater, Walter, on music 226
Phillips, Adam 219
philosophers, Hardy's reading of 10,
    201-202, 214-15
philosophy, Hardy's 226-28
poet, role, Paul Valéry on 121-22
poetics, Hardy's 139-146
Proust, Marcel
  on the artist's role 194, 207
  favourite Hardy novel 44
  and music 58n. 4
  on the past 198n. 12
  Remembrance of Things Past 194

reader response, and music 117-18
rhythm
  and music 146-49
  and the soul 148
  and time 184-192
Rutland, William R. 202

Sassoon, Siegfried, on Hardy 141
Schopenhauer, Arthur
  Hardy's reading of 212-13
  and music 211-12
Sherman, Elna 156
social criticism, and music 50-55
soul, the
  and the body 30
  Hardy on 19, 23-26, 109, 115, 198n. 9,
    208, 224
  and music 8, 16, 23-24, 26, 29, 80-81, 97,
    192
  physical expression of 9, 97
  and rhythm 148
sound, A.C. Bradley on 226
Stevenson, Robert Louis, on counterpoint
    141
Strachey, Lytton, on Hardy 137-38
Symbolism, Ernest Newman on 225-26
Symonds, John Addington, Essays
    Speculative and Suggestive 63, 227-28

Taylor, Dennis, Hardy's Metres and
    Victorian Poetry 139-40, 144, 184-87
Thomas, Edward 14
time
  and music 17-18
  and rhythm 184-192
tragedy, and music 46-9
transcendence, and music 109, 115
transformation, and music 72-74, 78-79
Turner, J.M.W., Hardy on 224-25
Turner, Paul 226

unconscious, the
  and Hardy 222-23
  and music 69

Valéry, Paul, on the poet's role 121-22

Warren, T. H. 138
Webb, C.C.J. 202-203
Widdowson, Peter 3, 4, 111, 145
Wittgenstein, Ludwig 222
Woolf, Virginia
  on Desperate Remedies 35-36
  on Hardy 38, 44, 77
Wordsworth, William, and Hardy 152n.
    18
writing, Hardy on 23, 108